D0113867

WITHDRAWN

Anonymous Gift

ALSO BY PETER J. SMITH

Make-Believe Ballrooms
Highlights of the Off-Season
A Good Family

ONWARD!

25 YEARS OF ADVICE, EXHORTATION, AND INSPIRATION
FROM AMERICA'S BEST COMMENCEMENT SPEECHES

∽∾

EDITED BY

PETER J. SMITH

SCRIBNER

New York   London   Toronto   Sydney   Singapore

SCRIBNER
1230 Avenue of the Americas
New York, NY 10020

Copyright © 2000 by Peter J. Smith
All rights reserved, including the right of reproduction in
whole or in part in any from.

SCRIBNER and design are trademarks of
Macmillan Library Reference, USA, Inc., used under
license by Simon & Schuster, the publisher of this work.

DESIGNED BY ERICH HOBBING

Set in Aldus

Manufactured in the United States of America

1   3   5   7   9   10   8   6   4   2

Library of Congress Cataloging-in-Publication Data
Onward! : 25 years of advice, exhortation, and inspiration from
America's best commencement speeches / [compiled by] Peter J. Smith.
p.   cm.
1. Speeches, addresses, etc., American.
2. Baccalaureate addresses. I. Smith, Peter J., 1959–
PS663.C74 O57 2000
815'.010892375—dc21   00-028473

ISBN 0-684-86452-5

Copyright information is continued on page 301.

PS
663
.C74
O57
2000

DEC 27 2009 ↑

CONTENTS

ONWARD!

INTRODUCTION

Commencement speeches have a bad reputation. Robert Novak, speaking at the University of Illinois at Champaign-Urbana, once remarked, "Graduation day—the high point of college. The commencement speech—the low point of graduation day." Garry Trudeau has noted that commencement speeches "were invented largely in the belief that outgoing college students should never be released into the world until they have been properly sedated." And James Reston once commented that the only people ever invited to speak at commencement exercises are "eminent bores."

Possibly as a result, not many people are able to remember their commencement speeches. For that matter, many commencement speakers make it clear that even *they* have no recollection of what was said on their own graduation day, back when. Oh, some might remember the speaker—*so cool that we have Bill Cosby! F. Lee Bailey! Mary Lou Retton!*—but as for the speaker's message, well, the graduates' minds were elsewhere that day, focused on tenses other than the present. For college seniors, graduation is a critical event, after all. They feel self-conscious in their mortarboard with the tassel, their warlock robes. There's a keg party following the ceremony, or else they want to hurry up and pack so they can go on that kayaking trip or that cross-country jaunt. Their parents and grandparents are crowded behind them in the audience, a blur of faces, hats, purses, breath mints, and Nicorette. What everybody—parents and graduates—wants out of the commencement speaker is brevity, wit (wit is always a plus), then a swift cut to the chase, amen, good-bye.

Unfortunately, most commencement speakers fail to meet this challenge. The best commencement speeches are abbreviated and funny, yes—but surprisingly few speakers say anything that hasn't been said at least two hundred times across the country, either that year or in a previous year. More speakers than you might imagine have a stump speech that they update every year, inserting new words and up-to-the-minute references, like performers who know from experience that local references will win over the local audience. The most common, and trying, commencement speech starts off with the speaker recalling the world as it was when he or she graduated from college—the cost of stamps, the films, the books, the political climate—then moves without surprise toward describing the world that current graduates face. The speech typically ends with two, no more than three, inspirational tidbits. The end. Another speech that typically annihilates the souls of college seniors is given by a politician who uses the commencement format as a means to praise the presidential or congressional or court administration for which he or she toils. There are few speeches that squirming graduates are less liable to remember at all.

In short, many commencement speeches *deserve* their crummy reputation. A commencement speech should not be a screed, a defense, an advertisement, or a labored attempt to compare now and then, and yet too often they are one or the other. But amid the trite, empty, long-winded orations that swell our college and high school auditoriums every year, there are pearls that stick out. While many speakers give canned recitals, many more find in the commencement speech an opportunity to look back upon their lives or careers, an opportunity to reflect on the lessons they may have learned (or ignored) along the way, an opportunity to reflect on what they might have done differently. Particularly nowadays—in a time of dismissive irony and cynicism, when the popular view is that the world is in bad shape and only getting worse, in a time when it seems uncool to profess hope or belief in much of anything—commencement speakers provide a welcome antidote to the fashionably ironic cultural shrug.

Part memoir, part summation of the year that's already gone by, part tribute to the person the speaker was at age twenty-two, part entertainment (you don't want to lose your audience, after all), part bulletin from the front (the work front, the adult front), and part sermonette, the commencement speech differs from any other type of speech. The best of them bring out the best in everyone. They instruct.

They warn. They reflect. They advise. They exhort. They persuade. They reassure. They impose an agenda. They update us, whether spiritually, socially, politically, or philosophically. And they inspire. Even the most blasé and media savvy of us sneak a glance at the excerpts from commencement speeches reprinted each year in newspapers in search of some telltale clue or explanation of our lives that maybe we've missed or overlooked. At the same time, commencement speeches are as personal as any formal speech delivered to three hundred or more people can be. Few other kinds of speech possess their peculiar authenticity.

Moreover, we endow our commencement speakers with the capacity to explain our times. They become emissaries, visiting representatives of the world that graduates are about to enter. We entrust our speakers to find a narrative in a world where most of us see disconnection or static, entrust them to carefully ally the past, the present, and the future. Succinctly, too (under twenty minutes, please). Considered together, commencement speeches can offer a singular perspective on how our culture has changed over the past twenty-five-plus years.

So, what has happened in that space of time? It is tempting to remark only on the negative things—the wars, the shootings, the terrorism, the political misdeeds—but that would be to overlook the end of the Cold War, the fall of the Berlin Wall, the dismantling of a brutal political infrastructure in South Africa, the pope's role in freeing Poland, the dissolution of the Soviet Union, and many other small and large miracles all over the world. The late writer and sociologist Christopher Lasch noted that the human impulse to chop time into decades—the 1970s, the 1980s, the 1990s—is artificially neat and misleading, though at the same time irresistible: how else to make sense of the baggy, crowded, contradictory novel of our times unless you divide it up into chapters? These days, some people cast a worshipful eye backward on 1970s artifacts—a popular compilation of songs from that decade is entitled, horribly, *Have a Nice Day*. We forget that, aside from the horrors of Watergate and Vietnam, the 1970s were, among other things, a tumultuous decade of recovery, one blindly focused on the self—self-realization, self-fulfillment, self-awareness. And the 1980s? Our culture became even less interested than usual in sitting still. What self? Show me the money! As our culture entered the middle eighties and the 1990s, fewer political figures, and more and more actors and actresses (and for some reason, television anchorpeople), began showing up on college campuses, a reflection of the increasing focus on celebrity in our lives.

The past twenty-five years have been marked by a gradual amnesia in our culture. We are an embarrassingly forgetful society. Overburdened by the bombardment of twenty-four-hour news stations and the Internet, we have started losing our memories. At the same time, the shelf life of our products has grown shorter. Very few things, or even ideas, last very long. Two or three weeks, it seems, is the current maximum time in the sun for any product before it is superseded by something else. Movies open and effectively close in a long weekend. Books come out, are reviewed, and then are promptly forgotten. Only a tragedy of some kind—a plane crash, a premature death, say, of Princess Diana or John F. Kennedy Jr.—manages to suspend our lives enough to allow us to sit still and engage in the kind of contemplation that most of us have no time for anymore.

Hence, some of the reasons for this collection of commencement addresses: to remind us all that just seventeen years ago, the United States was faced with nuclear annihilation, that just eleven years ago, Nelson Mandela was in jail, and that twenty years ago—can so much time have passed?—John Lennon was shot; to remind us why the generation that came of age in the seventies is so distrustful of authority; to bring us back to a time when we were not so litigious, and slightly less interested in money and in keeping score and in society's winners and losers; and most of all, to remind us of a period, unlike today, when many people felt they could make a difference or effect change in their worlds.

∽o∾

1975

As the United States prepared for its bicentennial celebration, the clouds of Watergate hung over the country's head. Early in January of 1975, former top Nixon aides H. R. Haldeman, John Mitchell, and Robert Mardian were convicted of conspiracy to obstruct justice. Concurrently, John Dean, Herbert Kalmbach, and Jeb Stuart Magruder, all former Nixon aides, were released from prison, while John Connally, Nixon's former treasury secretary, was acquitted of bribery allegations. Still, as America's two hundredth birthday approached, domestic unemployment was sky-high—nearly 9 percent, the highest percentage since World War II. It was little wonder that the American public chose to focus inwardly with transcendental meditation—that is, when they weren't reading Judith Rossner's Looking for Mr. Goodbar or E. L. Doctorow's Ragtime.

Against this backdrop, President Gerald Ford announced that American involvement in the Vietnam War was finally, blessedly over. Around the world, political change dominated. In Great Britain, Margaret Thatcher—a "grocer's daughter," the class-conscious British tabloids trumpeted, with their toxic mixture of envy and contempt—was elected the first ever female leader of the Conservative Party. Following the death of Generalissimo Francisco Franco, Spain's dictator for more than thirty-five years, Juan Carlos assumed the Spanish throne, but not before Franco's deterioration had been amusingly exhausted on a groundbreaking new comedy series called Saturday Night Live.

In Detroit, Michigan, Teamster boss Jimmy Hoffa was reported missing. His body, variously rumored to be at the bottom of the ocean or buried under the foundation of a sports stadium, would never turn up. The U.S. Supreme Court ruled that mentally ill persons could not be forcibly held in institutions if they presented no danger to the public at large and could live ably in society—thus helping to create a new American chaos (and tragedy) known as deinstitutionalization. Samuel Bronfman, the college-age heir to the Canadian distillery fortune, was released without harm after being abducted and held hostage. Authorities apprehended Lynette "Squeaky" Fromme, a former acolyte of Charles Manson, after she pointed a loaded gun at President Ford during his visit to Sacramento, California. By the end of the year, Fromme, to no one's surprise, had been sentenced to life in prison. In racially tense Boston, public schools began busing black and white students in order to achieve school integration. Miraculously, no violence was reported, though South Boston High School was placed in federal receivership for dragging its heels on desegregation. Patricia Hearst, a member of the California-based newspaper dynasty as well as a member of the Symbionese Liberation Army, was arrested by the FBI after a nearly two-year nationwide search and charged with armed robbery; a grainy video of Hearst wearing dark glasses and pointing a machine gun was endlessly replayed on the nightly news.

In hockey, the Philadelphia Flyers beat the Buffalo Sabres to win their second straight Stanley Cup. In baseball, the Cincinnati Reds defeated the Boston Red Sox to capture the World Series in a dramatic seven-game match, with Pete Rose, later to be banned forever from baseball, named as series MVP.

The beaver was named the national symbol of Canada.

∽ο∾

ART BUCHWALD
Newspaper Columnist
Vassar College

You are the generation of Watergate and Kahoutek. You were raised on *Bonanza* and *Kojak*. Walter Cronkite is your godfather, and Nixon was your president. You flopped at streaking, and you blew Earth Day, and you've seen war live and in color on television, and your previous president said he was not a crook.

Here are some things you can do right after graduation: throw a baseball to a little girl; ask your teacher for his or her autograph; take a shower with a friend; ask your mother or father to a dance; throw a kiss to a little old lady; and take a walk in the woods with someone you love.

∽∘∽

BUCKMINSTER FULLER
Architect
Hobart and William Smith Colleges

I'll leave you with this: the greatest thing of the world is love.

∽∘∽

DAVID BRODER
Columnist
Denison University

One hopes that in your years [here], you have acquired, along with other aspects of an education, the qualities that will serve you well as citizens:

- A mental outlook that is critical, perhaps even skeptical, about government and politics, but not cynical
- A tolerance for diversity that stops well short of acquiescence in ignorance or duplicity
- Optimism in your expectations; positiveness in your outlook, accompanied by steadfastness in the face of disappointed hopes; and cool courage in the face of massive disagreement with your own views

One hopes you will be actively involved in your community and your country—but not be so totally consumed by your desire to "set the world right" that you begin to use people as instruments of your design, rather than enjoy them for their own qualities.

I express the hope that you bring these qualities your country so much needs.

∽∾∾

Edward W. Brooke
U.S. Senator
Syracuse University

The greatest disaster in American foreign policy has at long last come to an end. And though the extent of our humanitarian aid there is still to be decided, the fact is that the Vietnam War is over!

In the four years since many of you commenced your college career, our country has endured a great deal of national trauma, more than enough for a lifetime. The final stages of the Vietnam tragedy, the Watergate scandal, and our present economic tribulations have taxed our strength and our capacity to maintain our equilibrium in a time of rapid change and uncertainty in the international realm. . . .

Nineteen seventy-six, then, presents a challenge to every individual, group, and institution. The bicentennial is more than a period of reflection or celebration. It is a time to redouble our efforts to achieve those values and goals which we profess to live by.

I believe I know the depth of your disillusionment with those of us who govern—of how bitter the revelation that the storybook vision of your country has turned out flawed.

But as William Faulkner once wrote of the South, "I think that one never loves a land *because*—you love despite, not for the virtues, but despite the faults." If you can accept the fact that *your* solutions too will be incomplete, and yet not let that possibility— that fear—paralyze you into inaction and indifference, you may still be able to achieve a safer and a better, if a still imperfect, world.

That is a far more modest wish than the traditional command of a commencement speaker to go out and save the world. But it is my wish for you, and *it is an honest one*!

ISAAC ASIMOV
Writer
Connecticut College

The day you stop learning is the day you begin decaying, and then you are no longer a human being.

∽∾∾

MAY SARTON*
Writer
Clark University

I hope to persuade you that in spite of entering adult life at a difficult time—jobs are scarce, the recession goes on, and the country has just suffered a confusing and confused military and moral defeat—you are going to find yourselves part of a subtle, but slowly rising, *gentle revolution*, and this gentle revolution will require every skill you have learned here, plus all your imagination and intelligence. I see signs of the gentle revolution every day, and wherever I go. It is the revolt against violence, against impersonal power, against mechanical solutions to human problems, against antediluvian ideas about military might. (It has been a salutary lesson, has it not, that although we threw more bombs on that tiny country than on Germany in the whole of World War II, we did not win.)

The gentle revolution springs from the imperative need to bring imagination, tenderness, human compassion to bear in regions where they have often been denied access. . . . The people engaged in this revolution will not be asking where the jobs are; they will be asking where the need is. Not piously, not as missionaries, but for reasons of job and self-fulfillment.

Among the gentle revolutionaries I feel sure you have heard of is Dr.

*Reprinted by the permission of Russell & Volkening as agents for the author, copyright © 1978 by May Sarton.

Leboyer, a French doctor who is changing our whole concept of how to treat the newborn infant. It seems incredible that no one until Frederick Leboyer came along had thought that to bring a newborn infant out into brilliant lights, hang him up by the heels, and slap him was bound to create trauma—we have all seen those faces, crumpled, bright red, screaming with fear at the hostile and terrifying world they find themselves in. "Newborn babies are ugly"—that is what we had believed.

Then Dr. Leboyer came along. Now we have seen the photographs of newborn babies perfectly serene and smiling . . . a kind of miracle, really, and all it took was someone with imagination, the imagination to *feel with*.

∽∘∾

Gerald Ford
U.S. President
University of Pennsylvania

We must increase the participation and influence of every citizen in the processes of self-government and the shaping of national consensus, and we will.

We must lead humanity's everlasting effort to live harmoniously with nature, employing the technology through the enrichment of spirit as well as body, and we will.

We must sustain and strengthen our alliances and partnerships with other freedom-loving nations as we seek cooperation and rational relations with all peoples, and we will.

We must maintain our vigilance and our defenses as a symbol of our undiminished devotion to peace in a lawful world, and we will.

Finally, perhaps more important, we must declare again the brotherly love in which this great commonwealth was founded. We must learn to trust one another and to help one another.

We must pledge anew to one another our lives, our fortunes, and our own sacred honor, and we will.

∽∘∾

NORMAN COUSINS
Writer
Lawrence University

Are we smart enough to survive? It seems to me that there are only two parties in the world, and these parties have no basic difference as to the facts. The two parties in the world today are, first, those who look at these problems and say no, there is nothing we can do, and thus become paralyzed, and those who say the problem is difficult but we've got a chance and no one knows enough to be a pessimist.

I would ask you to join that second party, because no one does know enough to be a pessimist. The uniqueness of the human race is represented by its ability to do that which it has never done before. The uniqueness of human life is that it has done, and can do, the impossible. The crisis is represented now by the problem; the crisis is represented by what goes on in our minds, by what we think is possible.

Are we smart enough to survive? Yes, we are.

❧

VINCENT BARNETT
Former President, Colgate Universtiy
Williams College

Almost everything is more complicated than it seems, but almost nothing is hopeless.

Everything is part of everything else, but you've got to start somewhere.

You are severely constrained by the "world you never made"— by "the system"—but you have meaningful choices within the system as well as modest opportunities to change it.

You ought to be judged—and you ought to judge yourself—by the way you exercise those choices.

The choices are your choices, and not the mere extension of the expectations of your parents, your professors, your favorite high school teacher, or the most admired members of your peer group.

To make such choices, you have to know who you are, what is important to you, and where you would like to go. (To be educated is not necessarily to know the answers to these questions, but to know that you must face them and try to answer them.)

If you don't know who you are, you'd better find out pretty soon; and in the meantime you'd better construct a working hypothesis, because you are in fact making these choices all the time, willy or nilly.

Beauty and meaning are not merely in the eye of the beholder, but also in the mind's eye of the creator and doer.

You count. You make a difference. You can add to the sum of beauty and joy and love and understanding in the world (for yourself, your family, your friends, your community however you define it), or you can subtract from those already scarce enough commodities. *What you do matters.*

∽୦∾

1976

What, precisely, did the bicentennial mean? If nothing else, it provided an opportunity for the United States to reflect on the decade it was living in, marked at midpoint by political corruption and an almost comical cultural solipsism. And a former governor from Georgia, Jimmy Carter, seemed to be what Americans needed to put the memories of the Richard Nixon White House firmly behind them.

At the Democratic National Convention, Jimmy Carter and Minnesota senator Walter Mondale accepted the party's nominations for president and vice president. At the Republican National Convention, Gerald Ford defeated former California governor Ronald Reagan to win the presidential nomination, and chose Kansas senator Robert Dole as his running mate. But the American public had had their fill of Republicans, and by the end of 1976, Carter and his wife, Rosalynn, were set to enter the White House. Internationally, 1976 saw little tumult, though the worst violence in South African history occurred when nearly a hundred black protesters rallying against a government regulation requiring the adoption of the Afrikaans language were killed. Elsewhere, José López Portillo was elected president of Mexico, the government of President Isabel Perón was overthrown in Argentina, and China mourned the deaths of Zhou Enlai, that country's premier for twenty-seven years, and Mao Zedong, chairman of the Chinese Communist Party.

Saul Bellow was awarded the Nobel Prize in literature. The Pittsburgh Steelers won the Super Bowl. U.S. secretary of transportation William T. Coleman Jr. decided that France and Great Britain could both fly the Concorde SST to New York City and Washington, D.C., on a trial basis. Aldo Moro retained the prime ministership of Italy, and in Innsbruck, Austria, the Twelfth Winter Olympic Games came to a close. In San Francisco, Patricia Hearst was found guilty of armed robbery and sentenced to prison for seven years. Ray Floyd won the Masters golf tournament. In Ohio, Republican Wayne Hayes acknowledged that he had had a "personal relationship" with a woman named Elizabeth Ray, but denied claims that Ray had received an annual salary taken from public funds. In tennis, Jimmy Connors won the U.S. Open, with Chris Evert walking away with the women's title. The Summer Olympic Games opened in Montreal, Canada. Clarence Kelley, the director of the FBI, retained his post despite his admissions that some of his home furnishings had been provided by the FBI without charge, and that he had been the beneficiary of gifts from some of his aides. Earl Butz, the U.S. secretary of agriculture, resigned his post after making a racist crack. Artist Alexander Calder died in New York City at age seventy-eight. And in a far-reaching decision, the Episcopal Church formally approved the ordination of women to the priesthood.

∽∘∾

Vernon Jordan
Civil Rights Leader
University of Notre Dame

In this bicentennial year, black Americans remind their fellow Americans that this land, America, is our land, too. America's soil is sprinkled with our sweat and watered with our tears and fertilized with our blood. Black people in America, lo these many years, have dug potatoes and toted cotton and lifted bale and sunk the canals and laid the railroad track linking the Atlantic and the Pacific. Indeed, black people helped build America's power and glory. We, too, like you, our fellow Americans, sing "God Bless America." We, too, sing "O beautiful for spacious skies, for amber waves of grain." We, too, pledge allegiance to the flag, and we died defending its honor. Crispus Attucks, a black man, was the first to die to make America a democratic nation. Black men and women have fought in America's every war, from Valley Forge to the rice patties of Vietnam, even in segregated armies. Even in the darkest days of slavery and separation and even on the tortured road to desegregation, we black Americans never wavered, never doubted. Rather, we kept our faith in America, and that faith has been like a tree planted by the rivers of water. It has not been moved.

So we say to America in this bicentennial year, sustain and concretize that faith. And we remind America that the issues of race are not just political, social, and economic. Indeed, it is a moral issue as well. We must recall Dante's great words that "the hottest places in hell are reserved for those who, in a period of moral crisis, maintain their neutrality."

We live in an age in which men have walked on the moon, have harnessed the vast power of nuclear energy, and have created enormous material wealth and riches. Yet our age is marked by ethical retardation, and by the passive tolerance of racism and poverty. Indeed, as Chesterton has written, "The Christian ideal has not been tried and found wanting. It has been found difficult and left untried."

And the result can be seen today in the cities and rural areas of our nation where the extremes of wealth and of poverty jostle each other in fear and loathing. While we preach the sermon of greed and indifference, we appear to have forgotten the Sermon on the Mount.

The question each of you must deal with is whether you will accept this situation—with all of its inequities and injustices—or whether you will struggle to help build a better, more humane society. Will you measure your success in terms of status and salary, or will you measure it by the efforts you make to overcome our society's heritage of discrimination and inequality?

∽о∾

ANDREW HACKER
Sociologist
Hobart and William Smith Colleges

Four years on this campus have been as ideal a life as our society will bestow on anyone. It has been a luxurious interlude: expensive, privileged, protected. So I congratulate you, members of the class of '76, on having had so enjoyable an experience. Pure pleasure is a rare commodity, as honorable as honest labor or the ethics of profit and production. To relax without guilt, to remain in bed without shame or apology, these are no easy achievements in a society so wedded to output. You look just fine to me as you are. Indeed, better than you will ever look again. But from this afternoon onward, you relinquish all your immunities. Within an hour, you will be on your own. Good luck. I have a feeling that some of you will need it.

∽୦∾

Martin Marty
Professor
Lawrence University

"I respond although I will be changed."

Fear of being changed by response holds some back. I prefer to call as witness John Henry Newman: "In a higher world it is otherwise, but here below to live is to change, and to be perfect is to have changed often."

∽୦∾

William Kunstler
Lawyer and Activist
Lawrence University

"If we have no memories, if we do not learn that evil is born and thrives in direct proportion to our own indifference to it, if we permit the Coliseum or its electronic equivalent to distract or divert us from the issues of the day, if fear rather than reason is our only catalyst, then the dark will indeed be upon the face of the earth once more and we shall deservedly slip silently back into the slime from which we so tortuously simmered up over the centuries."—George Santayana.

You must confront your environment with courage and rationality, or it will destroy you.

❧

WARREN E. BURGER
Chief Justice of the United States
University of Pennsylvania

Today we have peace in the streets; students are in classes and libraries without occupying them as hostile forces. No young Americans are on battlefields. And if all the world's leaders will lower their voices, but continue to talk with each other, perhaps we can maintain the world peace we now have, precarious as it is.

It may be too much to hope that a golden age of Pericles, or a modern version of the Renaissance, is "just around the corner," but if you demand that values of the spirit be given their rightful place, and demand that changes be made, a better life than has ever been known can be your lot in this, our third century—your century.

❧

1977

James Earl Carter Jr. was sworn in as the thirty-ninth president of the United States, naming a cabinet that included, among others, Cyrus Vance (secretary of state), Juanita Kreps (secretary of commerce), Joseph Califano (secretary of health, education, and welfare), Griffin Bell (attorney general), and Admiral Stansfield Turner (director of the Central Intelligence Agency). One of Carter's first acts of office: to grant an unconditional pardon to all American military draft evaders, as well as to lift the ban against Americans' traveling to Cuba, Vietnam, North Korea, and Cambodia.

Still, Nixon wouldn't go away that easily. Appearing on a series of televised interviews with David Frost, the former president denied he had committed any crimes associated with the Watergate scandal, admitting only that he "let the American people down." Elsewhere, the U.S. Supreme Court ruled that the Constitution did not forbid the spanking of schoolchildren by teachers or other school officials. In Los Angeles, Thomas Bradley was elected to a second mayoral term. Peter Jay was named the British ambassador to the United States, and Menachem Begin was elected the sixth prime minister of Israel. In Canada, prime minister Pierre Trudeau announced that he was separating from his wife, Margaret. A nightclub fire in Kentucky killed 160 people, a powerful earthquake struck Romania, and Great Britain marked the twenty-fifth anniversary of the accesssion of Queen Elizabeth II. Spain held its first free national elections on June 15, drawing an unprecedented 80 percent of that country's voters. A crippling power outage plunged New York City into darkness; massive looting ensued. In that same city, police arrested a twenty-four-year-old postal employee, David Berkowitz, and charged him with being the Son of

Sam murderer of six young women in the New York area. A Canadian assembly approved legislation establishing French as the principal language of Quebec. Legendary conductor Leopold Stokowski and crooner Bing Crosby died. The United States yacht Courageous *defeated the* Australia *in the America's Cup. Following controversy over his past professional dealings, U.S. Office of Management and Budget head Bert Lance resigned from office. The Yankees won the World Series and Tom Watson won the Masters. Two Irishwomen, Mairead Corrigan and Betty Williams, both active in the Northern Ireland peace movement, were awarded the 1976 Nobel Peace Prize; Amnesty International was awarded the Nobel Peace Prize for 1977. And Charlie Chaplin, the Little Tramp, died in Switzerland at the age of eighty-eight.*

∾⊙∾

George Plimpton
Writer
Harvard University

I have been led to understand that tomorrow you are going to graduate. Well, my strong recommendation is that you don't go. Stop! Go on back to your rooms. Unpack! There's not much out here. Chekhov tells the story of the traveler faced with three roads . . . if he takes the one to the right the wolves will eat him up, if he takes the one to the left he will eat up the wolves, and if he takes the one to the center he will eat himself up—all unappetizing choices.

The point is, we don't want you out here very much. . . . So go back to your rooms and stay. True, there may be some practical problems. The deans may come tapping at your door like hotel concierges, wondering about checkout time. Tell the dean through the door that you don't think you should go out into the world with a C minus in Economics 10. Great damage can be caused to the economic structure, and probably already has, by Harvard men out there who earned a C minus in Economics 10; you must tell the dean you don't want to compound such a situation.

The dean will say that he needs the room for the junior who is going to become a senior—the process must go on. Tell him there's no reason why the juniors can't stay juniors, the sophomores sophomores, and the freshmen freshmen. Tell him to stop the process. Why *should* the process go on? You've decided to stay. You're not going to budge!

After a while the dean will go away. Deans always go away. They go away to ponder things. They will assume that your parents will finally force the issue. They'll want you home. But I am not so sure. I have the sense that parents would rather not know what's being sent home to them these days from the colleges—not unlike receiving a mysterious package tied with hemp, addressed in rather queasy lettering from Dutch Guiana.

If your parents insist you pack up and come home, there are always measures. If you're a chemistry major, tell them that you've become very attached to something in a vat of formaldehyde. If you're prelaw, tell them that you're thinking of bringing home a tort. Your parents will probably have forgotten what a tort is, if they ever knew, and it *sounds* unpleasant—something that your mom wouldn't want to have stepping suddenly out of a hall closet. Surely, there is hardly an academic field of one's choice which does not have a nightmare possibility with which to force one's parent to pony up enough to allow nearly a decade of contemplation in one's room.

You'll remember the king in *Alice in Wonderland*. When asked, "Where shall I begin?" the king says, "Begin at the beginning, and go on until you come to the end; then stop." What I am suggesting is that you stop at the beginning, stop at your commencement. It's not very interesting to stop at the end—I mean everyone does that. So stop now. Tell them you won't go. Go back to your rooms. Unpack!

∽o∽

HUBERT HUMPHREY
Former U.S. Vice President
University of Pennsylvania

What an exciting time to be alive. The frontiers of science and technology are always being pushed forward. But it is in the political, economic, and social fields where mankind's ingenuity and inventiveness must now be directed.

Who are we to be afraid of trying? Experimentation and change are a part of the American character and of our history.

The message of the United States is not nuclear power, arms sales, and resistance to change. The message of the United States is a spiritual message, a statement of high ideals and perseverance in their achievement. It is the message of human dignity; it is the message of the freedom of ideas, speech, press, the right to assemble, to worship, and the message of freedom of movement of peoples.

It is the message of the Bill of Rights. It is the message of the Declaration of Independence, where we boldly proclaimed to a world dominated by monarchs and tyrants that "all men are created equal . . . endowed by their Creator with certain unalienable rights," and "among these are life, liberty, and the pursuit of happiness."

This is the message of America. This is the source of our power. This is the source of our strength.

Our nation's security lies in the strength of our people—our people at work, in prosperous communities, in sound mental and physical health. This is where our true national security lies. This is the source of our strength—moral, political, and economic. . . .

When our Founding Fathers met here in Philadelphia two hundred years ago, they gave us and the world a set of promises—promises toward a *more* perfect, not *the* perfect, union. America is a promise and a hope in the minds and hearts of all those who cherish liberty, justice, and opportunity.

We live by hope. We do not always get all we want when we want it. But we have to believe that someday, somehow, some way, it will be better and that we can make it so.

∾०∾

JUANITA KREPS
U.S. Secretary of Commerce
Duke University

I shall not exhort you with clichéd challenges to build a better world, to correct the mistakes we made. In fact, I find it offensive to depre- cate the achievements of previous generations. It was their efforts that moved this nation and a large part of the world to a position in which such a large proportion of us enjoy education and freedom of choice. In retrospect, many who preceded you would do some things differently, just as each of you in time will mourn past mistakes. But know how easy it is to avoid making mistakes: one has only to do nothing.

The only substitute for shouting is substance. Dwell, then, on knowing what you are about, for a knowing mind will ultimately win out, if anything can, against a loud voice.

Finally, I offer a plea that you treat yourself, as well as others, with respect, for you, too, are a special person. "Beyond a wholesome dis- cipline, be gentle with yourself." Hold on to what it was that brought you here, and all that you have added to it. Laugh as often and cry as little as possible. And know, always, that we care about you.

∞∾

MADELEINE L'ENGLE
Writer
Smith College

A friend of mine once commented that college freshmen (freshper- sons?) wander around holding their umbilical cords looking for someplace to plug them in. You're not freshmen now, and there isn't going to be another freshman year for you as there was when you graduated from high school. This is different. There's no plug for the cord; the apron strings are finally cut; and you're graduating as whole people. The problem is that most of the people you're going to encounter in the next few months and years aren't going to be whole; they're going to be broken, and I'm asking you to be menders, to heal the brokenness of the present generation. That's asking a great deal of you, but I do ask it—as a woman of other women, because women are uniquely gifted as healers.

I'm calling on you in a very special and desperately needed way, to be healers of the chasm which has come between intellect and intuition, conscious and subconscious minds, mind and heart.

We are meant to be whole creatures, we human beings, but mostly we are no more than fragments of what we ought to be, and the rift between conscious and unconscious mind has been slowly widening throughout the centuries. This gap is terrifying to some people, especially to men. It is so frightening that I have heard some men deny that it exists.

There is, too, the superstitious illusion of self-fulfillment. "I can't do this because I'm trying to *fulfill* myself." "This man isn't *fulfilling* me." "I can't feel free unless I *fulfill* myself." Whereas the paradox is that the only sure road to freedom and true personhood is self-abandonment—and I know this from experience. To write a book is an act of self-abandonment; to love a man is an act of self-abandonment; to listen to a friend, really and truly listen, is an act of self-abandonment. Think of the people you know who are most fulfilled, most free, most whole: I doubt if they waste time worrying about self-fulfillment. Probably they have learned through pragmatic observation that self-fulfillment turns out to be self-imprisonment. And it widens the rift between mind and heart; the heart does not know how to think in terms of self-fulfillment; the heart is made for love.

∽o∾

PAUL FREUND
Professor
Clark University

At commencement you wear your square-shaped mortarboards. My hope is that from time to time you will let your minds be bold, and wear sombreros.

❧

ROY WILKINS
Director, NAACP
Santa Clara University

What is integration of a people in a country such as America in the last quarter of the twentieth century? It is not the once popular "melting pot" conception of American society. It does not mean that a people loses its identity and takes on another. It does not mean assimilation. It does not mean that a race would lose its characteristics or cultural differences in an integrated society.

No, integration has to mean, in America, equality of each segment with every other segment.

If one citizen is not permitted, because of race or color or religion or national origin, to attain equal opportunity or achievement with other citizens of the country, then his group or religion does not have equality. It is below the status of other groups. . . .

To this struggle you will be asked to bring brains—technology, science, and the whole of human knowledge. It is a challenge that demands all of our energies, and there is no avoiding them because of their color.

❧

Shirley Chisholm
U.S. Congresswoman
Simmons College

I believe that the primary responsibility of the educated individual in our society is that he or she must translate the knowledge gained by the educational process into a commitment to share the opportunities which abound in this country. In other words, friends, your education has a context—not just a political one, but a social one and a moral one. Often when I look out into a youthful audience like this one and anticipate your hopes and dreams, I am struck by the potential which exists. And I believe that the key to maintaining social involvement and remaining idealistic throughout one's life is in maintaining a youthful attitude. The late Robert Kennedy, himself an example of young vitality, once defined youth in words which I believe are even more true today. He said, "Youth is not a time of life, but a state of mind, a temper of will, a quality of the imagination, a predominance of courage over timidity, of the appetite for adventure over the love of ease."

∾ତ∾

Studs Terkel
Journalist
Grinnell College

As we watch television's new and rising star, Richard Nixon, we are in a sense bearing witness—perverse though it be—to a being who can no longer tell right from wrong—if he ever could—whose fantasy has become reality. In short, someone who may possibly be autistic. We must ask ourselves the impertinent question: how was it possible that one such as he had been chosen as our commander in chief? We must ask ourselves the question: didn't we as a society become autistic and confuse our fantasy with reality? That we are number one among all people, that our way is the only way, and that there is no other. Surely Vietnam and Watergate did not evolve out of a vacuum. So it goes, if we have no sense of history. How can we recognize the challenge of now unless we remember the errors of then?

And when *they* say—they, up there—let's forget the past, let bygones be bygones, we must remember to say no. When they say let's put Vietnam behind us, we must remember to say no. When they say we must put Watergate behind us, we must remember to say no. When they say let's put all of our dark side behind, we must remember to say no so that we can better see the light that is within all of us.

It is difficult to be a young person today. It is difficult to be any kind of person today, but especially a young one, who feels there is more to life than things, more to life than making out in little boxes, ticky-tacky, little suburbs, ticky-tacky, and little country clubs, ticky-tacky, for the everlasting glory of the organization. Hush, little baby, don't say a word, Papa will buy you more than a mockingbird. Indeed, Big Brother will buy you an all-expense-paid round trip to Hawaii—if you behave.

But for the young person who will not behave, who insists there is more to life than this, who believes with the prairie poet that "youth when lighted and alive and given a sporting chance is strong for struggle," there are new adventures and new knowledge.

A few years ago, the phrase in vogue was "the silent majority." What an obscene phrase in an open society. To be silent is to be dead. The silent majority lies under headstones. To be alive is to be kicking. You know that piece old folk say: alive and kickin'. It isn't accidental. Much of folklore is based on truth. When a mother has a child inside her belly and she feels it kicking, she knows something is alive and aborning. When there is silence, there is terror. Silence is what the Germans of the thirties experienced, and what followed was inevitable.

This doesn't mean shouting from the rooftops, no. This doesn't mean defiance for defiance's sake, no. It means becoming aware of our possibilities, our individual possibilities and those of our neighbors—and our neighbors happen to live not in one restricted suburb or community. Our neighbors, in this small spaceship we all share—for better or worse—are all over this planet.

∽ᴑ∾

1978

Nineteen seventy-eight was a year of extreme weather and environmental disaster. In February, a horrendous blizzard with up to fifty inches of snow effectively shut down the northeastern United States; in Providence, Rhode Island, nearly five thousand cars were abandoned in the snow. If nothing else, the bad weather gave us all the opportunity to pretend not to read Mommie Dearest. In Alaska, a bomb exploded, spilling thousands of barrels of oil across the frozen tundra, and if that weren't enough, an American-owned supertanker, the Amoco Cadiz, broke up near Brest, in France, spilling countless gallons of oil along the French shoreline. Against this backdrop, at Camp David, Egyptian president Anwar Sadat, Israeli premier Menachem Begin, and Jimmy Carter signed a "Framework of Peace in the Middle East" accord following nearly two weeks of America-sponsored talks, preparing the way for a formal peace treaty between Egypt and Israel by the end of the year.

Affirmative action got a slap when the U.S. Supreme Court upheld a lower court order that required the University of California Medical School to admit a thirty-eight-year-old Caucasian engineer, Allan Bakke, who had protested that the medical school's minority-admission program had made him a victim of "reverse discrimination." Abroad, Jordan's King Hussein took a bride, twenty-six-year-old American Lisa Halaby. The body of Hubert Humphrey lay in state in the Capitol Rotunda. President Carter announced that his administration would raise the legal mandatory retirement age for most American employees to age seventy.

Abroad, the U.S. dollar plummeted. In Italy, former prime minister Aldo Moro was abducted; two months later, his body turned up in the center of Rome. The Pitti museum in Florence, Italy, was ransacked. Among the paintings stolen was Rubens's masterpiece The Three Graces. A second, much stranger ransacking: Charlie Chaplin's body, stolen from its grave in Corsier-sur-Vevey, Switzerland, was recovered and reinterred. In Rome, Pope John Paul I died after little more than a month in office. The following month, Karol Cardinal Wojtyla, the nearly sixty-year-old archbishop of Krakow, Poland, was named the first non-Italian pope of the Roman Catholic Church in nearly five hundred years. He took the name John Paul II. In the Soviet Union, Anatoli Shcharanksy, a leader of the Jewish emigration movement and a putative spy for the United States, was sentenced to a Soviet labor camp. In Lancashire, England, the first ever test-tube baby was born, weighing nearly six pounds. New York City suffered a newspaper strike of its three major dailies, including the New York Times, giving rise to the sudden appearance of tabloids with names like City News and the News World. Nearly three months later, the strike ended. American artist Norman Rockwell and anthropologist Margaret Mead both died, as did former prime minister of Israel Golda Meir. And in Jonestown, Guyana, more than nine hundred members of a group known as the People's Temple, led by the Reverend Jim Jones, committed suicide by drinking poisoned Kool-Aid.

Muhammad Ali lost to Leon Spinks, losing his title as the world heavyweight boxing champion. Bill Rogers, a thirty-year-old Massachusetts native, won the Boston marathon. Affirmed, ridden by Steve Cauthen, won horse racing's Triple Crown. In Tennis, Björn Borg, a limber, impassive Swede, won his third straight men's singles crown at Wimbledon; on the women's side, it was Martina Navritilova.

∽∘∾

ANTHONY LEWIS
Journalist
Williams College

Blindness to the humanity of other human beings—Jews or blacks or Asians or whomever—is a corrupting disease. Wherever it occurs, it endangers the peace and health not only of the victims but of those who close their eyes to the persecution. When Martin Luther King dreamt of being "free at last," it was freedom for whites as well as blacks.

Why is South Africa different? My point . . . is not about South Africa, but about us. An economist at the University of Capetown, Francis Wilson, explained to me why he stayed in South Africa. "The country," he said, "is us in microcosm. Each of us draws boundaries around himself and doesn't worry about those outside—the man in New Delhi does, the man in New York does. So it's not the good guys against the bad guys here in South Africa, it's the struggle within each of us."

Those of us who are not saints are bound to wonder, in the circumstances of this terrible century, what difference we can make. The belief that an individual can transform society is usually an illusion; newspaper columnists suffer from it, occasionally. But if wholesale transformation is unlikely, change does happen—and it usually comes because enough individuals refuse to live inside a compartment. Even in the overwhelmingly difficult circumstances of South Africa, one person can make a difference.

Do not turn your head away from injustice. Know the limitations of your country and yourself, but do not give up. Do not stop believing you can make a difference. Care!

∽○∾

EDWARD O. WILSON
Sociobiologist
Grinnell College

The reflective person knows that his life is in some incomprehensible manner guided through a biological progression, a more or less fixed order of life stages. He senses that with all the drive, wit, love, pride, anger, hope, and anxiety that characterize the species, he will in the end be sure only of helping to perpetuate the same cycle. Poets have defined this truth as tragedy. Yeats called it the coming of wisdom.

There has been an erosion of traditional religion and of the great ideologies, especially Marxism, which are the exact secular equivalents of religion. The price of this erosion of faith and failure of nerve has been a greater sense of helplessness about the human condition and a shrinking of concern back toward the self and the immediate future. The intellectual solution of the first dilemma can be achieved by a deeper and more truthful examination of human nature that combines the findings of biology, the social sciences, and the humanities. The mind must be more precisely explained as the product of the biological machinery of the brain. That machinery is in turn the product of genetic evolution in human populations that occurred over hundreds of thousands of years in the ancient environments of mankind. By a very careful extension of the methods and ideas of biology, a proper foundation can be laid for the social sciences, and the discontinuity still separating the natural sciences on the one side and the social sciences and humanities on the other might be erased.

JAMES V. CUNNINGHAM

Poet

Lawrence University

Endings need not be public, newsworthy events. Throughout your life, there will be many little endings, every day. It is these endings that somehow give shape to the fragments of your life that are called experience. And it is this "experience" that makes up one's life.

FRANCINE DU PLESSIX GRAY
Writer
Barnard College

In a world more and more polluted by the lying of politicians and the illusions of the media, I occasionally crave to hear and tell the truth. To borrow a beautiful phrase from Friedrich Nietzsche, I look upon my friend as "the beautiful enemy" who alone is able to offer me total candor. Friendship is by its very nature freer of deceit than any other relationship we can know because it is the bond least affected by striving for power, physical pleasure, or material profit, most liberated from any oath of duty or of constancy. With eros, the *body* stands naked. In friendship, our *spirit* is denuded. Friendship, in this sense, is a human condition resembling what may be humanity's most beautiful and necessary lie—the promise of an afterlife. . . . That marvelous Christian maverick C. S. Lewis tells us: "Friendship is unnecessary, like philosophy, like art, like the universe itself (since God did not *need* to create it). It has no survival value; rather, it is one of those things that give value to survival." And the great Jewish thinker Simone Weil focuses on the classic theme of free consent when she writes, "Friendship is a miracle by which a person consents to view from a certain distance, and without coming any nearer, the very being who is necessary to him as food."

‿oဟ‿

GEORGE PLIMPTON
Writer
Hobart and William Smith Colleges

We sense that you are all much brighter than we are. You speak a language that is almost foreign to us. You can read digital printouts. You know what astuteness reading is. And what is particularly disturbing is that you all come out at the same time—June—hordes with your dark graduation cloaks darkening the earth. Why is it, I ask, that you can't be squeezed out one at a time like peach pits?

Speaking as a writer who concerns himself largely with sport, I should warn you . . . that life has very little to do with the game. In J. D. Salinger's *Catcher in the Rye*, the English teacher says, "You must understand life is like a game," and Holden Caulfield says, "Yes it is, yes it is." But I think he's saying that to be polite, because in that intuitive wisdom of his, he knows better. Sports are fun and terribly important to us because they are an aside, a liberty. They are, as someone put it, deliciously ends in themselves. Even cads and cheats and decadents can play. There are no moral entrance requirements. No test for high seriousness. One of the difficulties is that the standards in sport are relatively clear compared to, say, the arts, and certainly life. Excellence is relatively uncontroversial as a judgment of performance, and that's what our appreciation of sports is mostly taken up with.

The judging of excellence in human performance in life is another matter.

∽∘∾

RAMSEY CLARK
Former U.S. Attorney General
University of Santa Clara

Graduations each year around the nation tend to take on a theme. And the theme this year, more than any others that I have heard, is of good times, even the best of times, how easy things are, and how much money we are going to make, and how happily we are going to live ever after. Particularly popular to compare this good year of 1978 with the worst of times ten years ago, 1968, when crime was paralyzing our cities with fear and the wildness and turbulence of our campuses seemed to drive reason off. The cities were in flames with the riots of those too long denied equality. The brutal and unbearable use of technology against life in Vietnam drove us to near distraction. But I suggest there was an element present then that is hard to find now. And it was an individual passion and belief that we can make a difference, that there are tasks to be done. The individual has a responsibility and a duty to act and work and exhaust himself in the effort to make this a better life for children.

Now look at 1978 briefly. Look at Europe. An authoritarianism rising in Germany. The trials of lawyers for representing unpopular people. Look at terrorism, the ultimate enemy of freedom. Shooting and killing and maiming in Italy; look at repression there clearly emerging. Look at the joy in France, as again its soldiers are being paratrooped from Zaire, as if nothing were learned from Indochina or Algeria. Look at Belgium, proudly marching down there again as if we cannot learn the lessons from history and are condemned to repeat them. Look at Asia, and wonder every day when the line between the north and south in Korea will be crossed and by whom, and what the consequences will be. Look at tyranny in the Philippines, that outpost of democracy where America had such an enormous investment. The terrorism of Marcos, whom we support, the guerrilla warfare on twelve islands, the repression of the Maryknoll priests and sisters, and all the rest. Look at Thailand, so similar to Vietnam in the early fifties and late sixties that you can hardly tell the difference; search and destroy, two-thirds of the provinces out of control. Look at Cambodia, with millions relocated, hundreds of thousands dead in the last several years. Beautiful, gentle Laos; look at the Plain of Jars, destroyed again. Afghanistan with a new military government, Bhutto on trial in Pakistan, with murder following conviction seeming inevitable; political vengeance. Look at India. Indira Gandhi emerging again. Latin America. The new military government in Peru the week before last. Argentina with ten thousand people missing, sixty disappearances the government will not acknowledge in the last week of May 1978. Pinochet with his heel on the throat of the people. Brazil, that great giant of human energy and imagination, under military government. Mexico, burgeoning with population and daily gunfire in the southern states. Africa, poor Africa, with all of its rich humanity: Idi Amin, Rhodesia, South Africa, and on and on.

And we think these are the best of times? Look at America. We turned our back on racism. Why is it that the overwhelming majority of our prison population is poor black? Does that make you angry? If not, then injustice does not trouble you. Why are Philip Berrigan and Allen Wood imprisoned today for opposing war and the war machine? What about Proposition 13—do we care? Do we believe in equality and justice and freedom in this society, or do we just want more comfort?

I am not worried about your economic future. I hope that does not seem insensitive to you, but look, this is a fat land. I am not worried about your economic future, I am worried about your moral vision and purpose. America has promises to keep. We are the luckiest people that ever lived, we have abundantly and manifestly the capacity to address human problems if we care. It is a matter of vision and courage and compassion. We can walk away from it, turn our backs on it, and if we do, God help this planet.

∽∘∾

1979

Nineteen seventy-nine was a year of political alliances and severings. The United States and the People's Republic of China formally opened diplomatic relations, and U.S. ties with Taiwan were formally ended. In Cambodia, the government of Pol Pot collapsed, and in Uganda, Tanzanian soldiers and Ugandan rebels toppled the government of Idi Amin. Exiled religious leader Ayatollah Ruhollah Khomeini returned to Iran from France. The shah of Iran, Muhammed Reza Pahlavi, left Iran ostensibly for a vacation, though many predicted, correctly, that he would not return. Later that year, the shah underwent gallbladder surgery and cancer treatment in New York City; by the end of 1979, he had relocated to Panama. And in Washington, Egyptian president Anwar Sadat and Israeli prime minister Menachem Begin signed a formal peace treaty that ended the thirty-one-year state of war between the two countries. President Carter served as a witness to the historic signing.

Elsewhere, the United States severed military ties with Nicaragua, and the Mexican government was openly critical of its relationship with the United States. Margaret Thatcher became the prime minister of Great Britain. Patricia Hearst was released from prison, having served slightly less than two years of a seven-year sentence for bank robbery. In the Caribbean, Saint Lucia gained independence from Great Britain. Good astronomical news: northeasterners viewed the last total eclipse of the sun they would witness until the year 2017, and the U.S. Voyager beamed down photographs of Jupiter. Bad astronomical news: Skylab, an unmanned U.S. space station, broke up in orbit, scattering debris over the Indian Ocean and southwest Australia. Earl Mountbatten, a war hero and a cousin to Queen Elizabeth, was *killed by an IRA bomb aboard his fishing boat off the Irish coast. Hurricane David left more than a thousand people dead, and in New York City, former U.S. vice president Nelson Rockefeller died of a heart attack under suggestive circumstances.*

The U.S. surgeon general, Dr. Julius B. Richmond, produced a report offering "overwhelming proof" that cigarette smoking causes lung cancer. Jane Byrne was the first woman ever elected mayor of Chicago. Lord Laurence Olivier was given an honorary Oscar at the Academy Awards ceremony, and in a California courtroom, Lee Marvin battled his former live-in girlfriend, Michelle Triola Marvin, over whether she was eligible for "palimony." Ultimately, the court denied her breach of contract claim. Spectacular Bid won the Kentucky Derby, and in Washington, some sixty-five thousand protesters marched from the White House to the Capitol in a peaceful demonstration against nuclear weapons. Domestically, the United States faced a gas shortage, with higher gas prices and long lines, and in car-crazy California, gas rationing was imposed in nine different counties. The estate of Karen Silkwood, a lab technician contaminated by radiation at an Oklahoma plutonium plant, was awarded $10.5 million. The Montreal Canadiens won the Stanley Cup, Pope John Paul II visited Poland, and actor-cowboy John Wayne died of cancer at age seventy-two.

∾᳁∾

ADRIENNE RICH
Poet
Smith College

We live in a society leeched upon by the "personal growth" and "human potential" industry, by the delusion that individual self-fulfillment can be found in thirteen weeks or a weekend, that the alienation and injustice experienced by women, by black and Third World people, by the poor, in a world ruled by white males, in a society which fails to meet the most basic human needs, and which is slowly poisoning itself, can be mitigated or solved by transcendental meditation. Perhaps the most succinct expression of this message I have seen is the appearance of a magazine for women called *Self*. The insistence of the feminist movement that each woman's selfhood is precious, that the feminine ethic of self-denial and self-sacrifice must give way to a true woman-identification, which would affirm our connectedness with all women, is perverted into a commercially profitable and politically debilitating narcissism. It is important for each of you, toward whom many of these messages are especially directed, that you discriminate clearly between "liberated lifestyle" and feminist struggle, and that you make a conscious choice.

∾

ART BUCHWALD
Newspaper Columnist
Georgetown University

It seems like centuries ago, but it was less than five years, that a president of the United States was forced to resign from office under the darkest of clouds, and he was asked to leave the office because he lied to the American people. I was at the White House that night to hear his resignation speech. And what impressed me more than anything else is that while one president was resigning, and another was taking his place, I did not see one tank or one helmeted soldier in the streets. And the only uniforms I saw that night were two motorcycle policemen on Pennsylvania Avenue directing traffic. Two hundred and twenty million people were able to change presidents overnight without one bayonet being unsheathed. And I believe that any country in the world that can still do that can't be all bad.

∾

E. L. Doctorow
Writer
Hobart and William Smith Colleges

When you get your jobs, you'll find that in the workaday world, you'll hardly ever be asked to perform at as high a level of accomplishment as was demanded of you as college students. In fact, the interesting suspense of your lives may very well be only how long, in whatever you do, it takes you to drop to the levels of prevailing practice. You may find that the ethical and intellectual standards of your parents and teachers seem quaint, or remote, and then inexpedient; and come to the conclusion that the more quickly you succumb to the sirens of incompetence, duplicity, conformism, the faster you will succeed.

You'll find yourself tending to take the point of view of the man or the institution who pays your salary. You will hear yourself laughing at his or her jokes a little more loudly than you laugh at any others. In return for this loyalty, you'll discover that you no longer have to define a moral issue apart from your own self-interest. If, for example, you work for a nuclear power company, you will righteously label that person a hysteric or possibly a radical who suggests that the concept of *permissible level of radiation* means the number of people you are willing to see die so that you may keep your job.

I think the point I'm making is that we all pay for our choices, and whatever life we choose determines the kind of payment we make. There really is a palpable moral component to our beings and it can be contaminated. Moral contamination almost never announces itself, it is always a very small, seemingly silent, inconsequential event, but it is like radiation, it accumulates, and there are no permissible safe levels.

∽∘∾

ELIZABETH DREW
Journalist
Reed College

If you think about life in terms of what you are going to do, what you are going to accomplish, you're leaving out big parts of it. Don't lose touch with your capacity to see absurdity, to laugh—including at yourselves—to enjoy, to take time out from striving, and just be. Don't lose touch with your capacity to love; in fact, nurture it, for you will find that it is something that can grow. Let yourself need people, and let them need you. Don't forget to take time out to look at the trees. If you do lose those things, you will have lost a great deal. And what are more commonly recognized by the outer world as accomplishments will have an emptiness.

∞

TOM BROKAW
Broadcaster
Syracuse University

You are the last class of this decade, the seventies, a curious time in American life. It began in turmoil. We were completing a convulsive period of risk-taking, experimentation, radical behavior on the right as well as the left.

Fifteen years of assassinations, bloody battles in the war against racial discrimination, another war that divided us deeply at home and cost us dearly in far-off jungles, a drug culture that confused our children and confounded their parents; a felonious vice president who had paraded before us as a model of piety; a president who promised to bring us together and then drove us apart with his disgraceful behavior, which ended with resignation.

It was stimulating, to say the least. It was in many ways the end of innocence, a milestone that coincided with the two hundreth birthday of the republic.

Generally, it left us so exhausted that when it began to wind down, we sat back and said to the world, "Go away. I'm not interested." Our exhaustion is reflected in so many ways: only about one in three voters bothers to show up at the polls on election day; for our popular culture we choose nothing more demanding than the reassuring repetition of disco rhythms or the escapist fantasy of *Star Wars*; our taste in journalism runs heavily to personality profiles and local television anchormen who are more at ease with a hot comb than with a typewriter. We gave life to a double negative: inactive disinterest.

I understand the temptation to shut it all out, to wish that the news would just stop. Well, there's nothing wrong with periodic personal relief, but the news would not stop entirely even if all of us willed it.

If television screens were to go dark and printing presses were to stop rolling, the world would not stop changing. There still would be the problems of racial discrimination, unemployment, overpopulation, nuclear proliferation. Those problems and all the others would not dry up. Indeed, they would grow at an alarming rate to the point where soon we would not be able to deal with them.

And so I suggest to you that a free press is an irreplaceable source of power to a free people. Further, I suggest to you that it is a fragile right that must be guarded zealously. I am counting on all of you to help.

∽o∾

TONI MORRISON
Writer
Barnard College

In your rainbow journey toward the realization of personal goals, don't make choices based only on your security and your safety. Nothing is safe. In the world of work, nothing is safe. In the world of family, nothing is safe. In the world of human emotions, nothing is safe. That is not to say that anything ever was, or that anything worth achieving ever should be. And I want to discourage you from choosing anything or making any decision simply because it is safe. Things of value seldom are. It is not safe to have a child. That is an extremely risky enterprise. It is not safe to want to be the best at what you do. It is not safe to challenge the status quo. It is not safe to choose work that has not been done before. Or to do old work in a new way. There will always be someone there to stop you. None of the things of real value are simply safe.

∽∾∾∽

JOSEPH CALIFANO
U.S. Secretary of Health, Education, and Welfare
University of Notre Dame

The question is this: how can we ensure that the knowledge we possess, our towering technological brilliance, will have decent, and not destructive, efforts?

For the last generation, that question took shape in the giant mushroom clouds that rose over the destruction of Nagasaki and Hiroshima.

For your generation, that question looms in the graceful hyperbolic silhouettes of the cooling towers at Three Mile Island. There, suddenly last March 28, technological genius threatened to melt uncontrollably into technological tragedy. There we have now created, however unintentionally, a huge container so filled with deadly radiation that it will be unapproachable for months, perhaps even years.

Nagasaki and Hiroshima were deliberate acts of wartime destruction. Three Mile Island was an accidental by-product of the peaceful use of nuclear power.

It is an ironic coincidence that on both occasions the question was expressed in nuclear terms. In fact, the question arises in many fields where our skill threatens to outrun our wisdom; not only in nuclear technology but in medicine, communications, agriculture, biology, and a host of other fields.

Will our scientific genius be informed with technological morality? Will technology—the commercial and industrial application of our scientific knowledge—be the servant of humanity, or its master?

Your generation will be called upon to ask and provide some answers to those central questions.

American science and technology, we should remember, has given the world the incandescent light, the automobile, surgical anesthesia, the airplane, hybrid corn and miracle rice, central air-conditioning, heart pacemakers, computers and television, the industrial assembly line—and human footprints laid forever on the windless surface of the moon.

If the march of technology also brought us traffic jams, crowded airports, mindless and debasing entertainment, unnecessary surgery, no matter: technology promised that human life, which for so many centuries had been "nasty, brutish, and short," could now be bountiful, comfortable, and long. Material progress might bring some inconveniences, but it posed few real dangers. What mattered was that technology promised to democratize plenty: to bring health and a comfortable standard of living to the many, not just to the few.

Today, as we stand in the long and foreboding shadow cast by the towers at Three Mile Island, that cheerful faith in the benevolence of technology seems naive indeed. The fire that warms can also burn.

∽o∾

1980

Can there be any person under the age of forty-five who doesn't remember what he or she was doing on December 8, 1980, when the news first broke that ex-Beatle John Lennon had been shot in New York City?

It was the culmination to a turbulent national and international year, a year in which Americans tried to put behind them memories of the political cynicism, as well as the focus on the self, that had marked the latter part of the 1970s, a time when a book on how to practice transcendental meditation topped the best-seller lists.

Domestically, a presidential race was heating up, while sitting president Jimmy Carter was forced to cope with the malfeasances of his roly-poly, beer-loving brother Billy, and later refused to participate in a televised debate between political opponents Ronald Reagan and John Anderson.

Elsewhere in the world, interferon was trumpeted as a natural virus-fighting weapon, and Indira Gandhi was restored as the prime minister of India. The Olympics got under way in Lake Placid, New York, and are perhaps best remembered for the five gold medals won by speed skater Eric Heiden. Dormant for over a century, Mount Saint Helens erupted in Washington State, and in response to the Ayatollah Khomeini's formal proclamation that the fifty-two Americans still being held hostage in Tehran would be kept under the control of militants and not taken into government custody, the United States severed diplomatic ties with Iran.

The Cold War dominated the news. As a result of the Soviet invasion of Afghanistan in the late seventies, as well as increasing tensions in the Persian Gulf, the U.S. Olympics Committee voted to boycott the Summer Olympic Games in Moscow, dashing the hopes of hundreds of homegrown athletes; ultimately, Canada, Japan, and West Germany would join the United States in the Olympics embargo. A massive transit strike in New York City closed down subway lines, causing millions of New Yorkers to rediscover the pleasures of walking and bicycling. Genuine Risk won the Kentucky Derby. Yugoslavian president Marshal Tito died. Miami, Florida, witnessed seventy-two hours of racial rioting, with nearly a thousand people arrested. President Carter declared a state of emergency when it was found that nearly a third of the residents in upstate New York had suffered some variation of chromosomal damage from Love Canal, a chemical dump site near Buffalo. Civil rights leader Vernon Jordan was shot and wounded in Indiana. Boatloads of Cuban refugees arrived in Florida and were promptly detained in a barracks in Arkansas, where some, angered at how long processing was taking, went on a rampage. Björn Borg won Wimbledon for the fifth consecutive time; in the women's finals, it was Evonne Goolagong Cawley. Bill Gates, a Harvard dropout, developed software known as MS-DOS, and sensibly decided to retain ownership.

"O Canada" was formally proclaimed Canada's national anthem. Sugar Ray Leonard defeated Roberto Duran, whose famous cry of submission—"No mas! No mas!"—was reprinted across the front pages of newspapers around the world.

But 1980 will be remembered, indelibly, as the year a former Beatle was killed by a fan. Returning from a recording session after a self-imposed hiatus from recording music, Lennon was gunned down as he opened the gate at New York City's Dakota apartment building on West Seventy-second Street, where he lived. Afterward, people stood in vigil in the chill of early December, holding candles and playing recordings of old Lennon-McCartney songs. It would be facile and insulting to the late President Kennedy to say that the moment of John Lennon's death left a mark as pointed as that of 1963. But culturally, it had a similar, time-stopping impact: for many, their youths had been wiped out.

∾⚬∾

ALAN ALDA*
Actor
Connecticut College

The best things said come last. People will talk for hours saying nothing much and then linger at the door with words that come with a rush from the heart.

We are all gathered at a doorway today. We linger there with our hand on the knob chattering away like Polonius to Laertes. Now remember, "Neither a borrower nor a lender be." And don't forget, "This above all: To thine own self be true."

But the very best things said often slip out completely unheralded, preceded by, "Oh, by the way." In real life, when Polonius had finished giving all that fatherly advice to his son—who probably wasn't paying much attention anyway—he must have said, "Oh, by the way, if you get into any trouble, don't forget you can always call me at the office."

As we stand in the doorway today, these are my parting words to my daughter. There are so many things I want to tell you, Eve.

The first thing is: don't be scared. You're being flung into a world that's running about as smoothly as a car with square wheels. It's OK to be uncertain. You're an adult in a time when the leaders of the world are behaving like children. Where the central image of the day is a terrorist one: humane concerns inhumanely expressed. And the only response to this is impotent fury. If you weren't a little uncertain, I'd be nervous for you.

Adulthood has come upon you and you're not all that sure you're ready for it. I think that sometimes I'm not ready for adulthood either—yours *or* mine.

The day before yesterday, you were a baby. I was afraid to hold you because you seemed so fragile. Yesterday, all I could feel was helplessness when you broke your nine-year-old arm. Only this morning you were a teenager. As I get older, the only thing that speeds up is time. But if time is a thief, time also leaves something in

*Copyright © by Alan Alda.

exchange: experience. And with experience, at least in your own work, you will be sure.

Love your work. If you always put your heart into everything you do, you really can't lose. Whether you wind up making a lot of money or not, you will have had a wonderful time, and no one will ever be able to take that away from you.

I want to squeeze things great and small into this lingering good-bye. I want to tell you to keep laughing. You gurgle when you laugh. Be sure to gurgle three times a day for your own well-being. And if you can get other people to join you in your laughter, you may help keep this shaky boat afloat. When people are laughing, they're generally not killing one another.

I have this helpless urge to pass on maxims to you, things that will see you through. But even the Golden Rule doesn't seem adequate to pass on to a daughter. There should be something added to it. Here's my Golden Rule for a tarnished age: be fair with others, but then keep after them until they're fair with you.

It's a complex world. I hope you'll learn to make distinctions. A peach is not its fuzz, a toad is not its warts, a person is not his or her crankiness. If we can make distinctions, we can be tolerant, and we can get to the heart of our problems instead of wrestling endlessly with their gross exteriors.

Once you make a habit of making distinctions, you'll begin challenging your own assumptions. Your assumptions are your windows on the world. Scrub them off every once in awhile, or the light won't come in. If you challenge your own, you won't be so quick to accept the unchallenged assumptions of others. You'll be a lot less likely to be caught up in bias or prejudice, or be influenced by people who ask you to hand over your brains, your soul, or your money because they have everything figured out for you.

Be as smart as you can, but remember that it's always better to be wise than to be smart. And don't be upset that it takes a long, long time to find wisdom. Like a rare virus, wisdom tends to break out at unexpected times, and it's mostly people with compassion and understanding who are susceptible to it.

The door is inching a little closer toward the latch and I still haven't said it. Let me dig a little deeper. Life is absurd and meaningless—unless *you* bring meaning to it, unless *you* make something of it. It is up to us to create our own existence.

No matter how loving or loved we are, it eventually occurs to most of us that deep down inside, we're all alone. When the moment comes for you to wrestle with that cold loneliness, which is every person's private monster, I want you to face the damn thing. I want you to see it for what it is and win.

When I was in college twenty-five years ago, the philosophy of existentialism was very popular. We all talked about nothingness, but we moved into a world of effort and endeavor. Now, no one much talks about nothingness, but the world itself is filled with it.

Whenever that sense of absurdity hits you, I want you to be ready. It will have a hard time getting hold of you if you're already in motion. You can use the skills of your profession and other skills you have learned here; dig into the world and push it into better shape.

For one thing, you can try to clean the air and water. Or you can try to make the justice system work, too. You can bring the day a little closer when the rich and privileged have to live by the same standards as the poor and the outcast.

You can try to put an end to organized crime—that happy family whose main objective is to convince us they don't exist while they destroy a generation with drugs and suck the life from our economy.

You can try to find out why people of every country and religion have at one time or another found it so easy to make other people suffer. (If you really want to grapple with absurdity, try understanding how people can be capable of both nurture and torture; can worry and fret over a little girl caught in a mine shaft, yet destroy a village and everyone in it with hardly the blink of an eye.) You can try to stop the next war now, *before* it starts, to keep old men from sending children away to die.

And while you're doing all of that, remember that every right you have as a woman was won for you by women fighting hard. There are little girls being born right now who won't even have the same rights you do when they grow up unless you do something to maintain them and extend the range of equality for women. The soup of civilized life is a nourishing stew but it doesn't keep bubbling on its own. Put something back in the pot as you leave for the people in line behind you.

There is plenty to keep you busy for the rest of your life. I can't promise you this will ever completely reduce that sense of absurdity, but it may get it down to a manageable level. It will allow you once in awhile to take a glorious vacation from nothingness and bask in the feeling that, all in all, things do seem to be moving forward.

I can see your brow knitting in that way that I love. That crinkle between your eyebrows that signals your doubt and your skepticism. Why—on a day of such excitement and hope—should I be talking of nothingness and decay? Because I want you to focus that hope and level that excitement into coherent rays that will strike like a laser at the targets of our discontent.

I want you to be potent; to do good when you can, and to hold your wit and your intelligence like a shield against other people's wantonness. And above all, to laugh and enjoy yourself in a life of your own choosing and in a world of your own making. I want you to be strong and aggressive and tough and resilient and full of feeling. I want you to be everything that's you, deep at the center of your being.

I want you to have chutzpah. Nothing important was ever accomplished without chutzpah. Columbus had chutzpah. The signers of the Declaration of Independence had chutzpah. Laugh at yourself, but don't ever aim your doubt at yourself. Be bold. When you embark for strange places, don't leave any of yourself safely on shore. Have the nerve to go into unexplored territory.

Be brave enough to live life creatively. The creative is the place where no one else has ever been. You have to leave the city of your comfort and go into the wilderness of your intuition. You can't get there by bus, only by hard work and risk and by not quite knowing what you're doing. What you'll discover will be wonderful. What you'll discover will be yourself.

Well, those are my parting words as today's door closes softly between us. So long, be happy.

Oh, by the way, I love you.

∽◦∾

ELIE WIESEL
Writer
Brandeis University

As a child, I lived in my own sheltered universe, shielded by my tradition and its legends of suffering and defiance; of the outside scenery I knew only the echoes of hate. We lived in parallel histories.

Now I know that human lives are not parallel; they form concentric circles, moving into the same direction, often at the same pace, to attain the same sense of fulfillment, power, or ecstasy. In other words: I have learned that human experiences, whatever their nature, must not be curtailed but shared; suffering itself ought not to become a prison but a vehicle. Despair is never the answer; despair is the question.

When I was your age, I had reasons to despair. Like most of my companions, I, too, was—for a while—tempted by silence. I, too, felt like surrendering. And giving up both on creation and its Creator. I thought: Night will last forever. Society has been—and will continue to be—unwilling to accept us Jews. Our children have been—and will continue to be—massacred, their parents humiliated, their old masters maimed, doomed. Why go on?

And yet. We choose to continue. How am I to explain this act of supreme affirmation on our part? I do not know. Like many other questions that I carry within me, this one, too, will remain unanswered. All I know is that somehow an entire generation has risen from the ashes, determined to build *on* and *with* ashes new homes for the homeless, new hopes for the dreamless.

❧

Francine du Plessix Gray[*]
Writer
Bryn Mawr College

Ritual is a complex system of structured gestures which provides a coherent affirmation of the reality about us, and thus reinfuses us with a heightened sense of our own identity and meaningfulness. In its deepest, most spiritual sense, ritual is a sequence of gestures which repeats a primordial act, such as the Christian rite of Communion, which symbolizes our brotherhood and sisterhood in sharing the body of the Godhead, or the rite of Passover, which symbolizes the miraculous survival of the Jewish people. Significant rituals are also those which fulfill our equally sacred need to reinfuse a family or a community with greater harmony and love. . . .

Recently, I ran across the most lugubrious example I've found to date of our renewed thirst for cult and ceremony. It seems that all over the nation, communities of teenagers and young adults are gathering at midnight on Saturdays to view a film called *The Rocky Horror Picture Show*. They chant litanic responses to the sound track, they hold lit candles in their hand, and some of them are seeing the film for the sixtieth, eightieth time in a row. In their desperate search for liturgical behavior, they're resorting to the most mechanical elements of ritual—mnemonic repetitions of sounds and gestures no more meaningful than disco dancing. *The Rocky Horror Picture Show* is one of the many cultic fads which prove how easily rite and ritual can be debased unto mere rote in a society deprived of genuine ceremonials.

∽∞∾

*Used by permission of Georges Borchardt.

JOHN KENNETH GALBRAITH
Economist
Haverford College

In the last few years, we have witnessed a celebration, even a sanctification, of self-concern. A person's highest duty, it holds, is to his own income. This attitude is a powerful attack on the least fortunate of our citizens. . . . Perhaps the disadvantages are now too few in the United States to make a revolution. But they could make life uncomfortable for all.

∽∘∾

THE LORD ANNAN
Member of Parliament
University of Pennsylvania

Never despise the acquisition of knowledge. However much the map of learning changes, you will find yourself at sixty living off some at least of the intellectual capital that you acquired when you were twenty. The kinds of things you thought important now, the conflicts, arguments, beliefs which you held or against which you reached, will mark you for life as belonging to the class of 1980.

∽∘∾

MAYA ANGELOU
Poet
Smith College

Courage is the most important of all the virtues because without courage you cannot be sure that you can practice any other virtue with consistency. So it is important to develop courage, the courage to love in an era, in a time, when love is almost synonymous with distrust, abuse, misuse, and in fact, negligence.

∾⚬∾

Pat Collins
Television Personality
Simmons College

I will leave you with one of my favorite quotes. "Through our great good fortune, in our youth our hearts were touched with fire." Oliver Wendell Holmes said that, and now I say it to you, not only for your benefit, but for my own. To begin with, that "fire" is only the start. To keep it there throughout a lifetime is the secret.

∾⚬∾

1981

A former actor named Ronald Reagan assumed the presidency of the United States on January 20, 1981, an electorate decision that ushered in not only an age of celebrity but an age of opulence and prosperity—at least (some critics noted) for the already rich. It was also a year in which the specter of a "limited" nuclear war hung gravely over the heads of American citizens, and election fanfare notwithstanding, the strained relations between the United States and the Soviet Union dominated the world's headlines.

By year's end, it had become clear that Reagan preferred to seek military answers to political differences of opinion, and European countries began to suspect that Reagan sought peace with the Soviets less than he sought to maintain the United States's hard-line dominance in the world. It had also become clear that the president didn't exactly suffer the poor gladly, as he commenced a series of maneuvers designed—or so it seemed to many critics—to punish the poor for being poor. Two assassination attempts made the news: the pope was shot by a Turkish terrorist in Saint Peter's Square, and in Washington, D.C., Reagan barely survived an assassination attempt by a depressive, baby-faced twenty-five-year-old named John Hinckley, who in the tortuous routes of his mind equated shooting the president with winning the heart of the actress Jodie Foster. That Hinckley won no hearts whatsoever—and ended up paralyzing White House press secretary James Brady, whose partial recovery later became a symbol for gun control—seemed evidence of a country, and a world, seriously out of balance. Elsewhere, violence continued in Northern Ireland. Bobby Sands, who had demanded that IRA inmates be recognized as political *prisoners and who refused any nourishment until authorities caved in to his demands, died in prison in Belfast.*

Nineteen eighty-one saw some sweet, nearly miraculous moments, too. In Poland, following a countrywide strike, the largest protest in Poland's history, a tentative agreement was reached between the Polish government and leaders of the labor movement, led by an unemployed electrician named Lech Walesa. Soviet dissident Andrei Sakharov ended a nearly three-week-long hunger strike following the Kremlin's decision to allow his stepson's wife an emigration visa to join her husband in the United States. After 444 days of captivity, the fifty-two American hostages were released on Inauguration Day and flown to Wiesbaden, West Germany. Egyptian president Anwar Sadat and prime minister Menachem Begin met in Alexandria to resume discussions regarding Palestinian autonomy. And Prince Charles of Great Britain finally took a bride, the seemingly diffident nineteen-year-old Lady Diana Spencer.

Elsewhere, Rupert Murdoch bought the Times *of London. U.S. postal stamps rose from fifteen cents to eighteen cents (by the end of 1981, it would cost twenty cents to send a letter). Journalism began its spiral into disrepute when Janet Cooke, a reporter for the* Washington Post, *agreed to return the Pulitzer Prize she had won for her moving but apocryphal story about a drug-addicted inner-city child. France elected its first-ever Socialist president, François Mitterrand. Elizabeth Taylor returned to Broadway in a production of Lillian Hellman's* The Little Foxes; *nothing stood between Brooke Shields and her Calvins; the character of Mad Max in* The Road Warrior *became a soot-faced apolcalyptic icon; and on June 12, baseball teams went on strike over the issue of free-agent compensation. When the season finally got under way in August, game attendance was down.*

Sandra Day O'Connor was nominated to the U.S. Supreme Court, and in the business world, E. I. du Pont de Nemours & Co. inaugurated what in the 1990s would become a frenzy of conglomeratization when it acquired Conoco. In New York City, Mark David Chapman was sentenced to twenty years to life for killing John Lennon.

✧

WILLIAM STYRON
Writer
Duke University

For free men, a hatred of communism should be as healthy and vital a response as breathing air. I think such a hatred has ever been of great political value in this country, since through the awful example of a captive society, we have sometimes energized our democratic institutions and perhaps even our capacity for generosity and brotherhood. But between hatred of communism and fear of it, as I say, there is a large and consequential difference. Fear of communism has more often than not poisoned us to our roots. Fear of communism degraded us by murdering Sacco and Vanzetti—whatever their technical guilt or innocence; fear of communism caused countless deaths and mutilations in the labor movement in the years before World War II; this terrible fear, inflamed by Senator McCarthy, turned friend against friend, wife against husband, brother against brother, and ruined the lives and reputations of hundreds of innocent men and women thirty years ago.

Most catastrophic of all, encouraged by industrial profiteers, our fear has led us into wars in places we never belonged, wars whose dismal outcome can show little or no gain, moral or physical, for the fact of our participation—hideous and bloody stalemates like Korea or, far worse, Vietnam, where thousands and thousands died utterly futile deaths, or returned home maimed and brutalized in body and spirit. We are still paying incalculable amounts—and not just in money—for that evil adventure.

I begin to feel that old unease when I see new manifestations of this fear. I see fear, for instance, on the face of Alexander Haig when he speaks, in nearly impenetrable language, of stopping the leftists in El Salvador or dealing with a worldwide Soviet terrorist conspiracy—a matter of doubtful reality. Those bulging eyes, those beads of sweat on the upper lip—this is truly craven fear, really, so desperately lacking in composure as to risk being called conduct unbecoming to an officer. Here let me not be misunderstood. Soviet power is as great and dangerous as our own, and I don't recommend for a minute that we relax a policy of vigilance, or that we assume the

Russians will not take advantage of any manifest weakness. What worries me is not that we will abandon our implacable opposition to communism, but that—like restless sleepers who mistake the threatening apparitions on the wall for corporeal monsters and strike out in aimless terror—we will confuse shadows with substance, as we have done so often in the past, and risk anew the old and lethal disasters.

∞∞

CHRISTOPHER LASCH
Sociologist
Middlebury College

Of all the divisions of historical time, the most arbitrary—and at the same time the most obviously indispensable—are the months and years of the calendar itself, which have no reference to events at all, yet unavoidably take on the coloration of the memorable occurrences with which they are associated in our minds. For some reason, American history, perhaps because it is so deficient in dramatic incident or because it is still so comparatively short, seems to be particularly susceptible to periodization by decades, which are the most unsatisfactory units of periodization of all—too short to be of any interpretive use, just long enough to retain a certain interpretive plausibility. . . .

Decades come in a variety of colors. Sometimes you get the impression that understanding American history has become an exercise in painting by numbers—the procedure in which the amateur artist simply applies a preselected color to a prescribed part of the canvas, instead of having to think about what he is doing or running the risk of making a mistake. We already have the Brown Decade, the Mauve Decade, and the Red Decade, and it shouldn't be too hard to fill in the rest of the landscape, now that we know the secret of how it is painted. . . . The seventies, of course, are the Me Decade; color them with skin tones, lightly bronzed by a judicious suntanning, with a healthy glow of overexercise left by jogging, ballet lessons, and other turns of strenuous self-improvement. The eighties? Too soon to tell, but the dominant colors so far seem to be red, white, and blue, raised aloft by something called the Moral Majority.

You see how easy it is to paint by numbers. Unfortunately, such paintings never convey much to the viewer aside from the sense of having seen them before. Unlike real works of art, they don't teach us to see the world around us; indeed, they prevent us from seeing it by distracting us with standardized images of familiar and immediately recognizable shapes, which we think we know better than we know them in fact.

Our collective understanding of the past seems to be failing even though our technical ability to re-create the past has reached an unprecedented level of development. Photographs and motion pictures and recordings, new techniques of historical research, the computer's total recall provide a rich documentary record of the past. We live surrounded by records, if anything overwhelmed with documentary evidence, bombarded by more information about history—and about everything else—than we can possibly assimilate. In some ways life today is like life in a museum. But then, that is exactly the point: once the past has been mummified, it no longer has any living connection with our experience today.

The notion of decades now allows us, in effect, to make instant history out of the present—that is, to make history *immediately* irrelevant to our present needs, without waiting for the slow passage of time. Formerly it took years—dare I say decades—to brew a good hot cup of nostalgia. Today you just add water and—presto!—you have nostalgia in five seconds: instant oblivion to everything in the past except for the sentimental afterglow. This new mixture, this latest wonder of modern technology, is every bit as refreshing as the waters of Lethe themselves, but just as poisonous in its effect on our collective memory.

Elizabeth Holtzman
Politician
Simmons College

Think of the sword of Damocles that now hangs over us as well as the rest of the world. We now have the capacity in effect to drop nine thousand nuclear bombs on any adversary, including the Soviet Union. (Each of those weapons is more explosive than the Hiroshima bomb.) But the Soviet Union has the capacity to drop six thousand nuclear bombs on us. And the number of nuclear weapons on each side is constantly escalating.

Humanity, in the form we know it now, cannot survive a nuclear war. We must put an end to nuclear weapons proliferation and begin to eliminate the nuclear arsenals of all nations. The threat of nuclear holocaust must be removed.

Silence in the face of injustice and wrongdoing encourages that injustice and fuels that wrongdoing. If *you* don't speak out, who will?

If I have talked to you about serious things, it is because I take seriously the high accomplishments that this day represents, and because you need to know how much your country is counting on you.

∾∘∾

Shirley Chisholm
U.S. Congresswoman
Mount Holyoke College

Be as bold as the first man or woman to eat an oyster.

∾∘∾

JANE BRYANT QUINN
Writer
Middlebury College

Let me tell you what I think is your chief risk. You risk becoming prisoners of your own vocabularies. For example: You may shake your head at your father the banker because you know in advance what he, as a banker, thinks about government spending. You may shrug off farmers because without even talking to them, you know that they favor higher farm-price supports. You know that a drug company executive thinks that the rules on new-drug testing are unreasonably burdensome. You know what a journalist thinks of the First Amendment . . . and a very fine amendment it is indeed.

Mark Twain said, "You tell me where a man gets his corn pone, and I'll tell you what his opinions are."

But all these people, the bankers, the farmers, the industry or political stereotypes, were once college graduates, like you, half listening to a commencement speaker and wondering what would happen to them. What happened is that they went into a particular business, learned its ways, and became its prisoner. A prisoner of its vocabulary.

Right now you are new graduates with minds supposedly open to many ideas and points of view. The great danger ahead is that when you enter an industry or a profession, your mind will pick up its ideas, then close, and sink like a stone. As an intellect, you may vanish without a trace. The next generation of students will perceive you as stereotypical bankers, ecologists, journalists, drug industry executives. You will have become the narrow-minded adults whose existence you once failed to understand. You have no idea how easy it is to pass that way, and how many of you will choose it.

Hannah Arendt wrote that the "inability to think is not a failing of the many who lack brain power, but an ever-present possibility for everybody—scientists, scholars, and other specialists in mental enterprises not excluded. . . ." "A life without thinking," she wrote, "is quite possible . . . but it fails to develop its own essence—it is not merely meaningless; it is not fully alive."

Our greatest living philosopher—Snoopy, in the cartoon strip

Peanuts—says that no problem is so big or so complicated that it cannot be run away from. As you grow older you will see all around you people running away from open inquiry. People who have learned to enjoy the simple art of doing without thinking.

I urge you to keep alive the spirit of inquiry which, with any luck, you have learned here. I urge you to keep your circle of acquaintance wide, so that you will always have fresh points of view. I hope that you will listen to your critics. If you can't answer them adequately, maybe they have something. I pray that you will worry if you start sounding like everyone else you know.

You are seeking what Dorothy Sayers called "the integrity of mind that money cannot buy; the humility in the face of the facts that self-esteem cannot corrupt." Put more crudely, where you stand should not depend on where you sit.

∽〇∾

Sam Nunn
U.S. Senator
Emory University

It has often been said that if we but educate the world's people, we will have *happiness* and *peace*. Modern history has proven, however, that education alone is not enough. In 1939, the Germans were among the most educated people in the world. Students flocked to the Third Reich for greater learning. Yet the Nazis who ruled Germany ultimately not only destroyed themselves but very nearly destroyed the civilization of Europe.

No—education does not develop your character until it merges with integrity and wisdom.

Yes—the future of our nation will be affected by our education, our wealth, and our technology, but our survival as a free society will be determined by our *wisdom*, our *integrity*, and our *character*.

The great football coach Vince Lombardi said, "The test for this century is whether we mistake a growth of wealth and power for a growth in strength and character."

During the Korean War, General William Dean was captured by the Communists, taken to an isolated prison camp, and told that he had only a few minutes to write a letter to his family before his execution.

"Tell our son, Bill," he wrote to his wife, "the word is 'integrity.'" He did not say "wealth" or "power," he said the word is "integrity."

∽o∼

VERNON JORDAN
Civil Rights Leader
University of Pennsylvania

I do want to say a few things to you directly. The first is to apologize for the world into which you graduate. It is in many ways a mean world: the superpowers rattle rockets at each other; television brings us, between commercials for expensive cars and clothing, pictures of some of the earth's starving millions; people still judge other people by the color of their skin; pockets of hate still pollute our human environment; and right here in the shadow of this great university, well over one out of five black people are out of work.

Yes, it is in many ways a mean, mean world. But it is not much different from the world we entered, and in some ways it is a better world. When I returned home after my college graduation, it was to separate drinking fountains, the back of the bus, and the denial of basic constitutional rights.

So the world has changed. Not nearly enough, but it has changed. And it changed because in the midst of that meanness, buried deep within the caves of injustice, there was the throbbing of the human spirit, the determination by millions of individuals that wrong is something to overcome, not to tolerate.

And so, many wrongs were overcome. The many that remain are ours together to overcome. But the prime responsibility must be yours, for you enter this brave new world unscarred by the battles we have fought, undaunted by the obstacles we have faced, and unburdened by the many myths we were taught to believe.

Your commencement marks the beginning of your acceptance of

what the writer James Agee called "the terrific responsibility toward human life."

You now share that responsibility fully. You are adults. You are our peers. From today onward, you will shape your own lives and your own destinies.

And you will help shape our nation's destiny—and the world's. I ask that you give to your children a better world than we give to you. I ask you to temper your striving for material success, for the glitter of things, with the drive to overcome injustice and misery that still stalk our nation and our planet.

I ask you to remember the worlds of Edward Everett Hale, who wrote:

> I am only one,
> But still I *am* one,
> I cannot do everything,
> But still I can do something,
> And because I cannot do everything,
> I will not refuse to do the something that I can do.

⋘⋙

Sissela Bok
Professor and Writer
Princeton University

My point of departure [is] the biblical injunction for those who go out into the world to be "wary as serpents and innocent as doves." To be wary and innocent, or as other translators of the Bible have expressed it, cunning and guileless: this seems to be paradoxical advice. Ordinarily, we think of the wary and the innocent as quite separate types of persons, each in their own way bound for pitfalls, either of excessive self-concern or of naive vulnerability. But if we try to unite these two qualities, and to strive for them jointly, then we see that together they delineate a state of integrity or whole-ness—the capacity to be wary enough to remain unharmed, and innocent enough not to produce harm; and we come to see that one is not truly attainable without the other.

∽୦∾

JAMES OLSON
Vice President of the Board, AT&T
DePauw University

Ladies and Gentlemen: Start your engines.

∽୦∾

1982

War, or the potential for war, was everywhere in 1982, concentrated not just on the Falklands (known in South America as the Islas Malvinas) but on Iran and Iraq, Israel and Lebanon, the United States and the Soviet Union.

The madness of the previous year's assassination attempts, as well as the iconic notion of the lone crazy, suggested that the illusion of control that many of us maintained about our world was just that, and that America's reputation as the land of freedom and opportunity had unleashed a peculiar type of homegrown lunacy; our faceless, fractured, overcrowded society seemed to have engendered an individual whose predominant desire was to be noticed. In the Midwest, someone laced bottles of Extra Strength Tylenol capsules with cyanide beads, killing seven people and forcing a recall of some 250,000 bottles. After being found not guilty by reason of insanity for shooting President Reagan, John Hinckley was remanded to a mental hospital in Washington, D.C. The antinuclear movement flowered across America and into Europe, at one point drawing five hundred thousand protesters into New York City. Unemployment was skyrocketing in the United States, the jobless rate affecting at one point 10.8 percent of the population.

In England, Princess Diana gave birth to a little boy, giving Prince Charles an heir. Claus von Bulow was found guilty on two counts of attempting to kill his heiress wife, Sunny von Bulow, who still rests in a coma in a New York hospital (later the verdict would be overturned on appeal). In Salt Lake City, a retired dentist named Barney Clark received an artificial heart. In Atlanta, a shy, bespectacled black man named Wayne Williams was convicted of the murder of two black boys, *though he was suspected in the deaths of many more. Lech Walesa was released from prison in Poland, though in response to continuing Soviet-backed martial law there, Great Britain joined the United States in imposing diplomatic sanctions against the Soviet Union. Leonid Brezhnev died and was replaced by Yuri Andropov. President Reagan announced that the draft would resume for eighteen-year-olds.*

Show business began to dominate our culture in a way it never had before. Released in the summer of 1982, Steven Spielberg's E.T. had moviegoers sobbing in their seats, and "E.T.—phone home" became a national mantra. In an adjoining theater, Sylvester Stallone's Rambo captured the fanatical attention of teenage boys. Actors Henry Fonda and Ingrid Bergman died, as did Princess Grace of Monaco, who was killed when the car she was driving went off a steep road in the hills above Monaco. The body of thirty-three-year-old John Belushi was found in a bungalow of the Chateau Marmont on Sunset Boulevard, a room that to this day certain guests still request in perverse homage.

But the sheer bizarreness of the Falklands War riveted national and international headlines. For the right to fly its flag, England unleashed a ferocious naval assault on the relatively small—eight-thousand-square-mile—cluster of islands, after Argentina had seized control of the Falklands, claiming they were part of its "national patrimony." The aftereffects: hundreds of Argentinian lives lost, and a somewhat dubious British victory.

The World's Fair opened in Knoxville, Tennessee, and the Dow Jones Industrial Average ended the year at 1,072.55, a record.

∽∘∾

Frances FitzGerald
Writer
Sarah Lawrence College

This is a piece of advice my father gave me when I was graduating from college. Actually, come to think about it, it came a couple of years after I'd graduated from college and was still lollygagging around quite unable to decide what I wanted to do. He said, "You must find a commitment."

At the time, I thought this was the most useless piece of advice I'd ever heard, because a commitment comes and finds you. But I didn't forget it, and it came to me most sharply after I was lucky enough to be found by a commitment. Because I then realized that it made all the difference. It's the difference between trying to, I don't know, push a piece of spaghetti through a tube and being pulled along.

I thought about my father's advice again while I was doing an article about a retirement community in Florida. The most depressing thing about this retirement community had nothing to do with age. It had to do with the fact that most of the people there had not found any fulfillment in their work. These people couldn't wait to retire—to retire and play golf. They had had jobs, and many of them had very good jobs, but they had no work. And so in later life they had nothing to do.

Here comes my piece of advice: watch out, watch out, as you go along, that what you're doing is not merely a job, not merely a career, but your work, the thing that you really want to do.

❦

DAN QUAYLE
U.S. Senator
DePauw University

As we seek discipline, whether it be in the arms race or the budget or assuming responsibility, a very useful guide to implement discipline is to demand of ourselves truth and reality. I happened to grow up in a newspaper family. Indelibly impressed upon me when I was a child, an adolescent, and even today, was to tell the truth. When people are dishonest, families are broken, individuals are ruined, governments are toppled. Many people today say that this country is going to hell, but as Hobbes said, "Hell is realizing the truth too late."

❦

Mother Teresa
Humanitarian
Georgetown University

Love begins at home—right there. And we must love until it hurts. And how do we begin to pray? God speaks in the silence of the heart. Listening is the beginning of prayer.

∽∘∾

Christopher Dodd
U.S. Senator
Connecticut College

Social responsibility . . . It's not a burden to be reluctantly shouldered. It's simply an invitation to enjoy life. "Not to participate fully in the action and passion of times," Oliver Wendell Holmes Jr. once wrote, "is to risk the judgment of not having lived at all."

∽∘∾

Elie Wiesel
Writer
Hobart and William Smith Colleges

You, for four years, were convinced that everything could be transmitted in words—philosophy, history, ethics, literature; it's words. Not true. There are experiences that cannot be transmitted in words, and I know something about it.

My friends, I could live my whole life and tell you only one sentence again and again, that one million Jewish children were killed. If I and you together would do nothing else but read their names, we would die before coming to the end of the list. Why? I don't know why. All I know is it happened.

Therefore, learn something from it, my friends: that culture is not enough, civilization is not enough; there must be an ethical dimension to whatever you study. Never accept abstractions as the ultimate truth. There is no such thing. If you take a human being and you turn that human being, him or her, into an abstraction, you will have no respect for that human being. Ultimately, you have already discarded her or his existence. On the contrary, take abstract notions and bring them closer to the living, to all living.

You have civil wars, dangerous wars in the Falklands, medieval wars in Ireland, and so many evils threatening us, but, my young friends, it is up to you. It is up to you to change, to disarm evil. In spite of what I lived through, I do have faith, and in spite of the fact that I know I cannot talk, I must talk, I must talk; I must share. I must tell you how great, how compassionate, how just the human being must be. It is our only hope.

∽◌◠

TED KOPPEL
Broadcaster
Syracuse University

You should be warned that it becomes increasingly easy, as you get older, to drown in nostalgia. In fact, you can almost measure where you are in life by the degree to which you have begun looking back, rather than ahead. Some, among the very old, lose themselves in the past, presumably on the grounds that they no longer care . . . or dare . . . to look ahead. Some, among the very young, lose themselves entirely in the future, presumably on the grounds that there is always promise in the unknown. Both are illusions.

Time doesn't pass—we do, hurtling across the face of a continuum. A snap of the finger is the passing of a generation. That snap of a finger is the span of your lifetime . . . and the difference between youth and middle age, or the passage from middle age to what is poetically referred to as the winter of our lives. And *what* you remember—or the fact that you remember it—is not necessarily indicative of how important it was. . . .

We are (and I know how depressing a thought this can be), we are more alike than different from one another. We—your parents, your grandparents, and I—are simply at different stages along the same journey as you.

Study us well. Among our number you will find Idi Amin and Mother Teresa, Ian Paisley and Isaac Stern, and if you look very closely, you will also find yourselves twenty or thirty or forty years from now.

Take comfort from the fact that we all know loneliness and sadness; draw strength from the fact that we are all subject to temptation and guilt. Take pride in the fact that, for all that universality, each of you carries within him or her a spark of uniqueness.

ॐ

1983

The world wasn't quite finished with terrorism yet. Dozens of people were killed in April of 1983 when a car bomb exploded in front of the U.S. embassy in Beirut. Later, in the same country, a truck bomb razed the U.S. Marine barracks, killing nearly 250 servicemen. There were bombings in Pretoria and Kuwait and Tyre, and during the height of the Christmas season, a car bomb exploded outside Harrods, London's upscale department store, killing five people.

As if taking a cue from Great Britain's invasion of the Falklands in 1982, American forces invaded the small Caribbean island of Grenada in October of 1983. In September, A Chorus Line became the longest-running show in Broadway history, having chalked up nearly four thousand performances. The art world lost many of its greatest practitioners, including Tennessee Williams, George Balanchine, and Ira Gershwin. Audiences flocked to see Meryl Streep and a surprisingly nuanced Cher in Silkwood. Karen Carpenter died of what would later be revealed to be anorexia nervosa. Troubled anchorwoman Jessica Savitch was drowned when her car slammed into a shallow canal. Sally Ride became the first American woman to travel in space, aboard the space shuttle Challenger. Gandhi swept the Oscars. The Cabbage Patch doll was by far the hottest commodity of the Christmas season, and a record television audience tuned in to the final episode of M*A*S*H. Rainstorms and mud slides devastated Malibu beachfront property owners. Elizabeth Dole was named to the Reagan cabinet as the new secretary of transportation. One hundred and twelve days after his artificial heart transplant, Barney Clark died at the University of Utah Medical Center.

In Germany, chemical tests revealed that Hitler's diaries, excerpted in Germany's Stern *magazine, were a hoax. The National Commission on Excellence in Education issued a brief report declaring that "a rising tide of mediocrity" in American high schools threatened America's future. Philippine opposition leader Benigno Aquino Jr. was assassinated at the Manila airport; his opposition-party followers pointed an accusing finger at the Marcos government.*

The most optimistic moment of 1983 came when Pope John Paul II visited his native Poland and met with former Solidarity leader Lech Walesa. Two months later, Polish leaders suspended martial law in Poland and released all political prisoners. In October, Walesa, the founder of Poland's trade union, Solidarity, was awarded the 1983 Nobel Peace Prize.

Back at home, two members of the House of Representatives were censured for sexual misconduct with congressional pages. Greyhound bus drivers went on strike for nearly two months. In Kansas City, Missouri, television news anchorwoman Christine Craft was awarded half a million dollars in a sex discrimination suit she had filed against station KMBC-TV, claiming she had been held back because of her age, her looks, and her inability to subjugate herself to the boys' club. A Korean Air 747 traveling from New York to Seoul was shot down after crossing into Soviet airspace; 240 passengers and 29 crew members were killed.

By the end of the year, Christine Craft's $500,000 jury award had been overturned.

∽○∾

Margaret Atwood[*]
Writer
University of Toronto

The year will come when you will wake up in the middle of the night and realize that the people you went to school with are in positions of power, and may soon actually be running things. If

[*]Copyright © 1983 by Margaret Atwood. Reprinted by permission of the author.

there's anything more calculated to thick men's blood with cold, it's that. After all, you know how much they didn't know then, and given yourself as an example, you can't assume they know a great deal more now. We're all doomed, you will think. You may feel that the only thing to do when you've reached this stage is to take up nail biting, mantras, or jogging, all of which would be recognized by animal behavior specialists as substitution activities, like scratching, which are resorted to in moments of unresolved conflict.

When faced with the inevitable, you always have a choice. You may not be able to alter reality, but you can alter your attitude toward it. As I learned during my liberal arts education, any symbol can have, in the imaginative context, two versions, a positive and a negative. Blood can either be the gift of life or what comes out of you when you cut your wrists in the bathtub. Or, somewhat less drastically, if you spill your milk you're left with a glass which is either half empty or half full.

What you are being ejected into today is a world that is both half empty and half full. On the one hand, the biosphere is rotting away. The raindrops that keep falling on your head are also killing the fish, the trees, the animals; and if they keep being as acid as they are now, they'll eventually do away with things a lot closer to home, such as crops, front lawns, and your digestive tract. Nature is no longer what surrounds us; we surround it, and the switch has not been for the better. On the other hand, unlike the ancient Egyptians, we as a civilization know what mistakes we are making and we also have the technology to stop making them; all that is lacking is the will.

∽〇∾

MERYL STREEP
Actor
Vassar College

Why did you ask me here to speak? What do you think I know? Or what do I represent that you want to know about? When I asked myself that, I said, "OK, you represent success to them. You went to

Vassar, got out, and did what you wanted to do, and are richly rewarded for it. Two Oscars, two kids, almost. They asked you here to speak because they imagine you know why this happened to you. They imagine it could happen to them, too, and please, could you please tell them how to set things up so that it does? Also, some of them would like to know how tall Dustin Hoffman is, and what does it feel like to kiss Robert De Niro? (You'll never know.)

What I would like to tell you about today is the unsuccessful part, unsuccessful in that I'm not finished with it yet. That is ... the investigation of my motives along the way, the process of making choices, and the struggle to maintain my integrity, such as it is, in a business that asks me to please just trip it off sometimes. I know I started from home with an advantage. My father's romantic heart and my mother's great, good common sense gave me a head start. But what you can take away from Vassar is a taste for excellence that needn't diminish. Sometimes I've wished it would go away, because some so-called important scripts are so illiterate, and the money is so good, that I've been tempted to toss all my acquired good taste and hustle. But there's always the knowledge, and this *is* from experience, that the work itself is the reward, and if I choose challenging work, it'll pay me back with interest. At least I'll be interested, even if nobody else is. That choice, between the devil and the dream, comes up every day in different little disguises. I'm sure it comes up in every field of endeavor and every life. My advice is to look the dilemma in the face and decide what you can live with. If you can live with the devil, Vassar hasn't sunk her teeth into your leg the way she did mine. But that conscience, that consciousness of quality, and the need to demand it, can galvanize your energies, not just in your work but in a rigorous exercise of mind and heart in every aspect of your life. I firmly believe that this engagement in the attempt for excellence is what sustains the most well-lived and satisfying successful lives.

Integrate what you believe into every single area of your life. Take your heart to work, and ask the most and best of everybody else too. Don't let your special character and values, the secret that you know and no one else does, the truth—don't let that get swallowed up by the great chewing complacency.

∞

WYNDHAM ROBERTSON
Former Assistant Managing Editor, *Fortune*
Hollins College

I know what you are thinking: you don't know what you want to do. Well, who ever did at your age? A few lucky men and women who really feel called, as to medicine, the ministry, or I suppose even accounting. But most of you don't know what's available, or even if it's available, what it is. So you go into advertising—what do you actually *do*?

Here's my no-nonsense plan. Take a few years to find out what you want to do. Take as many as five. I know it sounds like a lifetime to you, but believe me, it isn't: I still have items on my list of "things to do today" that I put there in 1978. Go out and get some job that has at least a whiff of a future. Something about it should appeal to you. The organization does something that interests you, the job looks like a stepping-stone to something you'd like, the company would pay to train you for something you think you'd like, or, another very good reason, the business is growing. Stay at least a year; it will take you that long to learn enough to make the experience worthwhile. One exception to the year rule: don't work for a company whose management, for some good and serious reason, you don't respect. If just your boss is a louse, maybe you should hang in there.

Really, it is happiness I wish you. The fact is that people who have studied happiness—*Time* calls them happyologists—have found that a satisfying job is important for happiness, but not as important as a good marriage (for those who have one) or a good relationship with friends.

My favorite clue on happiness comes from Bertrand Russell, who said about fifty years ago: "The secret of happiness is this: let your interests be as wide as possible, and let your reactions to the things and persons that interest you be, as far as possible, friendly rather than hostile."

∽∘∾

Susan Sontag
Writer
Wellesley College

I would urge you to be as impudent as you dare. BE BOLD, BE BOLD, BE BOLD. Keep on reading. (Poetry. And novels from 1700 to 1940.) Lay off the television. And remember, when you hear yourself saying one day that you don't have the time anymore to read—or listen to music, or look at a painting, or go to the movies, or do whatever feeds your head now—then you're getting old. That means they got you after all.

I wish you love. Courage. And fantasy.

∽o∾

Lewis Thomas
Scientist and Writer
Connecticut College

We need in a hurry some professionals who can tell us what has gone wrong in the minds of statesmen in this generation. How is it possible for so many people with the outward appearance of steadiness and authority, intelligent and convincing enough to have reached the highest positions in the governments of the world, to have lost so completely their sense of responsibility for the human beings to whom they are accountable?

Their obsession with stockpiling nuclear armaments and their urgency in laying out detailed plans for using them have, at the core, aspects of what we would be calling craziness in other people under other circumstances.

∽o∾

TERRY SANFORD
University President
Emory University

One could contend that there have been worse times in American history—for example, the long, bleak winter of Valley Forge, when the world's new and exciting experiment of self-government hung in awful suspense; or the spring of 1862, when General McClellan was locked in mortal checkmate with General Lee, and the survival of our nation was in daily doubt. Or more recently, within the memory of most of the immediate families who are here today, one might cite the dark days of Pearl Harbor, when the Pacific fleet was wiped out in one swift attack.

Those were all bad times. Those were the times, as Thomas Paine reminded the patriots at Valley Forge, that tried men's souls. But in each of those times, as well as during the ordeal of the Great Depression of the 1930s, America had not lost its way, not lost sight of itself. It knew where it had to go. It knew what it had to do.

Now, in 1983, we are not sure who we are or where we are going, and do not seem to know what we have to do. The road signs point to "extermination of mankind." Our military leaders and commander in chief tell us, almost daily, that the Russians can blow us off the globe, and imply that they are likely to do so. They keep us scared. Instead of calm confidence in our system and sturdy determination that we can surmount our problems, they are frantically spending the bulk of our earnings for weapons and more weapons. I do not believe our leaders know how to avoid war. That is why it is the worst of times. . . .

The United States, rather than a natural and confident leader that stands above the turmoil and the crowd, has been behaving like one of the ruffians in the school yard. We have methodically reduced our status to that of being just one more of the big, mean, thickheaded troublemakers. By adopting such a belligerent posture, we have destroyed our capacity for leadership and have created for ourselves the image of an insecure and ineffective bully. . . .

"The Russians are coming" is a paranoia that has engulfed this great, strong, free people of America for more than fifty years. The dread of the Yellow Peril kept us from speaking to the people of

China for some forty years. This national hysteria was exploited by Joe McCarthy to make himself a national figure, and it is the rationale for the present mindless buildup of military overkill. It is a blinding fear. Why should the people of the United States react in blindness to any challenge?

Instead of lurking behind the edge of the school building, peeking around the corner, picking up brickbats, looking nervously over our shoulders, screaming at the little ones who will not cluster around us with their own little pile of rocks and broken bottles, we should be walking across the yard with boldness and confidence in the sure knowledge that we were created to be a leader, not just another one of the pugnacious bullies of the school yard.

∽∾∾

E. L. Doctorow
Writer
Sarah Lawrence College

We are in thrall to our own bomb.

The time may be approaching when we will have to choose between two coincident reality systems: the historical human reality of feeling, of thought, of multitudinous expression, of life and love and natural death; and the suprahuman statist reality of rigid, ahistorical, censorious, and contending political myth structures that may in our name and from the most barbaric impulses disenfranchise 99 percent of the world's population from even tragic participation in their fate.

We've got to watch ourselves.

You may trust that I wish, that we all of us here wish, this wasn't the character of our age or the nature of our obligation on this day of your commencement. We are all here under this tent, this most ancient of structures, and it is indeed possible it may rain for forty days and forty nights. But there is a chance that it may not. And this is my good news. The presumption of your collegiate life here, the basic presumption, is that every life has a theme. It is a literary idea, the great root discovery of narrative literature—every life has a theme and there is human freedom to find it, to create it, to make it victorious.

You are in charge of yourselves: that is the underlying principle of the education you have received.

You may not have realized it, and we are somewhat embarrassed to have to say it, but willy-nilly and ipso facto, you commence this day in the name of civilization.

∽◦∾

ROBERT THURMAN
Professor and Writer
Hampshire College

Let me remind you that every day, today and every tomorrow, is an end in itself. We get so preoccupied with progress and responsibility, with getting somewhere and doing something; it can be another self-defeating form of self-preoccupation and we never somehow do catch up with the fact that we are here. And sometimes the trick of getting to a cherished goal on some final day . . . is to live fully each day to the full as an end in itself.

∽◦∾

JAMES LOVELL
Astronaut
Western Montana College

Every generation has the obligation to free men's minds for a look at new worlds, to look out from a higher plateau than the last generation. When I circled the moon and looked back at the Earth, my outlook on life and my viewpoint of Earth changed. By holding up my thumb at arm's length, I could completely blot out our planet. I suddenly realized how insignificant we are.

CORETTA SCOTT KING
Activist and Writer
Denison University

I hope you have a sense of the responsibility you have inherited.

You are the generation God has chosen to save this planet from destruction. Beyond the hallowed halls of this great university, a world in chaos is moving inexorably toward the final crisis. The situation is increasingly desperate, but not hopeless. As Martin Luther King Jr. said, "Every crisis has both its dangers and its opportunities." Our hope is that you who are graduating will seize the opportunity to make us a new world where peace, prosperity, and justice are secured for all people.

It is no exaggeration to say that the survival of humanity in this nuclear age depends on your generation. The great groundswell against the arms race that we have seen in recent years has been energized by people of your generation. People of all age groups have taken part in protesting this insanity, but I believe the young people have infused the moment with a new vitality.

The nonviolent civil rights movement which revolutionized American society was in many ways a youth movement. When Martin Luther King Jr. began his career as a civil rights leader during the Montgomery bus boycott in 1965, he was just twenty-five years old. Nine years later, he became the youngest person ever to win the Nobel Peace Prize.

In 1957, nine young black students braved a vicious gauntlet of angry, rock-throwing racists to integrate an all-white high school in Little Rock, Arkansas. James Meredith had a similar experience when he tried to integrate the University of Mississippi in 1962. So did the black students who faced George Wallace at the doorway of the University of Alabama in 1963. Students who are that determined could have gotten a good education somewhere else. Yet they risked life and limb for justice and for their brothers and sisters who would come after them.

༄ঔ

1984

Nineteen eighty-four failed to unravel as George Orwell had once imagined it would; though as Orwellians liked to point out, the author had chosen those four numbers simply by fooling around with the numerals 1948—the year he wrote about Big Brother. Instead, 1984 was dominated by a historic competition for the White House that saw incumbent president Ronald Reagan challenged not just by the Reverend Jesse Jackson—the first African American to make a serious run for the U.S. presidency—but by Walter Mondale and his running mate, a New York congresswoman named Geraldine Ferraro.

Jackson made a credible showing; and despite feminist pride about Ferraro, as well as countless editorials about how far American society had advanced, it soon became clear that toughness in a man was seen as advantageous, whereas toughness in a woman was viewed as rankling. By the end of the year, Ronald Reagan, who for many had taken on the role of a benevolent, armchair father from the West, had been reelected in an almost comical landslide.

Elsewhere, the U.S.-supported Contra forces made little headway against the Nicaraguan government, and as the year drew to a close, many American citizens found themselves dreading a war with a country few could even locate on a map. In India, Indira Gandhi was assassinated as a reprisal for the slaughter of hundreds of Sikh separatists; wary of her many enemies, the prime minister was doubtlessly surprised to find the fatal bullet emanating from one of her own bodyguards. Her son Rajiv was elected as her successor. In Britain, coal miners went on strike, and in Canada, Brian Mulroney was elected prime minister, replacing Pierre Trudeau, who stepped down after sixteen years in office.

Tensions continued between the United States and the Soviet Union. Though 1984 witnessed no arms control negotiations—Reagan failed to meet with Yuri Andropov's successor, Konstantin Chernenko—the defense budgets of each country continued to rise.

Nineteen eighty-four witnessed some good moments, too. Bishop Desmond Tutu, an outspoken opponent of apartheid in South Africa, was awarded the Nobel Peace Prize. The Winter Olympic Games took place in Sarajevo, Yugoslavia, a terrain the world would revisit, brutally, some fifteen years later, while the Summer Olympics were held in Los Angeles. The U.S. Supreme Court decided that noncommercial home use of video recorders did not violate federal copyright laws, thus opening the door to a thousand hastily scribbled sides of boxes tucked away in dark closets. Another Kennedy died, this time David, a son of the late senator Robert F. Kennedy, who was found dead of a drug overdose in a Florida hotel room. NATO marked its thirty-fifth anniversary. Vanessa Williams relinquished the title of Miss America after it was learned that several over-the-top nude pictures of her would be published in a men's magazine; less than twenty years later, when Williams had become a highly successful singer, pageant officials would ask her to host the proceedings (Williams said no). In Los Angeles, John De Lorean was found not guilty of charges that he'd sold cocaine. Moviegoers applauded Splash, *a movie about a beached mermaid; and in Chicago,* Donahue *was trounced in the ratings by* A.M. Chicago, *hosted by a newcomer named Oprah Winfrey.*

Nineteen eighty-four ended when Bernhard Goetz, a thirty-seven-year-old Manhattan resident, admitted to police that yes, he was the vigilante who earlier that month had opened fire on four teenagers who were mocking him on a subway train.

∞

MARIO CUOMO
Governor, New York
Iona College

It's clear to us that all the newly won power over space and time, the conquest of the forces of nature, the fulfilling of age-old challenges have not made us any happier or surer of ourselves.

We have built rockets and spaceships and shuttles; we have harnessed the atom; we have dazzled a generation with a display of our technological skills. But we still spend millions of dollars on aspirin and psychiatrists and tissues to wipe away the tears of anguish and uncertainty that result from our confusion and our emptiness.

Most of us have achieved a level of affluence and comfort unthought of two generations ago.

We've never had it so good, most of us.

Nor have we complained so bitterly about our problems.

The closed circle of pure materialism is clear to us now—aspirations become wants, wants become needs, and self-gratification becomes a bottomless pit. . . .

Do we have the right to tell these graduates that the most important thing in their lives will be their ability to believe in believing? And that without that ability, sooner or later they will be doomed to despair?

Do you think they would believe us if we told them today what we know to be true: that after the pride of obtaining a degree, and maybe later another degree, and after their first few love affairs, after earning their first big title, their first shiny new car, and traveling around the world for the first time, and having had it all, they will discover that none of it counts unless they have something real and permanent to believe in?

Tell me . . . are we the ones to tell them what their instructors have tried to teach them for years?

That the philosophers were right. That Saint Francis, Buddha, Muhammad, Maimonides all spoke the truth when they said the way to serve yourself is to serve others; and that Aristotle was right, before them, when he said the only way to assure yourself happiness is to learn to give happiness.

CHARLAYNE HUNTER-GAULT
Television Reporter
Grinnell College

I would be willing to bet that you have already had some experiences in having to perform delicate balancing acts. It is the quest not simply for a just balance that has preoccupied me from my college days; it is the quest for a total just balance. And it has become the focus of both my professional and private life because, over time, I have become profoundly convinced that a just balance is indispensable both to the conduct of one's personal affairs as well as to one's approach to a modern world that is often as frustrating in its folly as it is fascinating and rewarding in its genius and generosity....

It was Gandhi who articulated a formula for a just balance in describing the seven big sins of life. He said the first is "wealth without works." The second is "pleasure without conscience." The third is "knowledge without character." The fourth is "commerce without morality." The fifth is "science without humanity." The sixth is "worship without sacrifice." And the seventh is "politics without principle."

∽o∾

JULIUS LESTER[*]
Writer
Hampshire College

We live in a society and culture which does not value the quality of living. We are told that our reason for being is in achieving, and we are exhorted to do, to achieve, to create the great works of art, conceive the wonder drug that will cure illness and conquer death. And this passion to achieve infects everything we do, even our politics. Certainly it pains and angers many of us that our country should

*Copyright © 1984 by Julius Lester. Used by permission of the author.

provide such a safe haven for racism, anti-Semitism, sexism, poverty, and the many other assaults on our humanity. And the elimination of these becomes simply another goal to be achieved. And sometimes it seems as though many of us will be satisfied with nothing if we do not achieve Utopia. And we become obsessed by the desire to change the world, and never get around to assuming the almost unbearable responsibility for our own lives. But that is one of the dangers of a college education . . . a college education directs our attention to the heavens, and we forget that it is on the earth, in the mud and the rain as well as the sun, that we live. . . .

How can we be kind? Martin Luther King Jr. said that it is our responsibility not to knowingly add to the evil in the universe. This is such a simple statement, and we could delude ourselves into thinking that we understand it. But to take such a statement seriously means being wholly conscious of what we do in each and every moment of each and every day. It means being responsible for ourselves and our relationships, even the most casual ones, in such a way that we can be reasonably sure that if we have not increased the amount of good in the universe, we have not added to the evil. But it is possible to do this only to the extent that we accept our capacity for evil and accept responsibility for that capacity.

I would like to suggest that our appetite for achievement in the personal and political realms must be balanced by an active nondoing, by love of and passion for the useless, for that which has no social or political utility or application. It is in the realm of nondoing that we approach the counter pole to doing, which is Being, with a capital *B*. Only in Being can we find identity—that identity which is beyond race, beyond sex, beyond sexual orientation. "Identity in this deep sense," writes Thomas Merton, "is something that one must create for himself by choices that are significant and that require a courageous commitment in the face of anguish and risk. Identity is one's witness to truth in one's life."

∽∘∾

Jane Alexander
Actor
Sarah Lawrence College

The high-tech age that we have feared so much is actually going to free us enormously. I remember how amazed I was as a child when I once saw the Bible written on the head of a pin, in a museum (well, maybe not the whole Bible). Now, and in the years to come, the knowledge of the world will be available to me at the touch of my finger. What a space and time saver, and as it is estimated that fully 90 percent of the population may be engaged in informational occupations by the year 2000, it means there will be many options open in ways to live our lives. Do I wish to work in the north woods of Maine and rise at dawn to sit at my computer, or do I want the camaraderie of office life in a small community where pets and children aren't allowed but there is a common interest in quilt making?

Anxiety in the high-tech computer age has resulted in a confusion about values. What does endure? What do we carry with us into the future from our now-outmoded past? Are there any taboos left? Is there a morality? The spiritual vacuum many of us feel is an expression of this confusion, as is the rise of the new religions— many of them involved with being born again, or a resurrection of the old Christian values in the New Age.

Movies and plays lately have found heroes in our space cowboys, our pioneers to other galaxies, and in the gallantry of the afflicted of our society (*The Elephant Man, Children of a Lesser God*) and the terminally ill.

Next they dealt with our anxiety about the nonfeeling creatures we might become in the high-tech futuristic age. Films such as *E.T.* dispelled our fears; no matter how the human species may evolve in the future, *E.T.* assures us we will remain cuddly. One of the great lines in modern filmmaking must be "E.T.—phone home," because it is a reaffirmation that the old values will endure: the need to be rooted with those things we know and love best. There is currently a spate of movies on this theme, the forty-thousand-year-old-man in *Iceman*, Tarzan in *Greystoke*, the forthcoming *Starman*, to name a few; they are all different facets of us: aliens in a new environment, longing to be home again. . . .

The computer may store my bank account, my files, my writing, and even my reading someday, but it will not store the pictures of my family, or the drawing my niece made of her baby brother; those treasures will remain on my wall. Nor can I replace the bracelet Jane brought me from India, or the letter Tina wrote me on opening night, or the laugh of my husband. These things are unique to me and my perception of them. Love is the touchstone of the human experience, and it endures. We can count on that.

∞○∾

Barbara Kennelly
U.S. Congresswoman
Mount Holyoke College

I do *not* want to hope that one of you will be the first woman vice president. I do want to hope that long before you reach the age of eligibility for either vice president or president, the barriers will have been broken and the responsiveness of women to serve will have become so pervasive that we can stop speaking of *firsts* and insist that only our *best* be considered for high office.

∞○∾

Dan Rather
Broadcaster
Syracuse University

One of the things we are trying to conserve is the generous, compassionate spirit of American idealism.

James Agee captured it in his description of the old lady he talked to when he was doing his marvelous Depression piece *Let Us Now Praise Famous Men*. He found her out in the hollows of Appalachia— little shack with dirt floors, no heat, no plumbing. Agee asks the woman, "What would you do if someone came along and gave you some money to help you out?" Old lady rocks in her chair and shakes her head. She's thinking. Finally she nods and said, "I guess I'd give it to the poor."

That's the essence of the American spirit, that old lady, that generosity; that's our wealth, that's what we must all commit ourselves to conserving.

In the course of perpetuating our revolution and conserving the true spirit and wealth of this great country, large questions abound about the future of our public policies and the goals we should set for our society. They range from how best to prevent annihilation of the planet while defending ourselves to whether a college education should be the right of every qualified student.

Questions such as these demand the best thinking of our society.... I hope that those of you who are graduating today will recognize the investment you have in these public questions, and the responsibilities you have to our freedoms, and that you will devote an appropriate part of your talents to them. That you use your judgment, good sense, and perspective that you have developed at this university.

∞∞∞

HOWARD BAKER
U.S. Senator
Dartmouth College

I would like to see us stop selling candidates as if they were soap. I'd like to see the theatrics of political commercials eliminated. I'd like to see candidates on television talking to the American people, soliciting their support on the basis of merit and policy rather than enthralling them with Wagnerian music and Spielberg cinematography.

It may be too much to hope that Americans, so well conditioned by television, will base their political choices on issues rather than imagery, but it is not too much to ask that they have that chance.

It is not too much to ask that we begin consciously to reward civility and punish hostility in our political process, that we commit ourselves again to union as well as liberty in our national life, that we subdue the sense of narrow self-interest and restore our sense of nation.

We are not enemies but friends. We must not be enemies. There is animosity aplenty in this world without Americans attacking and destroying each other for political advantage or any other reason.

∽o∾

ROBERT COLES
Psychiatrist and Writer
Beloit College

Abraham Lincoln did not go to Gettysburg having commissioned a poll to find out what would sell at Gettysburg. There were no people with percentages for him, cautioning him about this group or that group or what they found in exit polls a year earlier. When will we have the courage of Lincoln?

∽o∾

ATHOL FUGARD
Playwright
Georgetown University

The level of our daily lives, one man or woman dealing with another man or woman, is finally the central arena of history.

∽o∾

Neil Simon
Playwright
Williams College

My first piece of sage advice is this: When you leave here today, it is *vital* that you take off those long black gowns. Very few businesses are going to hire someone applying for a job wearing a long black gown. Those who intend to go into medicine will find you will immediately lose your patients' confidence if you are examining them in a long black gown, wearing a pancake hat with a tassel hanging from it. Especially during operations—patients coming out of sodium pentathol, seeing a man over them wearing black, tend to have coronary occlusions. Future airplane pilots will discover passengers rushing for the exits when they see the captain getting into the cockpit in a long black gown and clutching a diploma. . . .

Advice number two: Upon leaving this day, do not tell any faculty member you think he's a creep. Faculty members have relatives everywhere. . . .

Advice number three: Do not take any classrooms with you. Mementos are nice, but try to leave the school the way you found it. Along this line, may I add, do not take home any girls that do not belong to you. For one thing, it is uncouth, and for another, she may one day be your employer.

Number four: When you return home to what you might call "civilian life" after four years away, there will be a certain period of adjustment. Therefore, you might want to look around and notice how the styles in clothing have changed since you left. People in big cities today tend *not* to wear their sweaters around their ankles. You don't have to drop completely the casual style of attire you've been used to, but you may want to start wearing shoes on the right foot as well as the left.

Number five: Studies have proved that students returning home after four years away at college tend to get agoraphobia when having to sleep in a room with less than fourteen people in it. If it's difficult at first, sleep in a YMCA dormitory for a few days, then try a small hospital ward with four to six people until you're ready to come back to a room of your own.

Number six: Do not take the very first job that's offered to you. Panic will only land you behind the counter at McDonald's. On the other hand, show some humility; don't walk into Chrysler and ask if they're looking for a replacement for Mr. Iacocca. . . .

Number seven: You are not obligated to marry the last person you had a date with.

Number eight: Those who intend to enter the highly competitive business of writing poetry should not expect to get rich quick. There is, of course, good money in poetry, but that's mostly because you save a good deal by not sending out your laundry or having to live in an apartment with heat. . . .

There is one last bit of advice I'd like to leave you with, and for this we move into more sobering territory. In an effort to find a phrase or a word that I would like to pass on as inspirational, I thought about what best expressed the theme of my own life. Passion! It's the force that has governed and motivated all my energies, that has given me the discipline that is mandatory to all creative efforts, and without it, life seems to me rather bleak and dismal.

In the play *Amadeus,* Salieri, the court composer, realizing young Mozart's genius when he hears his music for the first time, contemplates his own mediocre gifts by comparison and confides to the audience, "Is it enough just to have passion?" My daughter Nancy, who saw the play and was quite affected by it, talked to me about her own aspirations, and questioning her own abilities and talent, asked me the very same question: "Is it enough just to have a passion?" My answer was: "It's not only enough. It's everything."

∽∘∾

LORET MILLER RUPPE
Director, Peace Corps
University of Notre Dame

The entire question of peace—that beautiful five-letter word which we all treasure and say we crave—is up for grabs in the eighties. Is peace simply the absence of war, or is it really the absence of conditions that bring on war? The conditions of hunger, illiteracy, despair. . . .

When 50 percent of the children in a village die before they are five . . .

When a child dies of dysentery or measles for lack of medical attention . . .

When a woman, for lack of a well, has to walk five miles to a stream for water and then search for several hours for wood to cook with . . .

When a farmer or villager has no source of income . . .

When a village's youth and men flee to the cities which have no jobs for them . . .

When rain forests are stripped and no planting done . . .

When millions of refugees languish homeless . . .

When the latest news broadcast tells you that 150 million people only an ocean away are on the edge of starvation.

Then let's face it, America, the world is not at peace.

∽ perhaps ∽

1985

In 1985, the leaders of the two most powerful nations in the world finally agreed to a summit meeting to discuss arms control. Live Aid, a rock 'n' roll extravaganza filmed in Philadelphia and London and designed to raise money for African famine victims, proved to be one of the best rock concerts ever staged. The Titanic was discovered in the cold murk of the North Atlantic (a finding of which director James Cameron certainly must have taken note). And Rock Hudson died in a Paris hospital of AIDS.

Still, 1985 will be remembered, largely, as a year of continued terrorism.

Two attacks in airports in Rome and Vienna; a jetliner hijacked to Beirut by Lebanese Shiite Muslims; and in October, the Italian cruise liner the Achille Lauro, hijacked by Palestinians. Airplanes operated by Air India and Air Japan crashed. There were allegations of Soviet spying; among those charged, Americans John Walker and Richard Miller. Domestically, Ronald Reagan and George Bush began their second term in office. In March, following Konstantin Chernenko's death, Mikhail Gorbachev was named chairman of the Soviet Union's Communist Party; the lightning bolt on his forehead (actually, a birthmark) seemed mystical to a populace eager for any omens of where the arms control talks would go, though with the announcement of a planned summit in Geneva, Americans found themselves optimistic that perhaps the world might not disintegrate before their eyes after all. Meanwhile, President Reagan got himself in hot water in May of 1985 by visiting a German military cemetery in Bitburg, West Germany, containing, amid other graves, the remains of approximately fifty SS officers; blithely Reagan then continued on to Bergen-Belsen.

Rock Hudson's death cannot be minimized as a turning point in how Americans perceived the AIDS virus. It engendered a national call and response on a variety of topics: not just closeted actors and concealed sexuality, but about how AIDS failed to differentiate between the famous and the not famous. Hudson, after all, had romanced Doris Day in the movies. Elsewhere, Yul Brynner died of lung cancer, though not before taping a series of potent antismoking commercials that seemed to emanate from the grave. Coca-Cola introduced new Coke, then hastily withdrew the product when it flopped with consumers. Princess Diana continued to charm the world. In Illinois, an alleged rapist named Gary Dotson got his sentence commuted by the Illinois governor after his alleged victim, Cathleen Webb, claimed she had falsely accused him. In what would become a harbinger of confrontational television, the two appeared together on daytime television, with TV personality Phyllis George memorably enjoining them to "hug." Retried in Providence, Rhode Island, with countless stories swirling around him, Claus von Bulow was found not guilty of trying to murder his heiress wife, Sunny von Bulow.

By the end of 1985, Ronald Reagan and Mikhail Gorbachev met in summit in Geneva, Switzerland. Both men termed the talks promising.

∽∘∾

FRED ROGERS
Children's Television Host
Hobart and William Smith Colleges

All through our lives there are resignations of wishes. As children, once we learn to walk, we must resign ourselves to not being a baby anymore. If we just want to be taken care of and not make any effort to grow and do more and more for ourselves, then we can avoid that resignation and just stay a baby. . . .

In fact, you can see the excitement in children. As a child grows from creeping to standing up and walking . . . it's as though all of that child's energies are bound into that huge task of getting up and walking. Once that task is accomplished, once they're on their own two feet, they get this exciting surge of development in other areas. It's as if they are obsessed with that one task, and until it's accomplished, they can't concentrate on anything else. That's an enormous human task: standing upright and walking on our own two feet!

৵০৵

BEVERLY SILLS
Opera Singer
Smith College

Women are told today that they can have it all: career, marriage, and children. And I would like to tell you that if the word "all" means career, marriage, and children, then you can have it, but someone is going to pay for it. This "all" can bring you every kind of fulfillment, excitement, fun, rewards, but you really have to make a total commitment to making it work. You will need lots of give, lots of compromise, lots of humor. . . .

So, you can have it all, but there are two keys to this kingdom. The first is that you have to believe in yourself and you have to know that you can make it work. And the second is love. You're going to have to ooze it from every pore. You're going to have to love your work passionately—love it enough to feel it's worth the nightmare of days that are twenty-nine hours long. You're going to have to love your husband so that when he complains about your twenty-nine-hour day you will have the patience to soothe him, the desire to comfort him, and the ability to turn your twenty-nine-hour day into a thirty-hour day. The last hour for him alone. And you are going to have to love your child and not just hear its needs, but feel its needs, touch and hold and never let that child feel that anything is more important to you in the whole world. So what if the day is now thirty-one hours long? You can sleep in your old age if you live long enough to enjoy it.

৵০৵

Katharine Hepburn
Actor
Bryn Mawr College

Now here I am—I opted for myself—without children. I didn't feel I could do a great job on the kids if I worked. Right? Wrong? Who can say? But I do know, you just can't have it all. So I chose for myself, and I think I chose correctly. I chose to pig it.

∽०∾

Beverly Sills
Opera Singer
Dartmouth College

We must stop referring to the government as "they." They is us. This is not a monarchy. Those people in Washington are there by our good graces. If we like what they are doing, we should keep them there, and if we don't, we should get them out. We should let them know that we are watching them and that we know who they are. Therefore, it's quite important for us to know the names of our senators, our congressmen, our state senators, and our councilmen—all of them. You may feel that one voice, when a thousand are needed to make things change, is not enough. But you are wrong. One articulate voice can attract a thousand more. It is important for one of you out there to be that voice. You may feel that one vote when thousands are needed to make things happen is not worth the trouble to use. Use it and influence others. We are consumers and we can boycott the product. Don't be angry but be passionate. It is terribly important that you care about someone or something, but you must care to "help Charlie get his share." There are people who like to stick their heads in the sand. They forget that this only makes their backsides a bigger target. So if you are one of those who prefer being a spectator, that is OK. Nobody knows better than I that audiences are indispensable to performers. But if you are one of those people who like to get into the center of the ring and fight the bull in every sense of the word, I suggest you do it, because you can change the world.

∽○∽

PEARL BAILEY
Entertainer
Syracuse University

I do the best I can, always. Always. There was a wonderful lady in the theater called Sophie Tucker. She said to me once—I was young then . . . (Somebody just fainted over there. Listen, I wasn't born this tall, honey. I once was young.) "It ain't how good you are, Pearl." (And she did not mean me alone. It's you, out there.) "It's how long you can last."

I have got a friend now who is sick with double cancer. Double. On both sides. And I told her this story one day, and she laughed, this courageous woman. She said, "So right, Pearl. But may I add something to it?" She said, "You got to be *good* to last." That is the answer.

∽○∽

THOMAS WINSHIP
Editor and Writer
Marlboro College

You folks out there are needed like never before. I want to see all of you find genuine fun out of life. And the best formula for having fun is to be involved and useful—possibly even at a living wage. I have some ideas for you.

Become a journalist in some form or other. . . . For effecting change, zest, people helping and people watching, nothing can touch journalism. Is it hard to get a job on TV or on a newspaper? It sure is, but if the determination is there, so is the job. I know.

If you are a computer whiz, offer yourself to government, on the city, state, or national level. You will have more fun and make almost as much money as in the private sector. The computer is here to stay.

Go into the environmental protection business. It is a growth industry.

Go to graduate school. Borrow if you need to. Learn about aqua agriculture, fisheries management, or forestry, to name a few offbeat disciplines.

Man the refugee camps on the African and Asian fronts. Believe it or not, they pay in some of these lifesaving jobs.

Don't go to law school or into the investment business—unless you have limited talent and a lust for money. . . .

I have another piece of career advice, which came to me a few days ago from an unorthodox businessman friend. He is Warren Buffett, the investment genius who recently coughed up half a billion dollars to buy a piece of the ABC television network. I told him I was talking to graduates today, and asked if he had a thought for them. Without a moment's hesitation he said, "Tell them to go to work for the person they admire the most. Something good will come of it. Emulate your hero as best you can," he said. I like the thought.

There is nothing wrong with idealism, no matter what the cynics say.

⌘

DONALD REGAN
White House Chief of Staff
University of Pennsylvania

When you're born in America, so much comes free. By a lucky accident of birth, you inherit a brilliant and decent political tradition, you get a rich and varied culture, you get the freedom to make your own decisions, you get a society that still accepts the validity of spiritual beliefs and spiritual values—and you get all of this for free, just because you showed up. The way I see it, public service is a giveback.

⌘

1986

Turmoil in the Philippines (less, though, than might be expected), an end-of-year Icelandic summit between President Ronald Reagan and Soviet general secretary Mikhail Gorbachev, a nuclear accident at the Chernobyl power plant in the Ukraine, which spilled a cloud of toxic radiation into the atmosphere, and the explosion of the space shuttle Challenger were the major news stories of 1986, a year that will perhaps best be remembered for low-key political discord across the world.

It wasn't merely the transfer of power in the Philippines, the transition from the old rule of Ferdinand and Imelda Marcos (who fled the country after twenty contentious years of power) to the new, more soft-spoken rule of Corazón Aquino. It was also the transfer of power in Haiti, where President for Life Jean-Claude Duvalier, informally known as Baby Doc, was forced by antigovernment protesters to flee his country for France aboard a U.S. Air Force jetliner. It was also the presidential election in Austria of former U.N. secretary general Kurt Waldheim, who just three months earlier had been accused of having been a member of several Nazi organizations, as well as serving under a war criminal during the Second World War. It was also the shooting death of Sweden's prime minister, Olof Palme. And domestically, it was the charge that the Reagan administration had made covert arms sales to Iran, with the proceeds going to the Contras, rebels in Nicaragua. Yet with increasing public optimism over U.S.-Soviet relations, it must be admitted that none of these things felt unmanageable.

The explosion of the Challenger remains perhaps the enduring image of 1986. On January 28, the space shuttle lifted off into space, carrying among its seven-member crew a young, shaggy-haired schoolteacher from New Hampshire named Christa McAuliffe. One minute and thirteen seconds later, the Challenger malfunctioned and exploded in the sky, leaving a tail of smoke across the sky as frozen as the expressions on children's faces watching it. There really wasn't much to say.

Still, 1986 began promisingly, with Reagan and Gorbachev each delivering a five-minute-long message broadcast in each other's countries. Approximately two weeks later, in Geneva, the Soviets presented a proposal to ban nuclear weapons worldwide by the year 2000. That October, the summit in Reykjavik, Iceland, almost yielded a major arms control accord, but in the end fell apart over the issue of America's strategic defense initiative, better known, with turgid American playfulness, as Star Wars.

In the United States, Martin Luther King Day was for the first time officially observed as a major holiday. Vladimir Horowitz returned to the Soviet Union for the first time in sixty-one years. Nine people died in a blizzard atop Mount Hood in Oregon. A national extravaganza called Hands Across America, in which American citizens joined hands to create a chain across the fifty states, drew approximately five and a half million participants. Prince Andrew, the younger brother of Prince Charles, married Sarah Ferguson at London's Westminster Abbey. In Edmonds, Oklahoma, a part-time postal employee named Patrick Sherrill killed fourteen workers before turning the gun on himself. Nancy Reagan inaugurated a crusade against drugs and drug abuse, and Ivan Boesky agreed to pay a $100 million penalty for insider trading on Wall Street. Colonel Oliver North invoked the Fifth Amendment during a court appearance in which House and Senate investigators attempted to discover whether North had acted alone or with the consent of higher-ups during the Iran-Contra affair; the restoration of the Statue of Liberty was celebrated; and writer and activist Elie Wiesel was awarded the Nobel Peace Prize.

∾

TRACY KIDDER
Writer
Sarah Lawrence College

If you do feel a little worried, don't worry about being worried. You're heading out on an adventure, and you can always change your mind along the way and try something else. I know lots of people who have done that, and none I can think of who regret it. What some people I know do regret is the severing of connections between what they imagined themselves doing and what they've ended up with. Your generation has been advised repeatedly to go out and get an American Express card and have an interesting life. It's a tempting invitation, but in reality a cruel one. The odds don't favor your getting truly rich, not in your twenties, or your other decades either. And if you do single-mindedly pursue and achieve that state of grace, the unlimited line of credit, you may find you've thrown away that interesting life you were promised. You want work that is rewarding and altruistic, that is worth doing for its own sake, not just for the price it commands. The possibilities for that sort of work, for practicing craft, aren't especially numerous, but they aren't confined to such likely looking locations as the world of art either. Those opportunities can appear in unexpected places, and some of them, maybe the best of them, you have to invent.

∽◦∾

E. J. KAHN JR.
Writer
Marlboro College

I'm gloomily aware that however high the standards may still be in the academic world, in government, in business, and in many personal relationships, nobody seems to give a hoot anymore about ethical behavior, aside possibly from one taxi driver who the other day attemped to return to me the ten-dollar bill I had inadvertently passed along as a one. Practically everybody else I've made contact with lately seems far less concerned about an equitable distribution of the world's available assets than in the making of more and more money. I hope your generation can do something toward restoring balance and fairness and common decency to the nation's way of life. The generation just ahead of you certainly doesn't seem to have done it.

∽∽∾

LEE IACOCCA
Businessman
Duke University

Think for yourselves. Let me *repeat* it: *just think for yourselves.*

This isn't the first time you've heard it, but it's the *best* advice you'll ever get from me or *anybody* else.

By the way, you might just find it tough advice to take these days, because thinking for yourself doesn't seem to have much status anymore. Today, no matter what the problem, somebody has already worked out the solution, and *packaged* it.

If you're too fat, you can buy a thousand books to tell you how to get thin.

If you want to get rich, there are a million foolproof schemes.

And just think how lucky you people are—you've even got Dr. Ruth!

There's a little problem, though, with all these packaged solutions, *and* I should warn you about them: they generally only work for the people who *devise* them.

My generation's solutions worked fine for us, but they won't do much for you, I'm afraid. You'll have to figure out most of the answers for yourselves. My generation had to, and so will yours. . . .

When you think about it, we don't even have a *fundamental* ideology in this country. The genius of the Constitution is its tolerance of so many points of view and espousal of none. I don't think that's an accident. The Founding Fathers were too smart to try to tell us how to solve our problems, they just gave us a framework to work in. . . . You can read the Constitution all day long and you won't find a single answer to the big problems we face today. There's nothing to tell us how to protect the environment, whether we should trade with South Africa, what to do about the terrorists, how you put out a nuclear fire, *or how to compete in the world.*

We aren't leaving you a blueprint to solve your problems, but then nobody gave us one either. And if they had, it wouldn't have worked. Basically, we were on our own. And guess what? So are *you.*

∞∞

ELLEN GOODMAN
Journalist
Simmons College

I am told that you have spent the last weeks here in your two favorite occupations: worrying about the future and having as good a time as possible.

Well, as your emissary from the real world, let me tell you that all of this is pretty good preparation for postgraduate life.

I'll share a secret of that real world. This is what we do. Out here we function in the midst of doubt, we go through life adjusting and readjusting the course, questioning its value and our value. We go through life balancing work and play, our commitment to the present and the future, the short run and the long run. We may postpone pleasures and yet we are, as it says in the opening line of the traditional will, "mindful of the uncertainties of life."

It doesn't stop here. It doesn't stop today.

∞∞

DAVID MCCULLOUGH
Writer
Middlebury College

I want you all to go far.

I want you to see Italy, Florence in particular, at least once in your lifetime. I hope you can spend an hour in front of the great, incomparable Botticelli at the Uffizi—the *Birth of Venus*—an hour with that one painting, for the unparalleled pleasure of it, but also so you will have the experience to draw on whenever overtaken by the common hubris of our time, which is that our time outranks all others in all attainments. Botticelli lived five hundred years ago.

I hope by the time you are my age you will have been to Edinburgh, little Edinburgh, and walked its stone streets and read its great thinkers and considered their impact on our own Founding Fathers. And that you will be asking yourselves, as I do, how possibly so much creative vitality could have burst forth in so small and out-of-the-way a place and in such a brief span of time.

Why does a Florence happen? Why an Edinburgh? One explanation is that everyone was in touch with everyone—painters with lawyers, dramatists with engineers, philosophers with physicians. Quite the reverse idea, you see, from our age of specialization. Any suggestion that science and the arts are mutually exclusive would have been thought downright silly.

Go to Palenque—Palenque, the stupendous Mayan ruin in the beautiful Mexican province of Chiapas. Climb the long stairway of the central pyramid-tomb to the very top, and with the main palace and other monuments spread before you, try to keep in mind that what you are seeing is only a fraction of what once was and that all of it was built under the rule of one man who lived more than a thousand years ago, a king called Pacal, a name virtually unknown to North Americans, except for a handful of scholars, yet plainly one of the most remarkable leaders in the whole history of our hemisphere. He had to have been. You need only to see Palenque to know that.

I hope you go to Italy and Scotland and to places like Palenque because I think you will afterward see and understand your own country more clearly. That is an old idea, I know—that the country you learn most about by traveling abroad is your own—but then, some old ideas bear repeating.

∽∘∾

HENRY CISNEROS
Mayor, San Antonio
University of Texas at Austin

I visited with my dad a couple of weeks ago at home, and he had just come back from his high school reunion at Brighton High School in Brighton, Colorado, and he brought to me a paper that a woman had written for the graduation ceremonies there, and it really struck me. It struck me, what has occurred from 1936 to 1986, fifty years—just listen to this.

The lady writing the program for that event had taken time to write this piece. She said, "We were before television, before penicillin, polio shots, antibiotics, and Frisbees, before frozen food, nylon, Dacron, or Xerox. We were before radar, fluorescent lights, credit cards, or ballpoint pens. We were before computers, so, for us, time sharing meant togetherness, a chip meant a piece of wood, hardware meant a hammer, and software wasn't even a word." She goes on to say, "We were before panty hose and dryers and freezers and electric blankets, before Hawaii and Alaska became states. In our time, closets were for clothes, not for coming out of. Bunnies were small rabbits, and rabbits were not Volkswagens." She says, "We were before pizza, Cheerios, frozen orange juice, instant coffee. McDonald's was unheard of. We thought fast food was what you ate during Lent. We were before FM radio, tape recorders, electric typewriters, word processors, music, electronic music, disco dancing, and that may not have been bad."

Well, the point I'm making is when you stop and think on the sweep of change in that time period, your parents' lives, it says a lot of things. It says something about what the future may be. But to me it says a lot about what this country can absorb. There should be no fear, there should be no sense of self-doubt about it.

Mario Cuomo
Governor, New York
Syracuse University

In these hardheaded modern times, some people find it easy to dismiss the importance of dreams. As if, perhaps, they were the stuff of a softer, sweeter time. A time removed from the grim, world-shaking, myth-shattering events that seem to pursue us across our lives today—in headlines, broadcasts, the somber, always urgent tones of network anchormen. Libya, Chernobyl, deficits, South Africa, the danger of war, *Challenger* vanquished.

And don't believe it for a minute, graduates.

Of course there are problems.

But the truth is, there never has been or will be a time more suited for dreams.

All ages are the same when it comes to dreams. Each has its own share of hard and awful facts. What sweetness, beauty, and justice there is in the lives of men and women is always a triumph over circumstances. And triumph has always been possible.

Life has always been something of a struggle.

Ages before there were missile silos, there were saber-tooth tigers.

When men and women first ventured out of the safety of tree-tops onto the plains of the Serengeti, there were no welcoming committees.

And there have been precious few since.

Coming to this New World was a daring act for most of your parents, or grandparents, or great-grandparents.

A week before the inauguration of my term as governor, I was pondering the improbable hopes and long shots, and summed it up for myself by imagining this interview between my mother and an immigration official at Ellis Island.

"Where are you from?" the official would have wearily inquired of the young, timid immigrant woman—alone, with little more than hope, confused.

A. I'm from Provincia di Salerno. Tramonti.

Q. What do you do?

A. Nothing. I'm going to meet my husband in New Jersey.

Q. What does he do?

A. Nothing, he's looking for work.

Q. What kind of work?

A. Any kind.

Q. But what can he do?

A. Well, he has no skill, he never was educated. But he is strong and he can use his hands and he will work all day.

Q. Well, does he have any friends?

A. No.

Q. Any money?

A. No.

Q. How about you?

A. We have nothing, no friends, no money, just a baby.

Q. Well, with no friends, no money, no skills, no education, what do you expect of this country?

A. Not a lot. Not a lot. Work. A place to sleep. A chance to raise a family. And just one other thing—before I die, I would like to see my son the governor of New York State.

Imagine what kind of reception a dream like that would have received! And yet it describes a story that has happened over and over in this country. For those who dared . . . and who worked for their dreams.

ᘛᐧᘚ

JAMES BALDWIN[*]
Writer
Hampshire College

For me, too, it's a kind of ending. I've been teaching you this last year, and I learned a lot. Now, the first thing I had to learn was that my frame of reference was antique; that is to say, when I referred to

*Copyright © 1986 by James Baldwin. Reprinted by arrangement with the James Baldwin Estate.

something which happened twenty years ago or ten years ago, and I suddenly realized the blankness of the faces before me—that they did not know what I was talking about—I began to feel a little like somebody from ancient Rome. But I understood, I think, very quickly, that partly what I was confronting, what we were confronting, was the concept of time, time having very little meaning in this society. And the concept of history in this society, since everything is a little like last week's television show. Now, I then had to begin to see that my Malcolm X, or my JFK, or my Martin Luther King Jr. were creatures I had to, first of all, re-create in my own mind before I could reconvey them to the people younger than myself.

And this caused me to think about myself, really. And the great difference between myself and the youngster who might in some ways have been older than I. But one great difference, I think, is this: I was born twenty-one years before the atomic age was ushered in. I was born, whether or not I knew it then, no matter what my possibilities might have seemed to be—I was born to live a life, an ordinary life. I could dream of getting to be seventy or eighty if I could live that long. Behind me stretched, however disagreeably, or however beautifully, a sense of time, a sense of continuity. But I began to suspect that for anyone born in 1945 or after 1945, the sense of time which I had inherited was as remote for them really as ancient Rome is for me. . . .

We are living in the atomic age. We have failed to in any way whatever fulfill what we thought of as our promise. It would seem to me, then, that it might be up to your generation to excavate the things my generation thought we believed in and some of us did believe and do believe, to move us from where we are now to another place where the idea of color, the idea of freedom, the idea of race, the idea of love, the idea of joy, the possibilities of a human being will not be subordinate to the economic well-being of this society. It may be profoundly immoral to have a society in which if you get sick, you'd better have some money. If you are in trouble with the law, you'd better have some money. It seems to me that it is time in the world in which we live, given all the accidents that happen on the other side, on this side, given the fact that it is always easier to have an enemy without than to examine the chaos within. Given the fact that all of our lives are interconnected, and all of our identities are menaced because of that, and our potential, also because of that. And bearing in mind the reality in which we live, in which we live is a reality we have created. And it is time, my children, if I may say so, to begin the act of creation all over again.

∽o∾

FLORA LEWIS
Writer
Clark University

André Malraux said that the twenty-first century will be spiritual or it will *not be*. He didn't really explain what he meant, but I think it must be more a matter of faith than of religion, more a matter of thought than of reflex, more a matter of effort than of going along. Our society, I think, is losing the essential quality of enthusiasm, the interest which fires people and makes it unnecessary for them to ask, "What is the point of my life?" Some have it in abundance. They tend to be scientists, artists, educators, people whose driving concern is doing, not having. I think the greatest possible luxury is not to know for sure when you are working and when you are doing something else—to enjoy the pursuit of your concern so much that you'd probably be doing it even if you didn't think of it as your job.

It doesn't matter a great deal *what* you engage in. It's possible to make a contribution to the society in very many ways. But the spirit does matter. There's a problem particularly among young people now: too many of them unemployed and far too many of them seemingly doomed to remain unemployable. It's a problem that's likely to grow, as inventions, technology, automation reduce the need for muscle and unskilled, tedious labor to sustain us. Everybody is driven to find a place in society, even if it's only among the dropouts. And it's going to be harder and harder for all but the high achievers to find a place that is at once satisfying and constructive. So the need is to find ways to spread enthusiasm, create interest, provide the spark which gives life at work or at leisure its savorous point.

We've developed an enormous cultural passivity. We spend so

much of our time and attention as spectators, viewers, listeners, part of a vast, faceless audience. That can bring excitement, emotion, entertainment, but it makes for a synthetic kind of existence. Without personal participation, a sense of reality fades away, and then it becomes hard to identify values, set priorities, to think and feel with any depth. Taking part, whether it's doing something alone or in a group, generates the enthusiasm to learn more, to produce more, to create more, instead of just waiting to take what comes.

∞◦∞

GWENDOLYN BROOKS
Poet
University of Vermont

In Wednesday's *USA Today*, I noted a disturbing headline: "How to Help Your Teen in the Struggle to Fit In." Thousands of readers, I suppose, accepted the substance of that headline and went right on to read the timid little feature that followed, hoping for help. I shudder when I consider the possibility that some of you young people might be wondering how you are going to fit in. Planning to fit in. Look around us, look at the craziness, look at the fear, see the sickness. Into this you want to fit?

Do not desire to fit in. Desire to oblige yourselves to lead. Desire to oblige others—the timid, the static, the diseased—to fit into *your* intellectual reasonableness. Desire to cleanse, desire to extend—one of my favorite words—do not desire to follow. What is there to follow? What there is out there for you to follow these days is considerably dangerous, is considerably addled, is considerably itself uncertain.

∞◦∞

1987

On December 8, 1987, during the first day of a three-day summit in Washington, D.C., President Ronald Reagan and Soviet general secretary Mikhail Gorbachev signed a treaty eliminating intermediate-range nuclear forces. The world, and not just Americans and Soviets, let out a sigh of relief. It was a fitting reminder of a peril greater than what had been dealt the world in 1987, when the eighties finally came down to earth.

The prosperity that had marked the 1980s, and that would go underground briefly in the 1990s before the pursuit of money reasserted itself as our leading national cause, came to an end on October 19, 1987, when seven months after the Dow Jones Industrial Average exceeded the 2,000 mark for the first time, the stock market plunged 508 points. This day in October, which would forever be known thereafter as Black Monday, seemed in many ways a correction (economic and moral) of the eighties, since at the same time the market had been ascending, the federal budget had climbed over $1 trillion, and the trade deficit had risen higher than ever. As if Ivan Boesky's misdeeds hadn't been sufficient, the business world was stained once again when a thirty-eight-year-old investment banker named Martin Siegal pleaded guilty to insider trading.

In England and in Germany, Margaret Thatcher and Chancellor Helmut Kohl won reelection. As a result of his televised appearance during the Iran-Contra hearings, Oliver North was briefly considered a national hero, before the popular mood began to turn against him. Platoon, directed by another Oliver—Stone—swept the 1998 Academy Awards. Les Misérables opened on Broadway. Van Gogh's disturbingly undulate Irises, painted a few days after the artist entered a *mental hospital in St.-Rémy, France, sold at Sotheby's auction house for $53.9 million. In New York, alleged Mafia boss John Gotti was acquitted on federal racketeering and conspiracy charges. Nearly a quarter million black coal miners went on strike in South Africa. The pope visited America. Television evangelist Jim Bakker resigned his ministry after admitting to an extramarital affair with Jessica Hahn. Gary Hart quit the presidential race when it was revealed that he, too, had entered into an extramarital affair, with Donna Rice; several months later, Senator Joseph Biden resigned the presidential race amid charges that he had plagiarized speeches and falsified his vita. U.S. Supreme Court nominee Robert Bork was rejected by the Senate.*

Predictably, 1987 was marked by much blame-the-messenger hand-wringing about the role of the press in American life—or rather, its role in hunting down the dirt on public figures. Had the press done this to Roosevelt and to Kennedy? editorialists demanded. Was it fair? Was it relevant? As the members of the Reagan White House began to fall—Michael Deaver indicted for perjury; Lyn Nofziger, a Reagan political adviser, indicted for his lobbying attempts with the Wedtech Corporation—the answer seemed, for the time being at least, to be yes. Still, the worst was yet to come.

∽∽∽

TED KOPPEL
Broadcaster
Duke University

America has been Vannatized. Vannatized—as in Vanna White, *Wheel of Fortune's* vestal virgin. The young lady may or may not already have appeared on one of those ubiquitous lists of most-admired Americans; but if she has not, it's only a matter of time. Through the mysterious alchemy of popular television, Ms. White is roundly—indeed, all but universally—adored.

It seems unlikely, but lest there be among you someone who has not thrilled to the graceful ease with which Ms. White glides across our television screens, permit me to tell you what she does. She turns blocks, on which blank sides are displayed, to another side of the block, on which a letter is displayed. She does this very well, very fluidly, with what appears to be genuine enjoyment. She also does it mutely. Vanna says nothing. She is often seen smiling at and talking with winners at the end of the program; but we can only imagine what they are saying to each other. We don't hear Vanna. She speaks only body language, and she seems to like everything she sees. No, "like" is too tepid. Vanna thrills, rejoices with everything she sees . . . and therein lies her particular magic. The viewer can, and apparently does, project a thousand different personalities onto that charmingly neutral television image, and she accommodates them all.

Even Vanna White's autobiography, an oxymoron if ever there was one, reveals only that her greatest nightmare is running out of cat food, and that one of the complexities of her job entails making proper allowance for the greater weight of the letters *M* and *W* over the letter *I*, for example. Once, we learn, during her earlier, less experienced days, she failed to take that heavy-letter factor into proper account and broke a fingernail.

I tremble to think what judgment a future anthropologist, finding that book, will render on our society. I tremble not out of fear that they will misjudge us, but rather that they will judge us only too accurately.

We are nothing as an industry if we are not attuned to the appetites and limitations of our audience. We have learned, for example, that your attention span is brief. We should know—we helped make it that way. Watch *Miami Vice* some Friday night. You will find not only a pastel-colored world—which neatly symbolizes the moral ambiguity of that program—you will discover that no scene lasts longer than ten or fifteen seconds. It is a direct reflection of the television industry's confidence in your ability to concentrate. . . .

We now communicate with everyone and say absolutely nothing. We have reconstructed a Tower of Babel and it is a television antenna, a thousand voices producing a daily parody of democracy in which everyone's opinion is afforded equal weight regardless of substance or merit. Indeed, it can even be argued that opinions of real weight tend to sink with barely a trace in television's ocean of banalities.

Our society finds truth too strong a medicine to digest undiluted. In its purest form, truth is not a polite tap on the shoulder; it is a howling reproach. What Moses brought down from Mount Sinai were not the Ten Suggestions; they are commandments. *Are,* not *were.* The sheer beauty of the commandments is that they codify, in a handful of words, acceptable human behavior, not just for then or now, but for all time. Language evolves, power shifts from nation to nation, messages are transmitted with the speed of light, man erases one frontier after another; and yet we, and our behavior, and the commandments which govern that behavior, remain the same.

The tension between those commandments and our baser instincts provide the grist for journalism's daily mill. What a huge, gaping void there would be in our informational flow and in our entertainment without the routine violation of the sixth commandment: Thou shalt not murder. On what did the Hart campaign founder? On accusations that he violated the seventh commandment: Thou shalt not commit adultery. Relevant? Of course the commandments are relevant. Simply because we use different terms and tools, the eighth commandment is still relevant to the insider-trading scandal. The commandments don't get bogged down in methodology. Simple, to the point: Thou shalt not steal. Watch the Iran-Contra hearings and keep the ninth commandment in mind: Thou shalt not bear false witness. And the tenth commandment, which seems to have been crafted for the eighties and the "Me Generation," the commandment against covetous desires—against longing for anything we cannot get in an honest and legal fashion.

When you think about it, it's curious, isn't it? We've changed in almost all things: where we live, how we eat, communicate, travel. And yet, in our moral and immoral behavior, we are fundamentally unchanged.

Which brings me to the first, and in this day and age, probably the most controversial of the commandments, since it requires that we believe in the existence of a single, supreme God. . . . What a bizarre journey, from sweet, undemanding Vanna White to that all-demanding, jealous Old Testament God. There have always been imperfect role models, false gods of the appeal of success and fame; but now their influence is magnified by television.

∽○∽

THOMAS KEAN
Governor, New Jersey
Syracuse University

History may remember 1987 as the year in which America's major institutions—government, religious, and business—became engulfed in scandal. An epidemic of indictments has struck the privileged and the powerful.

You can't avoid the headlines.

Ivan Boesky and Dennis Levine may go to prison for stealing millions with inside information. City officials in New York stand convicted of lining their pockets with taxpayers' money. TV evangelist Jim Bakker is forced to resign his ministry for refusing to practice what he preaches.

In Washington, a former presidential assistant, Michael Deaver, stands accused of selling his contacts for cash. A congressional committee is trying to determine what happened to millions raised to free our hostages. The press, as represented by the *Miami Herald*, has taken to spying on the sex life of candidates for high office. And 50 percent of Americans believe the president of the United States is lying.

These things fill our newspaper, and yet the really important issues remain almost hidden.

There is still no peace on earth. There are still children suffering in America and around the world. Too many lives are plagued by poverty, injustice, and racial and religious hatred. An economic Dunkirk looms and there is still the impending threat of our own extinction through nuclear war. These are now the concerns of your generation, as well as mine.

You can choose to ignore these problems, entertaining the notion that someone else will take care of society's ills. But if you do, you run the risk that others will feel the same until there is no longer any common cause but only blind self-interest. Or, like the doers and dreamers of the past, you can choose to accept the responsibility and sacrifice for the common good that a democracy requires.

Our government, our laws, and by definition, our society are just as moral and just, or as corrupt and evil, as we choose to make them.

I was appalled, as I'm sure most of you are, by the actions of Ivan Boesky and by the clandestine behavior of Oliver North. But much more dangerous is the attitude held by many that this is business or politics as usual, and that the best thing to do is to turn away from public responsibility.

Never before have we needed people in government of greater wisdom and courage. And yet, it is one of the terrible paradoxes of our time, never have so many, particularly among the young, seemed so repulsed by government service or so apathetic to our social concerns. Too many seem to believe, in the words of David Byrne, of the group Talking Heads, that "compassion is a virtue, but I don't have enough time." Such an attitude will eventually lead to the death of democracy, not by ambush or assassination, but slowly, through apathy, indifference, and undernourishment. . . .

Long after all of us are gone, after fortunes are lost and won, after nations rise and fall, history will write the verdict of our work here based not on what we have done for ourselves, but on what we have done for children yet unborn.

∞

JOAN DIDION
Writer
Bard College

What I want to tell you today is not to move into that world where you're alone with yourself and your mantra and your fitness program or whatever it is that you might use to try to control the world by closing it out. I want to tell you to just live in the mess. Throw yourself out into the convulsions of the world. I'm not telling you to make the world better because I don't believe progress is necessarily part of the package. I'm just telling you to live in it, to look at it, to witness it. Try and get it. Take chances, make your own work, take pride in it. Seize the moment.

∞

KEN BURNS
Filmmaker
Hampshire College

I think our future lies behind us. In our past, personal and collective. In the last dozen years, I have learned many things, but that history is our greatest teacher is perhaps the most important lesson.

However, this enthusiasm is by no means shared by all. History, and its valuable advice, continues to recede in importance in schools all over. The statistics are now frightening. A majority of high school seniors do not know who Josef Stalin or Winston Churchill were. They did not know—of the Declaration of Independence, the Bill of Rights, and the Emancipation Proclamation—which came first. And a majority could not tell the correct half century in which the Civil War took place. The most important event in our past.

We Americans tend to ignore our past. Perhaps we fear having one, and burn it behind us like rocket fuel, always looking forward. And that's a bad thing. The consequences are not just ignorance, or stupidity, or even repeating. It represents the deepest kind of inattention, and it becomes a tear or a gap in who we are.

I think of what James Symington, a former congressman, said. Slavery, he said, was merely the horrible statutory expression of a deeper rift between peoples based on race, and this rift is what we struggle still to erase from the hearts and minds of people.

That rift stands at the very center of American history; it is the great challenge, to which all our deepest aspirations to freedom must rise. If we forget that, if we forget the great stain of slavery that stands at the heart of our history, we forget who we are, and we make the rift deeper and wider; and that's what forgetting is: making the human rift wider.

And we are forgetting it even now, on campuses and in suburbs and cities, forgetting that after all, only 127 years ago, 4 million Americans were owned by other Americans; that 630,000 Americans died over the issue, when our population was a mere 30 million. Two percent died.

We too often tend to think, and this is part of the forgetting, that those people, those Americans, were not the same as us, and thus we cut the thread of identity and responsibility that really binds us to them all the same. But they were very like us. They were health faddists and faith healers, into nature cures, water cures, free love, and women's rights; there was evangelical fervor, spiritual experiment, and religious movement of every kind. But they were worldly realists, too. Two days after the first battle of Bull Run in July of 1861, canny real estate speculators bought up the battlefield to make a second kind of killing as a tourist site.

It is alarming to reflect upon how many of the burning issues that for some reason seemed self-evident twenty years ago have faded from public concern in the past twelve, since I graduated here with my bare feet and my hair down my back. . . . What I am trying to say is that there is a profound connection between remembering and freedom and human attachment. That's what history is to me. And forgetting is the opposite of all that: it is a kind of slavery, and the worst kind of human detachment.

❦

BILL BRADLEY
U.S. Senator
Dartmouth College

Ultimately, it is you—alone with your conscience, your intelligence, your life's experience—who determine what you believe you owe to the rural poor, to starving Ethiopians, to refugees from tyranny, to concentration camp victims, or to the deinstitutionalized homeless who sleep on the street corners of our major cities.

Do you believe your responsibility to them is served by giving to a charity which will try to serve their needs? Do you believe that providing food, clothing, and shelter for them is a legitimate use of taxpayers' dollars? Do you believe that you should yourself go to work among the refugees of Southeast Asia or the street people of New York City? Or do you believe that you have no responsibility for anyone but yourself and your family?

How you think about the needs of strangers will determine the kind of society we become.

❧

Barbara Jordan
U.S. Congresswoman
Middlebury College

Think what a better world it would be if we all, the whole world, had cookies and milk about three o'clock every afternoon and then lay down on our blankets for a nap.

❧

Riccardo Muti
Conductor
University of Pennsylvania

There is a romantic idea that a musician should live in an ivory tower, where he has nothing to do with reality, no idea what is happening in the outside world. But that has *never* been the case. If we look at history, artists of *all* kinds—painters, sculptors, writers, and musicians—have always been among the most influential and the most deeply involved members of society. That is why in authoritarian states throughout history, the *first* people a regime tries to *silence* are the artists. There have been times in almost every country, including America, when artists were attacked and attempts made to silence them because the authorities somehow saw a threat in what they were expressing. Many of you will remember the blacklists of the 1950s, when musicians, actors, and writers were prevented from working here because of the controversial nature of their work.

In the Soviet Union, composers like Prokofiev and Shostakovich were punished by the authorities. Their work was considered anti-social. Among Soviet writers, the novelist Solzhenitsyn was subjected to suppression, imprisonment, and exile, and the poet Alexander Blok was tortured to death. The Nazis suppressed the music of Mendelssohn, Mahler, Hindemith. And we certainly have not heard the last of the so-called cultural revolutions in China, which include such signs of culture as silencing pianists by breaking their hands.

So it has been through *history.* The musicians and all other artists have always had to struggle against *censorship.* Yet if music truly has nothing to do with reality, why should the thoughts of these composers be so important that they must be kept silent?

What the censors have always understood is that music is one of the most effective ways to bring people together. And what makes music *most dangerous* to the tyrants and the totalitarian is its ability to *express* issues, to confront them, in ways that politicians cannot get away with.

∽⚬∾

MAYA ANGELOU
Poet
Simmons College

You must take time out to look at the world you are walking into. We are offering you an all-time-high rate of divorce and single-parent homes, more often than not headed by women. We are offering you political leaders whose approach to morality seems to be simply to ignore its existence as an ideal. We are offering you professionals who deny the orders of their professional oaths to serve mankind because service is out of fashion and might even be dangerous. We are offering you men and women whose ancestors fought for the right to vote, but who will not register, and if they register, more often than not, will not vote. We are offering you a society rife with racism, sexism, and ageism. We are offering you a world which has become exiled to things, material things. We give you streets rampant with

crime, children dazed with drugs, old folks ignored, the ill abandoned, the youth uninformed. And yet we have loved you.

Someone survived so that you could come to this day to say,
"Alleluia." It is time now for you to start to think about taking time
out. How will you make this indeed a better world? The charge upon
you is no small matter: it is to make this country more than what
James Baldwin calls these "yet-to-be United States." And courage is
the most important of all the virtues, young women and men,
because without courage, you cannot practice any other virtue with
consistency. You cannot be consistently kind, or true, or fair, or generous, or honest, without courage. I wish I had said that first; actually, Aristotle said it. . . .

Young women, young men, this is the time. Since life is our most
precious gift, and since it is given to us to live but once, let us live so
we will not regret years of useless virtue, and inertia, and timidity.
And in living your lives each of you can say, "All my conscious life
and energies have been devoted to the most noble cause in the world:
the liberation of the human mind and spirit, beginning with my
own."

∽০∾

MARIO CUOMO
Governor, New York
Grinnell College

The story of America has been told millions of times and you'll be
its next chapter. You'll be successful lawyers, executives, business-
people, teachers, engineers, respected by your colleagues. You'll have
a car and then two cars, and a house and a summer place, and travel,
just about everything you want. It's all there before you, the shining
city on a hill. And it may even be enough for you. It has been for
many Americans. So no one should disparage this version of the
American dream, and I certainly won't. I'm not going to put it down.

But there is something more. Sooner or later for *some* of you, the
house, the travel, the feeling of having made it as an individual will

not be enough to leave you fulfilled. *Some* of you, just some of you, will need to feel that your life has touched, has influenced for the better, a world larger than the one that ends in your own backyard. For some, this need to reach beyond yourselves may spring from religious or cultural seeds that were planted in you a long time ago—from a faint remembrance, perhaps, or from strong convictions about mankind's mission in the world. Some of you may be old-fashioned, mushy-headed liberals, inspired by a reading or by the voice and the picture of John F. Kennedy or the dreams of Martin Luther King Jr. or the words of a professor. . . . Others will just feel it. They'll feel revulsion when they see people living in cardboard boxes, huddling in telephone booths, seeking shelter from the winter against the grating of a building's warm-air exhaust. They'll feel threatened by acid rain menacing our forests and lakes and streams and wildlife, by toxic wastes seeping into the earth, fouling our life-giving waters. They'll feel sickened when they see in their own nation an infant mortality rate that is the shame of the developed world, when they realize that for all of our power and affluence and progress, we've now reached the point where we have become the only industrialized nation in the world's history in which the children are poorer than the rest of us.

Or maybe they'll be appalled at the absurd paradox of a world desperately in need of every penny of its wealth to properly house and feed, to educate and protect its people, wasting trillions of dollars on nuclear weapons that can never be used because to fire even one is to doom our very existence. Or perhaps one day, after all the headlines, all the radio and television reports, one more story on corruption in high places in Washington or Wall Street, it will all reach a kind of emotional, critical mass and give them the uneasy feeling that something fundamental is awry in this world.

And some will see all of this and they will feel that they must do something. They must get involved in the effort to change and improve things, not because anyone will force them to—God forbid, not here, not in America—no, they'll become part of the important group of Americans who seek to influence the nation's direction because they want to, because they choose to. And so they will listen and they will study and they will vote and they will advocate. They may even, some of them, become public officials affecting directly the policies to be pursued, the goals to be set, the commitments to be made.

And eventually you're going to have to make your choice, one way or the other, as I and millions of other people before you have. For myself, at one point in my life not long ago, I chose to get involved. I chose to participate, to lend my efforts, however ineffectual they might be, but with a full heart and an eagerness, a real eagerness, to make a difference, out of gratitude for all that this country has meant to me and my family, and out of a sense that that's the way this place has to work—those of us who have benefited sharing the fruits of our good fortune with others—because the American dream, it seems to me, would be a cruel hoax if it were a dream that ended only with you and me. I hope some of you will agree.

∽○∼

1988

If the 1980s had seen its share of political tension, turmoil, and out-
right bellicosity, 1988 witnessed countries and their leaders coming to
their senses. Most critical of all was the ratification of the agreement
between the United States and the Soviet Union banning the use of
intermediate-range nuclear forces—which didn't mean that concilia-
tion and truce-making didn't take place elsewhere, too. Iran and Iraq
agreed to a truce in the Persian Gulf; the Soviets began removing their
troops from Afghanistan; in Nicaragua, the Sandinistas and the Contras tentatively agreed to talks; and across the Soviet Union, Mikhail
Gorbachev's policies of perestroika, or restructuring, seemed to have
altered the foundations of what had previously been viewed as a
country highly resistant to change.

Politically, there were changes in the United States as well. George
Bush and Senator Dan Quayle, sailing on the triumphs and prosperi-
ties of the Reagan years, handily defeated their opponents, Michael
Dukakis and Senator Lloyd Bentsen. Quayle swiftly proved to be
something of a political liability, and in short order got himself into
trouble as a skilled mangler of words and ideas. Eventually, the vice
president disappeared from sight, where his verbal affronts could be
kept under control, or at least under wraps.

Elsewhere, Oprah Winfrey, by now the undisputed doyenne of daytime television, appeared on television in skin-tight jeans and a black
belt, sixty-seven pounds lighter. An international group of historians
concluded that Kurt Waldheim, the president of Austria, while surely
aware of war crimes, had not committed any crimes himself. Who
Framed Roger Rabbit, the first ever full-length movie combining animation with human characters, attracted scads of moviegoers, though

predictably, Bertolucci's stately The Last Emperor took home most of the Academy Awards. In Israel, a court convicted John Demjanjuk, identified by some Holocaust survivors as Ivan the Terrible, of participating in SS concentration camp murders during the Second World War; Demjanjuk was promptly sentenced to death. Australia began its bicentennial in Sydney harbor. The Winter Olympics took place in Calgary, Canada, and the Summer Olympics took place in Korea. Chilean voters ousted President Augusto Pinochet, and in Pakistan, opposition leader Benazir Bhutto was appointed the first ever female leader of a Muslim nation. The Securities and Exchange Commission charged so-called junk bond king Michael Milken and his brokerage firm, Drexel Burnham Lambert, with insider trading; ultimately, Drexel agreed to cough up a $650 million fine. The space shuttle Discovery lifted off from Cape Canaveral. Philip Morris acquired Kraft, and Kohlberg Kravis Roberts acquired RJR Nabisco. Twenty-five years after Martin Luther King Jr. delivered his famous "I have a dream" speech, editorial writers began asking themselves aloud whether America's racial problems had improved; as Reagan left office, another question was left hanging: was America winning the drug war? The answer, obvious even to kindergartners, was a resounding no.

When unemployment records were released, the United States had the lowest unemployment record in fourteen years. Black Monday notwithstanding, the party of the 1980s seemed set to continue.

~∞~

Malcolm Forbes
Industrialist
Syracuse University

The only advice I would give to you—you've been getting it; by tomorrow you can start giving it—is that when people ask what makes for success, I think there is only one very simple answer. You have to do, in your life and with your life, what turns you on. Anything else is a waste of time. If you know where your own button is, press it.

We're not put on earth to be clones of our parents or our siblings. The only way anybody succeeds is to love what he's doing. It doesn't mean it will be easily done. It's picking out what you like to do that's sometimes the problem. But doing what you want to do in your life is what your life is all about, and nothing could please a parent more. You know, they might be impressed if you go to work in a bank, or become president of the bank or something, but if that doesn't do it for you, it's an absolute waste.

We've got little enough time; you don't realize until you're running out of it how little time you have. So I would say to you, in the time you have left, make the most of it by making the most of yourself, which is doing what means the most to you and not to somebody else.

∽◦∾

James Gannon
Editor, *Des Moines Register*
Coe College

If you don't have a philosophy of life yet, let me warn you that the world you are about to enter is a dangerous place to go looking for one. I am told that there's a popular new bumper sticker that says "I shop, therefore I am." In a society in which many people seem to define themselves by their purchases, that's only half a joke.

I went shopping for signs of the 1980s philosophy in some of our popular magazines recently. You can tell a lot about this culture from its advertising. For instance, there was one ad that carried this headline: "You Can Never Be Too Rich or Too Thin."

Oddly enough, it was an ad for a candy bar. A rich, thin candy bar with a foreign-sounding name. I don't know if this candy bar is any good, but I'll bet that a lot of people nod and smile at its slogan, which seems to capture the values of the eighties succinctly.

∽◦∾

Marian Wright Edelman
Founder and Director, Children's Defense Fund
Dartmouth College

What can you and I do?

One: Resist despair. This is a time to go to work to meet the challenges that threaten our children, families, and entire nation. But it will take time, energy, leadership, and a sustained investment of private sector and public resources. Every American must speak out against and help redirect the misguided national investment priorities of this decade, which have placed missiles and bombs ahead of mothers and babies and families. Since 1980, each American has increased spending on the military by 37 percent, on the national debt by 81 percent, and decreased spending on all programs for low income families and children by 2 percent. And we let politicians blame spending on the poor for escalating deficits.

Two: Each of us must actively struggle to inform ourselves and pay more attention to what our political and private sector leaders *do* rather than what they say, and hold them accountable. Convenient ignorance is a more deadly threat to the future of America than AIDS. It absolves us of responsibility to act and feeds a continuing politics of illusion and cheap redemption. And we must watch out for quick-fix or politically cosmetic solutions to complex problems that we can solve only with patience and effort. There is no cheap grace.

Three: Understand and be confident that each of us can make a difference by caring and acting in small as well as big ways. Democracy is not a spectator but a participatory sport. Don't ask, in the face of growing child and family suffering, political timidity, and private sector indifference and corruption, Why doesn't somebody do something? Ask, Why don't *I* do something?

Sojourner Truth, a black slave woman who could neither read nor write, pointed the way for us. Once a heckler told Sojourner that he cared no more for her antislavery talk "than for an old fleabite." "Maybe not," was her answer, "but the Lord willing, I'll keep you scratching."

Through your votes, your voices, your service for the poor and young, in whatever job you choose or role you decide to play in life, you can be a flea for justice. Enough fleas biting strategically can make even the biggest dog uncomfortable.

⤖⤖

SISSELA BOK
Professor and Writer
Clark University

You are graduating at a time when you hear all around you how the nation is deteriorating morally, how young people are not as principled or as cultured as their elders, how civilization is on the skids. And I hope that you recognize such vast generalizations for the superficial claptrap they really are—the very same tirades that nostalgia has generated among those no longer young since time began, or at least for as long as we have written records.

Some who issue such vast condemnations look back at the prime of their own lives as a kind of Golden Age; others have located that age much farther in the past. But most of these commentators have surveyed their own societies with the gravest misgivings, either as culturally exhausted or as morally corrupt. Among them, one of my favorites is a wistful Egyptian scribe two thousand years B.C., cited by Professor Walter Jackson Bate in his illuminating book *The Burden of the Past*. This scribe wrote in sorrow about how there was no fresh, new way left to say things; all possible phrases had already been used by "men of old" to the point of growing stale. His complaint is all the more astounding to us, as Bate points out, since none of what we now take to be the world's great works of literature had been composed at the time.

If all the pessimists of the past had been right in speaking of their society's running out of creative possibilities, or going to ruin, civilization would indeed have ground to a halt long ago.

⤖⤖

Toni Morrison
Writer
Sarah Lawrence College

I'm not sure [happiness] is all it's cracked up to be. I know, of course, that its pursuit, if not its achievement, is a legal one, amended into the Constitution. I know that whole industries are designed to help you identify, attain, and feel it. One more article of clothing? Or the ultimate telephone. The best-appointed apartment, a boat, an instantly timeless camera taking hundreds of shots meant to outlast the ages. The fastest diet, or best of all, the perfect ice cream with all of the pleasures of sugar and cream and none of their dangers . . .

Still, I'm not interested in it—not yours, and not mine, and not anybody's. I don't think we can afford it anymore. I don't think it delivers the goods. But most important, it's getting in the way of everything worth doing. . . . Focusing on it now has gotten quite out of hand. It's become a bankrupt idea, the vocabulary of which is frightening. Money and things and protection and control and speed and more and more and more.

I'd like to think about and substitute something else for its search, for its pursuit. Something urgent. Something neither the world nor you can continue without. . . . I want to talk about the activity you are always warned against as being wasteful, impractical, hopeless. I want to talk about dreaming. Not the activity of the sleeping brain but rather the activity of the awake and alert one. Not idle, wishful speculation, but engaged, directed daytime vision. Entrance into another space. Someone else's situation, sphere, projection if you like. By dreaming, the self permits intimacy with the other without the risk of being the other. And this intimacy that comes from pointed imagining, it should precede all our decision making, all of our cause mongering, and our action. We are in a mess, you know, and we have to get out.

And I believe it is the archaic definition of the word "dreaming" that will say this. That definition is to envision a series of images of unusual vividness, clarity, order, and significance. Unusual vividness, clarity, order, and significance. If we undertake that kind of dreaming, we can avoid complicating what is simple, and simplify what is complicated. We would avoid substituting slogans like "national will" for "national perception." What kind of national will? Informed? Uninformed? Obstinate? South African national will? Nineteen-forty Germany's national will? We can avoid hanging on to destructive theses simply because we developed them half a century ago. We can avoid comic book solutions to biblical problems in nuclear times. We should visualize, imagine, dream up, and enter the other before we presume to solve their problems or ours. We might as well dream the world as it ought to be.

⌒∞⌒

WILLIAM ZINSSER*
Writer
Wesleyan University

The sportswriter Red Smith was one of my heroes. Not long before his own death he gave the eulogy at the funeral of another writer, and he said, "Dying is no big deal. Living is the trick."

Living is the trick. That's what we're all given one chance to do well. One reason I admired Red Smith was that he wrote about sports for fifty-five years, with elegance and humor, without ever succumbing to the pressure, which ruined many sportswriters, that he ought to be writing about something "serious." Red Smith found in sportswriting exactly what he wanted to do and what he deeply loved doing. And because it was right for him he said more important things about American values than many writers who wrote about serious subjects—so seriously that nobody could read them.

Another story about writers. When I was teaching at Yale, the poet Allen Ginsberg came to talk to our students, and one of them asked him: "Was there a point when you consciously decided to become a poet?" And Ginsberg said: "It wasn't quite a choice; it was a realization. I was twenty-eight and I had a job as a market researcher. One day I told my psychiatrist that what I really wanted to do was to quit

*Copyright © 2000 by William K. Zinsser

my job and just write poetry. And the psychiatrist said, 'Why not?' And I said, 'Well, what would the American Psychoanalytical Association say?' And he said, 'There's no party line.' So I did."

We'll never know how big a loss that was for the field of market research. But it was a big moment for American poetry. There's no party line. Good advice. You can be your own party line. If living is the trick, what's crucial for you is to do something that makes the best use of your own gifts and your own individuality. There's only one you. Don't ever let anyone persuade you that you're somebody else. . . .

Never be afraid to be different. Don't assume that people you'd like to work for have defined their needs as narrowly as you think they have—that they know exactly who they want. What any good executive is looking for is general intelligence, breadth, originality, imagination, audacity, a sense of history, a sense of cultural context, a sense of wonder, a sense of humor, far more than he or she is looking for a precise fit. America has more than enough college graduates every year who are willing to go through life being someone else's precise fit. What we need are men and women who will dare to break the mold of tired thinking—who just won't buy somebody's saying, "We've always done it this way. This way is good enough."

Well, obviously it's not good enough or the country wouldn't be in the mess it's in. I don't have to tell you all the areas where this wonderful country is not living up to its best dreams: poverty, inequality, injustice, debt, illiteracy, health care, day care, homelessness, pollution, arms spending that milks us of the money that should be going into life-affirming work. There's no corner of American life that doesn't need radically fresh thinking. So, sell yourself as the person who will do that fresh thinking. Don't shape yourself to a dumb job; shape the job to your strengths and your curiosity and your ideals. . . .

One of the themes I've been talking to you about this morning (though I haven't used the word) is separation. It's very much on your mind today, and it will be many times again, and it will always be painful; none of the changes that I've told you about in my life were anything but scary at the time I made them. But there are two ways to think about separation: as a loss, or as a beginning. To separate is to start fresh.

For you, I hope today will be the first of many separations that will mean the putting behind you of something you've done well and the beginning of something you'll do just as well, or better. Keep separating yourself from any project that's not up to your highest standards of what's right for you—and for the broader community where you can affect the quality of life: your home, your town, your children's schools, your state, your country, your world. If living is the trick, live usefully. Nothing in your life will be as satisfying as making a difference in somebody else's life.

∽∾∾

STEPHEN KING
Writer
University of Maine

I am not *addressing* you, because you are not letters. Even if you were put in a large package and could be sent bulk mail, I would have nowhere to send you. I am not *commencing* anything. I did that when I began to talk. *You* are not commencing anything, at least in the aggregate; I am aware that *individuals* are *always* commencing something: some of you are commencing respiration, commencing efforts to stifle yawns, commencing to feel the need for a beer. But as a group, you're just sitting there, and you commenced that already. . . .

I refuse to offer homilies in spite of an almost insurmountable urge to talk about what will happen as you row the canoe of your life down the river of the future, encountering the sandbars of confusion and the rapids of adversity. I'll save that bullshit for the Jim and Tammy Bakkers of the world. They can say it because they believe it. If you're anything like me, most of the time you feel more like the transmission of your prospects just fell out on the New Jersey Turnpike of your existence. I'm not here to tell you you're lost without a compass and headed up shit creek, but I'll be damned if I'll stand here and tell you everything's going to be fine if you work hard, because no one knows that. I'm saying I'm too dumb to lie, but at least I'm smart enough to know it. . . .

Nor can I be a role model. Role models only exist in small, intimate groups—families, friends, sometimes people thrown together in a situation where survival may be in doubt. I'd like to be a role model to my kids. My wife is one to me, someone who shows me how I might live better, do better, and think quicker. When she said, "I guess no one has to follow *Reagan* around to see if he's screwing models, huh?" my heart fell at her feet. She said something I'd felt but hadn't been able to coalesce in my own mind.

To people who don't know you, the function of role model is replaced by its hollow substitute, celebrity. Going somewhere to see a celebrity is, in my book, as intelligent as counting how many dogs pee on a fire hydrant in a twenty-four-hour period. Celebrity is some sort of crazy invention which grows in direct ratio to its uselessness. When I am asked for my autograph, I give it if I can, but I always wonder the same thing: *Why does somebody—anybody— want me to deface a sheet of paper with my name?* A name is all it is. . . . When a guy in a Western says, "What's yore handle, pard?" I can relate. A name *is* a handle. Your face is something you have so your significant others can recognize you in a crowd of species where everyone has two eyes, two ears, one nose, and one mouth. Talent has nothing to do with names or faces. Talent is possibility; ability is the knack of getting a certain thing right more often than you get it wrong; creativity is a mixture of both. Celebrity is to talent what a carbuncle is to normal flesh. The perverse thing is that many people have somehow been convinced that *this* carbuncle is not only not wrong, or even just normal, but actually *desirable*. Which is a way of saying that I have no idea where the seeds from which the likes of John Travolta, Charo, Vanna White, and Dick Clark grew, but I wish someone would find out and spray the area with defoliant. . . .

You will work at good jobs or bad ones, you will meet Mr. or Miss Right, or their counterparts, Mr. and Miss Wrong. You will be political or apolitical. Some of you will grow cynical. Some will find the courage to husband your hopes. But simple statistics show that most of you will be all right. I do not say this in a rah-rah, cheerleading sort of way; I am not selling success the way guys sell Ginsu knives and Slim Whitman records on TV. I am only telling you the fact that happy endings are the rule rather than the exception out of the experiences of my own life and the observation of my eyes and mind. The way of the world is no river of experience, but it is no mean blind alley of hopelessness, either. It's just this street that goes someplace.

There is no canoe. There is no river. Your ship will not come in. You will not win the megabucks lottery or the Publishers Clearing House sweepstakes. No one will give you the key to any city, and if they did, it wouldn't even open a can of cat food. No one is going to put you in the pace car of the Tournament of Roses Parade, and no one is making a movie of your life. Am I telling you everything you don't know? I doubt if I am. . . .

There is no metaphor for your life. There is only one single man and one single woman living a life with the earth under and the sky over and all the worlds of possibility in the head existing between the two. You want to know what is going to happen to you. You want to know what to do next. I don't know the answer to either question. But I know as surely as I know summer follows spring that *you can,* and that most of you *will.*

∽∘∽

1989

Few years in the twentieth century would prove to be as extraordinary as 1989. Much of the warfare of the previous few years had subsided, or even ended (though fighting continued in El Salvador), and 1989 proved to be a year in which critical reverberations took place in Eastern Europe.

Domestically, George Herbert Walker Bush was sworn in as the forty-first president of the United States, the very same year that television celebrated its fiftieth birthday. Internationally, Poland, Hungary, Czechoslovakia, and East Germany all established brand-new governments. The Berlin Wall fell in November of 1989, though 1989 also saw violence in China, as Red Army troops fired at scores of prodemocracy demonstrators in Tiananmen Square. In the Philippines, Corazón Aquino narrowly survived a coup attempt, and Emperor Hirohito died in Japan. In the United States, President Bush took military action to rid the world of Panamanian dictator General Manuel Noriega. Hurricane Hugo pummeled the U.S. Virgin Islands. An enormous oil spill occurred in Alaska, the Exxon Valdez the culprit. Medical experimentation with the anti-AIDS drug AZT offered new hope to sufferers of the disease. Pete Rose was forever banned from baseball for gambling on games. Kareem Abdul-Jabbar and Chris Evert retired from their respective sports, basketball and tennis. Batman drew enormous crowds at the box office, and Japan's Sony Corporation, wanting a piece of Hollywood action, made what would turn out to be a very expensive fumble: buying Columbia Pictures. Lucille Ball, Lord Laurence Olivier, and Vladimir Horowitz died. Three nights of rioting and looting followed the shooting of a black motorcyclist by a Miami police officer. Serial killer Ted Bundy was exe-

cuted at a Florida State prison, and Lyndon LaRouche was sentenced to fifteen years in prison for attempting to defraud the Internal Revenue Service out of $30 million.

Elsewhere, Education Minister Frederick W. de Klerk was appointed the acting president of South Africa, following President P. W. Botha's resignation. Playwright and human rights activist Václav Havel was elected interim president of Czechoslovakia. Iran's Ayatollah Khomeini declared that The Satanic Verses *contained virulently anti-Islamic sentiments and that Salman Rushdie, its author, was a marked man. Rushdie ultimately went into hiding, along the way becoming the most celebrated writer in the world. Another Reaganite, Robert McFarlane, was sentenced to two years probation for withholding information from Congress during the Iran-Contra hearings.* Rain Man *swept the Academy Awards. Ninety-five people were killed, and roughly two hundred injured during a soccer match in Sheffield, England. An explosion aboard the USS* Iowa *killed forty-seven American soldiers. C. Everett Koop resigned his position as the U.S. surgeon general. Massachusetts democrat Barney Frank admitted hiring a male prostitute as his personal aide. Irving Berlin died (he was 101), and so did expatriate Samuel Beckett.*

Transforming the world, however, was the opening of the Berlin Wall in November of 1989. All borders were opened, allowing citizens to travel and emigrate freely within Germany and elsewhere for the first time since World War II. The world suddenly seemed very, very new.

∽∘∾

Patricia Schroeder
U.S. Congresswoman
Simmons College

Your parents have given you wings. In the eighties, the big thing was to give people things. Wings are a whole lot more important than things. If you keep exercising them, you're going to do a great thing for your country, and a great thing for yourself. . . .

We've got to have rootedness. You can be out trying your wings all day long, but at some point during the day, you've got to coalesce and sink your roots with the group that you live with. If we're all detached particles banging around in the universe, then we really lose what society, community, and this country are all about. Try to give your spouses, your family, your children the same things your family gave you. Try to give them wings.

To get the wings you need the roots. If you can just keep those two things centered in your mind as you get hurled around through different career options, and different things that will happen to you, I think you'll find it a wonderful compass for how to guide the rest of your life....

We are closing out the eighties. The eighties have been a decade where the trilogy was me, myself, and I. We've got to start thinking about us, our community, our country, and how we're going to compete.

We shared the eighties together. It's 1989 ... who were you glad you shared this decade with? When I ask at most universities, of course I get Madonna and Bruce Springsteen, but when you really push this question, it comes down to Gorbachev. When I ask, "Why Gorbachev?" they say, "He's modernizing global strategy, and we're doing the same old modernizing of weapons." I don't think there's another decade when young people would have mentioned someone who wasn't an American.

And that's the challenge to you. Get these wings out, get them moving, and let's get back into the world-leadership mode. The world isn't going to wait for us to decide when we want to lead; they're going to move right around us and go right on without us if we don't get out there.

You are living in incredibly exciting times. Take your wings, be prepared for change, keep your rootedness, and go out there.

∽○∽

Leonard Lauder
Businessman
Connecticut College

There is a man named Viktor E. Frankl who owes his life to his ability to project himself. He was a renowned Viennese psychologist before the Nazis threw him into a concentration camp. "Look," he said, "there is only one reason why I am here today. What kept me alive in a situation where others had given up hope and died was the dream that someday I would be here telling you how I survived the Nazi concentration camp. I have never been here before. I have never seen any of you before, and I have never given this speech before, but in my dreams, I have stood before you in this room and said these words a thousand times."

Anatole France said, "To accomplish great things, we must dream as well as act."

∽◦∾

Tracy Kidder
Writer
University of Massachusetts at Amherst

Teaching . . . can be an exhilarating job. At the very least, those of you who have chosen to teach won't usually get bored, which is more than can be said for many other jobs. Every day, at least one child in your class will do something to keep you feeling alive: will say something hilarious, or commit some act of extraordinary kindness, or just when you thought it would never happen, catch on to long division. Many days a student will also do something appalling or reveal to you the wounds of growing up in an unhappy household. The grim statistics on child abuse say that you're bound to have at least a couple of severely mistreated children in your room; you probably won't be able to prove it, but most of the time you'll know. On days when you come in already tired out, you'll find that you can't hide; in fact, the slightest suggestion you convey of wanting to withdraw will probably make the children all the more insistent that you attend to them. Teaching does wear many people out. I'm sure that every school has some teachers who have lost their enthusiasm and their fondness for other people's children. Teaching isn't an easy job, but then again, easy jobs get old long before you do.

And teaching matters. Always potentially and often in fact, it is one of the lofty professions. Teachers have the job of awakening and cultivating minds. In part, that means delivering academic lessons, but the job doesn't end or really begin there. The good teacher creates, both in the class and individual child, the conditions under which academic learning can take place—the conditions without which academic learning has little meaning anyway. The good teacher, especially the good elementary school teacher, becomes the mayor of a village. She shows children how to get along in a community. She tries to help all of them begin to discover who they are and who they might become.

Some people find it easy to imagine unseen webs of malevolent conspiracy in the world. As we know from the news, they are not always wrong. But there is also an innocence that conspires to hold humanity together, and it is made of people who can never fully know the good that they have done. Teachers rarely get to see the long-term effects of their work. They rarely find out that they have made a lasting difference in a child's life, even in cases where they've made a dramatic difference. But good teachers are part of that benevolent conspiracy. Over the years each good teacher redirects hundreds of lives.

∽∾∽

SANDRA DAY O'CONNOR
U.S. Supreme Court Justice
Rockford College

The . . . final thought I will leave with you is one attributed to Winston Churchill:

Success is never final;
Failure is never fatal;
The only thing that matters
Is courage.

Each one of us achieves some success as we go through life. . . . But our successes when they come are never final. More challenges always lie ahead. Each one of us also suffers some failures in life. We may fail to receive a grade we thought we deserved, or a job opportunity we wanted, or a marriage may fail. These failures are not fatal. We must put them behind us and go on to do our best with the opportunities at hand. And always, with each decision we are called upon to make in life, we must face it with courage—courage to do what we think is right and just and fair. May each of you also develop the courage to accept life's challenges and make from them a life worth living.

∽∾∾

Michael Eisner
CEO, Disney
Denison University

While you're setting goals, don't be afraid of failure. Fear of failure is a far worse condition than failure itself, because it kills off possibilities.

His one-sentence lecture on the subject was "Don't try something unless it is manifestly important and nearly impossible."

Norman Vincent Peale adds, "The trouble with most of us is that we would rather be ruined by praise than saved by criticism." Accept criticism with open arms, except from your mother. If your mother criticizes you, you are probably hopeless. . . .

The worst thing that can happen if you risk failure is that you will fail. But the fact is that most of the world's truly successful people fail many times over the course of a lifetime.

A man who worked on cartoons at my company for a while had earlier run a small film studio in Kansas City. He was such an enthusiastic novice that he went broke.

Penniless, he came to the West Coast and created a successful cartoon character. It was stolen from him.

After two such failures, many people would have given up. Instead, he tried again . . . and created a cartoon character that became enormously successful. The character was Mickey Mouse. The cartoonist was Walt Disney. Today I am grateful to both of them for my job.

ഇ∞

JOHNNETTA COLE
Anthropologist
Williams College

One hundred years ago, Gaius Charles Bolin graduated from this distinguished liberal arts college—the first African American to do so. . . . Today, one hundred years from the graduation of Gaius Charles Bolin, what are the prospects for millions of African-American youth? Will they, like Bolin, leave a fine liberal arts institution to pursue a career in law or some other profession, enjoying a life of prominence and the rewards of serving others?

Certainly a few will; and in this graduating class, there are those whose lives will be twenty-first-century versions of Bolin's. But unless we as a nation discover not only the will but the means to positively intervene in the lives of millions of black youngsters, they will be wasted. And a human mind—like a body and like a soul—is a terrible thing to waste.

Today, one in every five black youth is at risk of becoming a teen parent. One in seven of these is at risk of dropping out of school.

Today, there are ten-year-old kids who make $1,000 a day carrying drugs for those who are prepared to use our children in their traffic of death.

Today, there are more college-age black men in America's prisons and jails than in the dormitories of our colleges and universities.

Today, between 30 and 40 percent of all black American youngsters drop out of high school. The consequence of dropping out is captured in the fact that each additional year of secondary school reduces the chance of being on welfare by 35 percent. . . .

Today, in 1989, in our rich land, over one-third of all black Americans are living in poverty. While the life expectancy of white Americans continues to rise, for the very first time, between 1984 and 1986, that of black Americans declined. African Americans' rates of hypertension are 40 percent higher than that of white Americans; and the cancer rate is 20 percent higher.

Today, the leading cause of death for black males between fifteen and twenty-five years old is homicide. Black men are only 6 percent of the total U.S. population, but they make up 40 percent of the state and federal prison population. Black women head 41.5 percent of all black households in America.

On a day of great joy and happiness, why should you have to listen to descriptions of the plight of African-American youth? Quite simply because, in the words of Martin Luther King Jr., "Until all of us are free, not a single one of us is truly free!"

Then what might you do to help address the conditions of Bolin's descendants? What might you do for Gaius Charles Bolin, and for ourselves?

In tribute to Gaius Charles Bolin, for his descendants, indeed for all of us, I ask of you quite simply to give of yourselves. Regardless of the next steps for you, regardless of what career you devote your life to in the coming period, could you give a little of yourself for others? I don't mean that kind of giving that is built on noblesse oblige—feelings of guilt for the less fortunate. I mean the kind of giving that comes from that place inside each of us where our humanness resides. I mean the kind of giving that makes ordinary men and ordinary women great human beings.

I leave you with words from the Igbo people of Nigeria, words which I am convinced Gaius Bolin could have spoken:

> Not to know is bad.
> Not to want to know is worse.
> Not to hope unthinkable.
> Not to care unforgivable.

∽∽∽

RICHARD T. CUNNINGHAM
Attorney and Emeritus Trustee
Kent State University

Who is the successful person? Last year, Michael Milken, the king of junk bonds, made more than $500 million. He literally changed the structure of corporate America. He also got himself indicted and is presently facing criminal charges.

Let's compare that "success" with a true story about a good friend of mine. John is an outstanding teacher and educator in the local area. After I told him that I was going to be a commencement speaker, he handed me a letter and said, "Commencement is a very special time for me. On my son's commencement day, he gave me this letter which you may read."

John is an outstanding teacher, but not a famous person or one that has ever made $500 million a year, much less $50,000. Nevertheless . . .

It reads:

> Dad, I don't think we have ever had a very vocal father/son relationship. However, I think a mutual love and respect has evolved without the words. It is important to me that I express some of these inner feelings I have toward you. Most of the friends I speak with talk of how they would like to exemplify this or that characteristic of their father.
>
> It isn't like that for me.
>
> Dad, you are the type of person I hope to be like in every respect. I have yet to meet—and doubt I ever will meet—a person who doesn't have the highest respect for you as both a teacher and a person.
>
> It was not too long ago that I naively assumed that all people held the high moral and ethical standards that you do.
>
> Thank you for your role model; it will undoubtedly be the key factor in my future decision making when moral and ethical issues arise.
>
> Someday I will marry, and how do I know how to be a good husband?

One thing I'll never forget is how you said that your wife is your best friend.

But I think I could have guessed that from the way you and Mom are together.

The third hat you wear is that of a father. To rear me is a feat most fathers would have given up on. You have instilled a motivational force in me—a force that will not allow me to accept mediocrity.

In closing, let me just say thank you—thank you for being an exceptional role model, a caring father, and a close friend.

Who do you think is successful? Michael Milken, or my friend John?

∽∾∽

Joseph Brodsky[*]
Poet
Dartmouth College

A substantial part of what lies ahead of you is going to be claimed by boredom.

Known under several aliases—anguish, ennui, tedium, doldrums, humdrum, the blahs, apathy, listlessness, stolidity, lethargy, languor, torpor, etc.—boredom is a complex phenomenon and by and large a product of repetition. It would seem, then, that the best remedy against it would be constant inventiveness and originality. That is what you, young and new-fangled, would hope for. Alas, life won't supply you with that option, for life's main medium is precisely repetition. . . .

When hit by boredom, go for it. Let yourself be crushed by it; submerge, hit the bottom. In general, with things unpleasant, the rule is, the sooner you hit the bottom, the faster you surface. The idea here, to paraphrase another great poet of the English language, is to exact a full look at the worst. The reason boredom deserves such

*Used by permission of Farrar, Straus & Giroux

scrutiny is that it represents pure, undiluted time in all its repetitive, redundant, monotonous splendor.

In a manner of speaking, boredom is your window on time, on those properties of it one tends to ignore to the likely peril of one's mental equilibrium. In short, it is your window onto time's infinity, which is to say on your insignificance in it. That's what accounts, perhaps, for one's dread of lonely, torpid evenings, for the fascination with which one watches sometimes a fleck of dust aswirl in a sunbeam, and somewhere a clock tick-tocks, the day is hot, and your willpower is a zero.

Once this window opens, don't try to shut it; on the contrary, throw it wide open. For boredom speaks the language of time, and it is to teach you the most valuable lesson in your life—the one you didn't get here, on these green lawns—the lesson of your utter insignificance. It is valuable to you, as well as to those you are to rub shoulders with. "You are finite," time tells you in a voice of boredom, "and whatever you do is, from my point of view, futile." As music to your ears, this, of course, may not count; yet the sense of futility, of limited significance even of your best, most ardent actions, is better than the illusion of their consequences and the attendant self-aggrandizement. . . .

This is what it means—to be insignificant. If it takes will-paralyzing boredom to bring this home, then hail the boredom. You are insignificant because you are finite. Yet the more finite a thing is, the more it is charged with life, emotions, joy, fears, compassion. For infinity is not terribly lively, not terribly emotional. Your boredom, at least, tells you that much. Because your boredom is the boredom of infinity.

This is not to say that you have been conceived out of boredom, or that the finite breeds the finite (though both may ring true). It is to suggest, rather, that passion is the privilege of the insignificant.

So try to stay passionate, leave your cool to constellations. Passion, above all, is a remedy against boredom.

∽o∾

WENDELL BERRY*
Writer
College of the Atlantic

Our most serious problem, perhaps, is that we have become a nation of fantasists. We believe, apparently, in the infinite availability of finite resources. . . . We have an economy that depends not upon the quality and quantity of necessary goods and services but on the behavior of a few stockbrokers. We believe that democratic freedom can be preserved by people ignorant of the history of democracy and indifferent to the responsibilities of freedom.

Our leaders have been for many years as oblivious to the realities and dangers of their time as were George III and Lord North. They believe that the difference between war and peace is still the overriding political difference—when, in fact, the difference has diminished to the point of insignificance. How would you describe the difference between modern war and modern industry—between, say, bombing and strip mining, or between chemical warfare and chemical manufacturing? The difference seems to be only that in war the victimization of humans is directly intentional and in industry it is accepted as a trade-off.

Were the catastrophes of Love Canal, Bhopal, Chernobyl, and the *Exxon Valdez* episodes of war, or of peace? They were, in fact, peacetime acts of aggression, intentional to the extent that the risks were known and ignored.

We are involved unremittingly in a war not against foreign enemies, but against the world, against our freedom, and indeed against our existence. Our so-called industrial accidents should be looked upon as revenges of Nature. We forget that Nature is necessarily party to all our enterprises and that she imposes conditions of her own.

Now she is plainly saying to us: "If you put the fates of whole communities or cities or regions or ecosystems at risk in single ships or factories or power plants, then I will furnish the drunk or the fool or the imbecile who will make the necessary small mistake."

*Used by permission of Farrar, Straus & Giroux

JAMES B. STEWART
Writer
DePauw University

I want to explore with you an aphorism attributed to the Spanish saint Teresa of Avila: "More tears have been shed over answered prayers than unanswered prayers."

First of all, embedded in that statement is the assumption that one has prayers. That is something today that I'm afraid can't be taken for granted. I think I've had no more chilling experience recently than having attended a cocktail party for some college graduates in New York City, graduates of Ivy League schools. It took place in a Park Avenue apartment. It was given by extremely wealthy parents and these were young people who have literally had everything money could buy all their lives. What I encountered was boredom. They had Armani outfits, they had trips to Europe, they had cars, they had everything. I couldn't find out what they wanted, and they certainly did not seem to know.

If you have not yet developed any prayers of your own, now is the time to start, and I hope some of my remarks can help. I have some reassuring words to those of you who in fact have prayers that have already been dashed. There is no question in my own mind that failure is the foundation on which the greatest prayers are built, and that one can never fully savor the satisfactions of accomplishment unless one can contrast the feelings of hopes dashed or goals missed, by way of contrast.

Freud in many of his great writings mentioned that part of the process of becoming an adult is learning to embrace failure, to accept it, to bounce back, to grow from it, and to use that to develop new and perhaps even obtainable goals. Once you've decided that in fact it is time to focus on some prayers, and I use that in the broadest sense to mean dreams, aspirations, goals, desires . . . how do you get them? I think the process begins by exploring yourself internally and not going immediately outward.

How dramatically things have changed today. . . . I do not think that this is going to be necessarily an easier world in which to live. Again, the studies of nationalism persistently show that identities of nations are often forged through the presence of an enemy. And in the United States during all my lifetime, our national identity has largely been defined by the presence of a Soviet enemy. If you take this enemy away, I can predict, I think, with some confidence, there is going to be a scramble to find another enemy. Will it be the Japanese? That question will be decided by you and your generation. Will we turn internally for enemies? Or will we perhaps, idealistically, actually take human nature to a higher plane, where our own identities do not in fact depend on the presence of an enemy? The answer to these questions will have the profoundest implications for the world in which you are going to live; there will be no easy answers.

I wouldn't be here had I not gone out, done something I love (which really in and of itself probably would have been enough), achieved some measure of recognition, and indeed I hope in doing so, reflected well on this community, on family, and the many teachers and other people who made this possible. I have only one exhortation for you today. And that is to go now, go out into this huge, crazy, wonderful world and let your imaginations go. If you haven't before, start having dreams. Have lots of them. Have great dreams, have small dreams. I think I can tell you with a near certainty that some of those dreams—not all of them, but some of those dreams—will come true. And if there are tears, they will be tears of joy.

∽◦∾

Helen Vendler
Professor and Writer
Marlboro College

To those of you in the social sciences: you are our guides, not only to the global human past, but also to the human other. Our first great American poet, Walt Whitman, announced that there would speak through him "many long dumb voices," and the long-silent voices speak not only through poets but also through social scientists. Majority and minority alike are inchoate masses until a historian researches and writes, an anthropologist enters and participates, a psychologist listens with what Freud called the third ear, a sociologist draws heterogeneous data into intelligibility. You are the investigators who can replace prejudices with facts, tribal suspicion with global communication. You can give a human face to the statistics we necessarily are. In the last poem of his last book, Robert Lowell uttered a warning to poets that applies as well to everyone working with human beings en masse; besides our transient appearance as statistics, he said, we need to be described as living souls:

> We are poor passing facts,
> Warned by that to give
> Each figure in the photograph
> His living name.

As social scientists, you will remember that behind every statistic, every set of passing facts about any group—Republicans, mothers, people with AIDS, the unemployed, college graduates—there lie multitudes of living names.

To those of you in the humanities and arts it falls to create an American aesthetic culture. We are one of the youngest nations in the world; we have been here only two hundred years. The Holy Roman Empire when it was three hundred years old had not yet invented what we call European literature, art, and music. We probably have barely begun to invent American literature, art, and music, and the words to describe them through criticism, art history, and musicology. . . .

You are enjoined, by your reading here in the great naked modern books—Dostoyevsky, Kafka, Eliot, Beckett—to make the new Whitmans and Dickinsons of the twenty-first century welcome. "His country absorbs him," said Whitman of the poet, "as affectionately as he has absorbed it." You will be our makers and absorbers both.

⟳

1990

The threat of warfare and destruction in the world, which had disintegrated since the ending of the Cold War, revved up again in midsummer of 1990, when Saddam Hussein's military forces overran Kuwait, igniting an international crisis. The United Nations, considered by many a beneficent but undynamic organization, took immediate charge, passing twelve resolutions against Iraq, and the United States readied itself for what commentators were already referring to, with prophetic show business pizzazz, as the "showdown in the Gulf."

Ironically, 1990 was also the year East and West Germany became a unified nation for the first time since World War II; Mikhail Gorbachev was awarded the Nobel Peace Prize; Lech Walesa was elected president of Poland; and black nationalist leader Nelson Mandela was released after twenty-seven years in prison to a jubilant reception in his native South Africa. Even more promising, on February 2, South African president F. W. de Klerk announced that the South African government was lifting its longtime ban against the African National Congress, or ANC (the principal black organization determined to end white minority rule), and easing apartheid laws. Mandela arrived in New York for a nearly two-week tour, and by the end of 1990, he and de Klerk were engaging in formal talks between the South African government and the ANC.

Elsewhere in the world, Boris Yeltsin was elected president of the Russian Federation, and there was civil war in Liberia. George Bush broke his promise—"Read my lips"—that he would not raise taxes, announcing that the U.S. government would be unable to balance the federal budget without a tax increase; later that year, Bush would nominate David Souter to the U.S. Supreme Court. Another lone-gunman shooting took place in Jacksonville, Florida. On Broadway, A Chorus Line *finally closed*. Tom Cruise and Nicole Kidman tied the knot. Thieves broke into the formidable Isabella Stewart Gardner Museum in Boston, Massachusetts, stealing artwork valued at approximately $200 million. In Cincinnati, Ohio, the Contemporary Arts Center was acquitted on charges of obscenity arising over its exhibition of a Robert Mapplethorpe retrospective. Buster Douglas knocked out Mike Tyson. Mary Robinson was elected the first female president of Ireland, and in Great Britain, John Major became prime minister, succeeding Margaret Thatcher. Moviegoers turned to romantic films, including Ghost *and* Pretty Woman, *and younger audiences delighted in the notion of* Home Alone. *At the Oscars, Jessica Tandy took home the best actress Oscar for* Driving Miss Daisy. *Ken Burns's documentary on the American Civil War was PBS's most popular show ever. AIDS killed Halston, the designer. The arts world also lost Sammy Davis Jr., Leonard Bernstein, and Muppets creator Jim Henson. And in New York City, Greta Garbo died as secretly as she had lived.*

The aftereffects of the 1980s resonated. Another former Reagan appointee, John Poindexter, was convicted of five felony charges for his role in the Iran-Contra affair. Michael Milken pleaded guilty to securities fraud and was sentenced to ten years in prison. And in Washington, D.C., Mayor Marion Barry was convicted on a single misdemeanor drug charge, having been caught on videotape.

∽∘∾

TOM BROKAW
Broadcaster
Duke University

You are educated. Your certification is in your degree. You may think of it as the ticket to the good life. Let me ask you to think of an alternative.

Think of it as your ticket to join the revolution. Democracy is already here, you may say. I have what the others want. True. You also have certain assumptions, and you're not alone. Among them:

There will be more of everything. More affluence, more freedom, more rights because it's our due. As a society, we have come to believe what we have is maintenance-free.

It is not. It requires vigilance and nourishment. That is your responsibility and mine. It is the obligation of all, but it is especially the responsibility of the educated. A. Bartlett Giamatti characteristically said it well when he addressed a Yale graduating class: "When we are fatigued—or believe we should be; when we are frustrated because we are shackled, not redeemed by our best hopes, the tension between perfectibility and fallibility breaks us apart—and we share only a desire to lie low." This is not a time to lie low.

You are privileged. . . . You leave here armed with an education your generational counterparts in Eastern Europe, the Soviet Union, China, South Africa envy. What do you think a young Soviet citizen would do with your education? Or a young black South African? Or a Chinese?

Would they clutch it to their breasts? Would they lie low, in the words of Bart Giamatti? Or would they use it as a national resource for the common welfare?

It is a national resource, and there is much to be done.

∽◦∾

DESMOND TUTU
Archbishop
Wesleyan University

I stand here as an emissary from those who have been victims of one of the most racialist systems the world has known, stand here to say thank you to all of you for helping us in our struggle for a new and democratic and nonracial and nonsexist South Africa. Thank you for your love and for your prayers.

I would want to pay at this time a very warm tribute to young people, because young people in this country, in their concern for justice and for peace, helped to get this country out of the Vietnam War. You might have thought that there was a measure of self-interest in their concern, since it was their brothers who were dying in that war, and they themselves were due for the draft, some of them. But I was quite taken aback on one occasion when I came to this country and visited a number of university campuses and found there students campaigning for disinvestment in South Africa—doing so at a time when students should have been more properly worried about good grades and examinations—and saying they were concerned about people ten thousand miles away, saying by their actions that there were some things that were more important perhaps than good grades, than making it in the rat race. And my faith in humankind was restored by that spectacle. . . .

We live in extraordinary times, in stirring times. . . . It is truly extraordinary times when you think that in September of last year, our people could not walk on the beaches in South Africa, which were segregated, because the army came out onto the beach. And trying to walk on the beaches because we said we were going to defy unjust laws, since an unjust law does not oblige obedience, we had to run the gauntlet of police dogs, tear gas, and bullets.

When you think that last year, September, in our country, they had a racist election in which the government was painting the ANC as demons incarnate, it is extraordinary times when a Mr. de Klerk can, as he did on February 2, make what can only be described as an epoch-making speech. And then on February 11, we saw that extraordinary spectacle when the world was glued to their television sets to watch one prisoner emerge from prison and Nelson Mandela walked free. And the world, expecting someone who would be spewing forth hatred, bitterness, and revenge, were amazed at the man that they encountered, so full of humaneness, compassion, caring, deeply committed to a truly free, truly democratic South Africa.

And one wants to ask, "How come? How did all of this happen?" And I want to suggest a few reasons for why freedom is breaking out in so many unlikely places, with dictators and totalitarian rules biting the dust all over the place, doing so ignominiously. Why has it happened in our country when it seemed so unlikely only a few months ago? I think the first reason is that the government of South Africa discovered that there is an incredible resilience in a people, that you may for ages tread underfoot the dignity of persons, that you can rub their noses in the dust for an incredible length of time, and yet there is something in the human spirit that refuses to be quenched. That human beings are created freely for freedom. And so our people said to the South African government, "Despite all of your repression, despite all of your violence against us, you have had it. We are made for freedom, and our march to freedom is unstoppable." And the South African government recognized that freedom in the end is cheaper than repression.

And you saw something of the nobility of the human spirit, didn't you, when a student on Tiananmen Square in Beijing kept standing in front of the tanks, preventing the tanks from moving in one direction, and when they changed course he would come in front of them. And today, tomorrow, we think back a year ago to those events. And I have no doubt myself that that kind of indomitability is something that no ruler, however powerful, will be able to overcome.

But I believe, friends, much the most important, in a sense, reason why the kind of things that are happening at home are happening is that this is a moral universe. Right and wrong matter. Injustice and oppression and evil and exploitation will not ultimately have the final say. This is God's world and God is in charge. Moral decisions influence the way things turn out. Standing for truth and for right matter, and ultimately make a difference. . . .

Friends, we say we have no doubt we are going to be free in South Africa. We do not say perhaps it is a matter under discussion. We don't say, ah, maybe. . . . And so, dear friends, we say we are preparing the celebrations of a new South Africa. Truly democratic, nonracial, nonsexist, a South Africa where human beings count, not because of the biological irrelevance of their skin color, but because they are people of infinite worth, created in the image of God. We say we're going to be free, all of us, black and white together, for there is no other way in which we can survive, except together, black and white. There is no other way in which we can be human, except together, black and white. There is no other way in which we can be free, except together, black and white. And we say, we want to invite you, come and celebrate with us our freedom.

∽○∽

Barbara Bush
First Lady
Wellesley College

I hope that many of you will consider making three very special choices.

The first is to believe in something larger than yourself . . . to get involved in some of the big ideas of our time. I chose literacy because I honestly believe that if more people could read, write, and comprehend, we would be much closer to solving so many of the problems that plague our nation and our society.

Early on, I made another choice, which I hope you will make as well. Whether you are talking about education, career, or service, you are talking about life . . . and life really must have joy. It's supposed to be fun!

One of the reasons I made the most important decision in my life . . . to marry George Bush . . . is because he made me laugh. It's true, sometimes we've laughed through our tears . . . but that shared laughter has been one of our strongest bonds. Find the joy in life, because as Ferris Bueller said on his day off, "Life moves pretty fast. Ya don't stop and look around once in a while, ya gonna miss it."

The third choice that must not be missed is to cherish your human connections: your relationships with family and friends. For several years, you've had impressed upon you the importance to your career of dedication and hard work, and of course, that's true. But as important as your obligations as a doctor, lawyer, or business leader will be, you are a human being first, and those human connections—with spouses, with children, with friends—are the most important investments you will ever make.

At the end of your life, you will never regret not having passed one more test, not winning one more verdict, or not closing one more deal. You will regret time not spent with a husband, a child, a friend, or a parent.

Whatever the era—whatever the times—one thing will never change: fathers and mothers, if you have children, they must come first.

You must read to your children, hug your children, and you must love your children. Your success as a family—our success as a society—depends not on what happens in the White House, but on what happens inside your house.

✧✦✧

JILL KER CONWAY
Writer
Dartmouth College

Here you are—conscious of gifts and talents—burdened by student debt—by family expectations—ready to rush to Wall Street, to the nearest consulting firm, to the best specialty—to be rid of all those debts, financial and personal. For it is easy to value our talents as young graduates or beginning professionals as the market does.

And I am here to say—don't do it. At least don't do it without a lot of thought—if you want to keep on growing as a person—finding the meaning of those talents—striving to tap your deepest motivations—and your real sources of creativity. That is a long-term endeavor with high long-term yields.

I am *not* telling you to scorn the market, and capitalist incentives. It is clear that over the long haul, they are the most effective means of mobilizing energy and distributing goods and services. I *am* telling you to search for your real vocation—that full expression of your talents—that connection between your moral and spiritual self—which will keep you developing.

Our society's problems of productivity come, in part, because our young no longer think of work as a vocation, and because they are so burdened by debt that they rush unthinkingly to the highest-paying entry-level job. But a true vocation brings our best talents to bear on tasks society needs, and through working on them, we focus our most creative energies.

So, look for that vocation. Forget the starting salary, and remember that your biggest debt is to your talents—and to the people who have helped you foster them so far.

Ben Cohen
Cofounder, Ben & Jerry's
Hampshire College

I've been, I think accurately, described as a "hippie dropped-out industrialist." You can find articles about me in both the *New Age* and the *Wall Street Journal*. But the latest magazine that was interested in talking to me is *Success* magazine, and so I've been thinking a little about the idea of success lately, and I noticed that my definition of success doesn't really jive with *Success* magazine's idea. You know, people in general look at me as a successful ice-cream businessman. I think it's important to know that it would be just as true to look at me as a failure as a potter. I spent six years of my life trying to become a potter. I love pottery, and I really wanted to become one, but I found that I enjoyed doing pottery a lot more than people liked buying my pots. So I really wasn't able to make it as a potter. You know, it occurs to me that success is not a place, but it's a process. Success is a path, a journey, lifelong learning, evolution, and growth. If Ben & Jerry's were to go out of business tomorrow, would that make me a failure? I feel like success is a spiral with trying, failing, learning, and growing, and that's what excellence is also. You know, we never achieve excellence, we always fail, but the process of failing, and learning, and growing, and coming closer and closer, to me that's excellence, that's success.

And I need to tell you that I would much rather fail at something new than succeed at something old. You know, I wonder why this society in general has such a strange and inaccurate definition of success. And I think part of it might be because we tend to concentrate on that which we can measure, and the things which we tend to measure most are those which are easiest to measure, or most quantifiable. The ironic part is that things which are easiest to measure are the least important. It's the intangibles—caring, spirit, joy, intuition, love, warmth, trust—those are the things that matter most, and those are the things that our society values least because we can't quantify them.

✌︎⊙✍︎

JOHNNETTA COLE
Anthropologist
Grinnell College

Think globally and act locally.

Our world obviously grows smaller and smaller as technology connects us one to the other. Compared to the old days, even think about language now as people run around talking about "faxing" each other. Consumers in our nation are keenly aware these days of international products. The profusion of products in American lives that are made in Japan, Taiwan, and Brazil, for example, and Haiti, gives us at least some awareness of a commercial world beyond our borders. Of course, to be an informed American citizen one ought to know that people don't speak Spanish in Brazil, and Zimbabwe and Zambia aren't the same.

But I am calling for a way of thinking that is far more profound than knowing that your shoes were made in Brazil, or that the capital of Burkina Faso is Ouagadougou. I'm talking about a new way of thinking that rests on the assumption that you cannot fully understand your own life and events which surround you without knowing and thinking beyond your life, your own neighborhood, and even your own nation. I'm calling for learning to think globally in a way that rests on related assumptions from the field of anthropology, and that is, that we learn a great deal from the comparative method. I think that I now know more about American education because I am exploring how it's done in Japan, and I submit that nothing quite instructs us on the nature of persistent racism in America like seriously studying apartheid in South Africa. For me, one of the most compelling reasons why I urge you, the first graduates of this decade, to continue to think globally is that thinking globally is the antithesis of thinking provincially, chauvinistically, ethnocentrically. . . .

How does one learn to think in global terms? Is it magic? Is it difficult? Is it doable? Yes to each of the above. It's as magical as having a lightbulb go off over your head when you finally open your eyes and ears and mind to the ways of another reality. It is as difficult as it has always been for a person to give up a prejudice, to shed bigotry.

But it is as doable as anything else that draws on the human capacity to learn. . . .

I believe that we learn to think globally by engaging in that special exercise called human empathy. Not sympathy, but empathy. It is human empathy that will allow you to know what it's like to be a homeless kid in Palestine and a homeless kid in Atlanta, Georgia. Human empathy will permit you to know the plight of an untouchable in India and a victim of AIDS in the United States.

What, then, is the connection between learning to think globally and acting locally? Perhaps no one has ever put it better than Malcolm X when he said, "You won't ever change Johannesburg until you change Mississippi. And changing Mississippi will help you to change Johannesburg."

⧉

Paul Newman
Actor
Sarah Lawrence College

The best thing you can give yourselves for graduation is the gift of possibility. And the best thing you can give each other is the pledge to go on protecting that gift in each other as long as you live.

Now, I'm a late learner and I've spent a lifetime rummaging around in my head to see if I could discern a plan, a diagram—could perceive, even dimly, some design in all those incidents I've bumped into, or that have bumped into me. And the event that glued it all together started, mystically enough, in a cellar full of bottles. There, at the pinnacle of my success, my twenty-five-foot image vibrating with desire—and desirability and gratitude—an idea arrived that would permit me to use the pulpit of my achievement not only for the betterment of humankind, but also to recycle the bottles. An old pal joined me, a plot was hatched: we would bring to the beleaguered of the world something they longed for more than home, more than redemption, more even than immortality: salad dressing.

In that dark cellar, on that propitious night, illuminated fitfully by a scudding moon, we conceived, in an ecstasy of garlic and puree of onion, a character that we named Salad King. "My own, my own!" I sobbed as I watched it birth itself in a puddle of vinegar there on the dank cellar floor. "It's *alive!*" we shouted as it bestirred itself. We stood it up on its spindly legs, aimed it toward the ladder of success, and commanded it to climb!

Well, it fell flat on its face. It had "tacky" written all over its forehead, and as a matter of fact, so did we. We decided then and there that it wasn't its ingredients that were making it falter on the first rung; it was its purpose in the world; and we pledged to each other that if rewards should ever accrue, they would be given forever in charity.

Would you believe, at that exact instant, the spunky little bugger gathered itself up, welded on its knuckles, and started slugging, kicked the bejesus out of all available contenders! The *Kid!* The salad kind! Packed the supermarkets coast to coast. Knocked 'em silly— off the shelf. With a mind of its own it went way beyond any authorship of mine—buckets to give away each year; it began to invest in communities everywhere.

In a camp for children with catastrophic blood diseases—a place on a lake that looked like a turn-of-the-century logging camp. A lunatic idea. But it rallied everyone—from the medical team at Yale to the Navy Seabees, from the people who build swimming pools to the king of Saudi Arabia—and so many volunteer counselors there wasn't room to let them all in.

It was for sick children, but you know who's recovering? Us. Some kids have their miracles, too, and the rest have a very good time. But the biggest beneficiaries, as near as we can tell, are the staff, the crews, and the counselors....

There is a counselor at the camp, a teacher in real life at the University of Connecticut. One day he was with a young boy about eight years old whose immune system began rejecting his own extremities—his hands, his feet, little by little. They were sitting on a rock by the lake, this counselor and this boy, because the boy wasn't strong enough on that particular day to go fishing, or whatever he was scheduled to do, and they were talking about God, and whether there was one. The boy said he wasn't too conversant with God, but he did know about the big bang theory. And it fascinated him that in the expanding universe, force is balanced and finite—that whatever energy you exert in one direction is precisely what comes back from another. And the counselor said he was glad that the camp was different from the rest of the universe because, at least for him, he got back a good deal more than he put into it. The kid wrangled that one awhile, and said, "Well, maybe *that's* God." So—if not God, as close to heaven as I'd ever hope to get.

Congratulations. You are much loved. Go get 'em.

∽○∾

CATHLEEN BLACK
President, Hearst
Simmons College

We live in a time when success is too often measured in numbers and letters.

Think of the measures we assign to people's lives that we equate with value: salary; what our apartments or homes are worth; the number of job offers received; titles.

It's a mistake to think that numbers or letters in themselves are measures of success. They describe certain forms of achievement, that's all. It is ridiculous to think that a $90,000-a-year investment banker is more successful than an elementary school teacher who makes just enough to live on.

It is equally ridiculous to think that a married woman is more successful than an unmarried woman, or a woman with three kids is more successful than a woman with no kids. Or that a mother who has a career outside the home is more important than a woman who chooses to be at home with her children.

When we try to quantify success this way, we sell ourselves—and everyone else—short. The point of all the change we, as women, have witnessed in the last decade, is to provide choices in life. Ones that we control and determine.

A few months ago, I heard John Brademas, the president of New York University, speak on "The Difference Between Success and

Excellence." He quoted Thomas Boswell, a sportswriter for the *Washington Post*, who believes that we have an obsession with winning because we confuse success and excellence.

Success, says Boswell, "is measured externally . . . by comparison with others; success is often beyond our personal control, and moreover, it is perishable.

"Excellence, on the other hand, is an internal quality, a consequence in large measure of the capacity and of the commitment of an individual. Excellence, therefore, endures."

That's what I wish for you—and I encourage you to wish for yourselves—excellence. Excellence is found in self-esteem, in pride, in ethical behavior. In sharing riches . . .

If we believe that excellence is an internal quality, as Boswell suggests, and not a result to be judged externally, then we need to know how to *nurture excellence in ourselves.*

I believe that excellence begins with self-esteem. It's knowing what your special talents are, and taking pride in them. Society thinks of some talents as more important than others. We admire singers, doctors, dancers, mathematicians, lawyers, and artists. We speak of professionals as being "talented."

But what about women who make beautiful quilts? What about women who tell wonderful stories which can transform a noisy group of children into a rapt audience? What about women—and men—who bake fabulous cookies? Or nurse their aging parents?

What about the mothers in the inner city who are their neighborhood watchdogs, activists, and social service providers? What about social workers? And community volunteers? What about simply being a good listener, a good confidant, a good friend?

These are all special talents. These are all things anyone can be good at and should be proud of. To undervalue our human talents as not important, lucrative, or creative enough is to undermine self-esteem.

It is a myth that the sum of your talents is equal to the sum of your paycheck. Talent, like success, is what you define it to be. *Excellence is doing your best at what you do best.*

∞

Carl Sagan
Astronomer and Writer
University of Illinois at Champaign-Urbana

I never once said that phrase. I mean, I said that there are hundreds of billions of stars in the galaxy, I said that there are billions of trillions of stars in the universe, but I never once said billions and billions. . . .

We've explored many dozens of worlds, if you include the moons as well as the planets. We have seen magnificent landscapes. We have learned an enormous amount of information, but there is not a hint of anything alive. We have not landed on most of those worlds; there may be something living that we haven't been smart enough to detect yet, but at least as far as we know, there is no life on any of those worlds. You can have dozens of worlds and have life on only one of them. And so it seems natural to me, after this twenty-five-year period of exploration that I've been involved in, to turn my attention back to this world, the only one we know that is graced by life.

Spacecraft have enhanced our appreciation of this world: they have provided the first pictures of the whole Earth. Most striking were the first such pictures, the color photos of the Earth taken by the Apollo astronauts on their voyages to the moon. What we saw was a small, beautiful, blue-and-white jewel-like world set against the velvet backdrop of space. You look at those pictures and, unbidden, the thought arises that this is a fragile and vulnerable place. If you look closely, you can see on the daylit hemisphere a kind of corona, a kind of aura of blue, and that's just the scattering of sunlight off the atmosphere. What is so striking about it (many astronauts have commented on it) is how thin it seems. Indeed, the thickness of the Earth's atmosphere compared to the diameter of the Earth is about the same as the thickness of the coat of shellac on a school globe compared to the diameter of the globe. There is hardly any air there.

When we started out, we humans, in East Africa a million or two years ago, our numbers were very small, our technological abilities extremely limited. The idea that we might influence the environment of the planet on which we depend could never have arisen in the most prescient of our ancestors of that time. But today, there are 5.3 billions of us (truly billions and billions). Our technology has reached formidable, indeed even awesome, proportions. Today we are fully able to make catastrophic changes in the environment that sustains us, not only on purpose, but also inadvertently, accidentally. If we don't watch what we're doing, we can make great troubles for ourselves.

∽∾

Wendy Wasserstein
Playwright
Mount Holyoke College

I know there are those of you here today who dissected a squid in freshman zoology and immediately knew, "This is bliss." But my guess is that the majority of us aren't that fortunate or that fond of squid. Most of us find our roads in a more circuitous way.

I began my playwriting career my junior year when I was taking Victoria Schuck's political science course and studying to be a congressional intern and kept falling asleep on the *Congressional Digest* in the library. A friend of mine asked me why I was doing that when we could take playwriting . . . and then go shopping. And although I loved the theater, it was really the shopping that got me. . . . But that playwriting class was the first time I realized that you could get credit in life for something you liked to do.

There are so many shoulds for women of your generation. And there are so many catchphrases. Thank heavens, ones like the "Mommy track" and "having it all" seem to be on the way out. But I am constantly hearing that the future happiness of young women's personal and professional lives depends on "juggling" and "balancing." But in the midst of these circus acts is a self that has been nurtured here, that will lead you to what you really want to do. There is no one plan that is workable. There isn't one way of doing it that is best. But there is something to be said for passion. There's something to be said for caring deeply.

In playwriting terms, today the curtain is going up and the action begins. Take all the goodness, honesty, intelligence, toughness, and wit that you learned here and don't compromise them. So much has been written about the women of the nineties. My response is, the women of the nineties have yet to make their mark. Go out there and do something remarkable. Don't live down to expectations. The women of the nineties are you.

∽०∾

Gary Larson
Cartoonist
Washington State University

I wish you much weirdness in your lives.

∽०∾

1991

Following the failure of talks between U.S. secretary of state James Baker and Iraq's foreign minister, Tariq Aziz, 1991 witnessed the first ever "live" war: the United States versus Iraq, televised in real time from Kuwait. To many Americans, the war felt like nothing less than a football game taking place in the air, a game that ended a month and a half after it started when the allied forces, led by General "Stormin' Norman" Schwarzkopf, liberated Kuwait.

By year's end, it was a domestic debate that people would find it difficult to forget: a drawn-out congressional hearing pitting a black Supreme Court nominee named Clarence Thomas against a young black law professor named Anita Hill.

Internationally, the world scene was changing swiftly, without apology and without, it seemed, looking back. The leaders of Hungary, Poland, and Czechoslovakia agreed that their nations would thenceforth become free-market economies. Macedonia, Croatia, and Slovenia declared their independence from Yugoslavia. The U.S.S.R. again dominated world news, as Mikhail Gorbachev relinquished his presidency and the country the world had always known as Russia fractured into a Commonwealth of Independent States. All charges against Oliver North for his role in the Iran-Contra affair were dropped, leaving North free to pursue a career as a radio talk-show host.

In Milwaukee, Wisconsin, thirty-one-year-old Jeffrey Dahmer was arrested after police found human heads in his apartment. Magic Johnson, the Los Angeles Lakers' basketball star, announced that he had contracted the AIDS virus. Theatergoers flocked to see Miss Saigon, and Katie Couric joined the Today show. Eastern Airlines ceased operations, as did Pan American Airways. In Los Angeles, a *grand jury indicted four white police officers for the beating of a black motorist named Rodney King.* Dances with Wolves *swept the Academy Awards. Another lone gunman went on a shooting rampage in Killeen, Texas. The body of media kingpin Robert Maxwell was found floating off the Canary Islands. In the Louisiana gubernatorial election, Governor Edwin Edwards defeated former Ku Klux Klan leader David Duke. Martha Graham died at age ninety-six. Winnie Mandela, the wife of Nelson Mandela, was convicted of kidnapping and sentenced to six years in prison. Indira Gandhi's son Rajiv was assassinated near Madras, in India, and Boris Yeltsin was elected to the brand-new position of executive president of the Russian Federation. In Haiti, president Jean-Bertrand Aristide was overthrown in a coup. The Chicago Bulls won their first ever NBA championship. Theodor Geisel—aka Dr. Seuss—died in La Jolla, California.*

But while the war took the headlines, it was the Clarence Thomas–Anita Hill affair that took a cultural center stage, introducing to the world lexicon the term "sexual harassment"; concurrently, another term, "date rape," entered the lexicon. In the end, however, Clarence Thomas was elevated to the U.S. Supreme Court (succeeding Thurgood Marshall) by a narrow vote in the Senate of 52 to 48. William Kennedy Smith, the nephew of the slain president, was tried and acquitted on national television on sexual battery charges—for allegedly raping a young woman in front of the Kennedys' beachfront mansion in Palm Beach, Florida.

∽○∾

John Clendenin
Professor
Georgia State University

In all things, be willing to listen to people around you. None of us is really smart enough to go it alone.

∽○∾

JOHN NAISBITT
Writer
Syracuse University

We get lost in the details that each day's newspaper brings us. But if you look at the decade as a whole, there is cause for much optimism. How can I not be optimistic when I see democratic governments with free-market economies being set up all over Eastern Europe? How can I not be optimistic when the Soviet Union is no longer a threat to America? How can I not be optimistic when I see that all over the world the shift is from authoritarian regimes to democracy, laying the political groundwork for more economic growth?

In our new information global economy, our human resources are the competitive edge. That's why education is so important. There is nothing on America's social agenda, nothing on America's economic agenda, that is more important than attending to our education systems.

We are living in the time of the parenthesis, the time between eras, the time of transition. We haven't fully left the old industrial era and we aren't fully up to speed in the new information electronics global era. We are astraddle these eras in this time of the parenthesis. It's a time of great change, a time of great uncertainty, and we must make uncertainty our friend. In stable eras, everything has a name and everything knows its place and you and I can leverage very little. But in the time of the parenthesis, we have extraordinary leverage and extraordinary influence, individually, professionally, and institutionally, if we can get a clear sense, a clear vision of the road ahead. And that's why I say, what a fantastic time to be alive, what a fantastic time to graduate.

೧౦౦

Elizabeth Dole
Chairman, American Red Cross
Dartmouth College

Material possessions rust away, wear away, or depreciate. Character alone will never tarnish.

Whether on the floor of Congress or in the corridors of a big city hospital, there is no body of professional expertise and no anthology of case studies which can supplant the force of character. Character provides both a sense of direction and a means to fulfillment. It asks not what you want to be but who you want to be. For in the final analysis, it is your moral compass that counts for more than any bank balance, any résumé, and, yes, any diploma.

∽∾∾

Chinua Achebe
Writer
Hobart and William Smith Colleges

You might say, "We have no power." But is that really so? When the pop singers of England and then America . . . raised their voices together in concert some years ago, did they not discover for us new isotopes of power? And is this really such a surprise? The power of creation is there in all its magnificence in the myths and legends of the world. The power of the word, the power of the mind. The power of cooperation, of love and compassion.

Here is a celebration of that power in an Inuit poem:

> That was the time when words were like magic
> The human mind had mysterious powers
> A word spoken by chance
> Might have strange consequences
> It would suddenly come alive

And what people wanted to happen could happen
All you had to do was say it.

Note the last two lines particularly:

And what people wanted to happen could happen
All you had to do was say it.

∽○∾

MADELEINE L'ENGLE
Writer
Wellesley College

Don't fall into martyrdom! That's a choice, too. So is being a victim. I don't like that word. When bad things happen, it is up to me to choose to be a victim or to get on with it. Terrible things can happen to us— rape, accident, bereavement—all precarious and full of the unexpected; but we do not have to become victims, no matter what happens.

∽○∾

FREEMAN DYSON
Scientist and Writer
Haverford College

The purpose of science is to create opportunities for unpredictable things to happen. When nature does something unexpected, we learn something about how nature works. It used to be said before the recent era of revolutionary discoveries that science was organized common sense. In the modern era, it would be more accurate to say science is organized unpredictability.

So the great task before us now and before you as citizens of the world is to learn how to organize our societies in such a way that unpredictable things have a chance to happen. A number of revolutions in our thinking are long overdue. We need a collapse of nationalism and a rising commitment to international institutions. We need a collapse of greed and a commitment to decent treatment of the poor. We need a collapse of military rivalry and a commitment to a worldwide effort to preserve our planet as a fit home for mankind and other living creatures. The conventional wisdom says that none of these revolutions will happen. But we have seen in the last two years a number of revolutions that the conventional wisdom had declared impossible.

The overdue revolutions are unpredictable, but not impossible. It is your task, both in science and in society at large, to prove the conventional wisdom wrong and to make your unpredictable dreams come true.

∾∽

BARBARA EHRENREICH
Writer
Bryn Mawr College

I am talking about the habitual meanness that seems to require us to have an enemy in order to define our identity. When the Cold War ended, were there celebrations in Washington? No, there was a search for a new enemy to replace what we lost. First drugs. We had a war on drugs. Why a war? Why not a public health campaign against drugs and a war against poverty? And, may I ask, what does it say about us, that drugs are illegal and guns are not? Yes, drugs can kill and destroy lives, but guns have no other purpose but to kill and destroy lives.

Then, in the search for an enemy, there was Manuel Noriega. A few of you might remember him. Then Saddam Hussein. Both, admittedly, tyrants who were former allies, though transformed overnight into embodiments of evil. Is it too seditious to ask why they were our allies in the first place? Or to ask why our foreign policy now seems to be conducted like a rogue police operation, focused on individual miscreants with so little regard for the larger populations at risk?

I am talking, too, about the escalating violence of our culture and entertainment spectacle. Consider this. Last fall, a museum director in Cincinnati was brought to trial for exhibiting the works of Robert Mapplethorpe, which some people found offensive because of the homoerotic themes. Fortunately, the museum director was acquitted. But my point is that at roughly the same time, Hollywood was bringing us works like *Total Recall, Predator II, Terminator Ten* or *Fifteen,* whatever it is, and no one even thought of bringing a Hollywood producer to trial. Now, what can we conclude? That images of men loving men are suspect at best, but men killing men, decapitating men, mutilating and dismembering men, that's all right, that's entertainment.

∽∾∾

WILLIAM CHACE
President, Emory College
Wesleyan University

Now let me talk about a metaphor. This metaphor, with which you are all familiar, is that of "the level playing field." That is the field of competition where we all want to play. The game, we think, will be fair there. You who are about to enter the world of competition in professional schools, in the workplace, and in developing your careers would like to play on the level playing field.

I am here to tell you that, for you, it won't be level. This is because you are about to enter competition with most all of the advantages on your side. . . . To put it very bluntly, there will be certain people with whom you won't have to compete. They just won't be around.

Consider these grim, sad facts:

The United States ranks last among nineteen nations in its infant mortality rates, and nonwhite infants are more than twice as likely to die as white ones. Moreover, one in four homeless people in cities is a child. The early dead and the homeless won't be competing with you. The contest is easier. That's regrettable.

And if some people live, they don't live for long. Life expectancy for young black males in American cities is lower than that for males of equivalent age in Bangladesh. In 1987, black males between the ages of fifteen and nineteen were ten times more likely to be shot and five times more likely to be murdered otherwise than white males of similar age. You won't have to compete with the urban dead and wounded.

And many of those who survive will be locked up. The rate of incarceration in the United States has doubled during the 1980s, and is expected to double again by the end of the century. We lock up a lot of people, more so than does the Soviet Union or South Africa. Those people won't be competing with you.

Among the children who do survive these grim realities, some don't learn enough to compete. Half of this country's seventeen-year-olds are not good enough in math, reading, and science to be able to perform such simple tasks as summarizing an editorial in a newspaper or calculating decimals. Such folks won't offer you much competition. That is true, tough, and regrettable.

I ask you, then, to consider the absences. They are many. You are not on a level playing field. You are staring down from a mountain.

Or I can put it in yet another way. The mountain is staring down at you.

∞∞

BOB EDWARDS
Radio Broadcaster
Grinnell College

Failure is intensely interesting.

What's interesting about failure is how you handle it. A few years ago, PBS did a program about half a dozen middle-aged men who had been classmates at Yale. My memory is that maybe one of them was somewhat happy with his lot in life. The others had lots of reasons why it turned out wrong. . . . No episode of *Thirtysomething* had as much whining as this program had. But as Kipling said: "We have forty million reasons for failure, but not a single excuse." "No excuses" is a great slogan and deserves better than display on the butts of blue jeans. "No excuses" should be our national motto—though I'm kind of fond of *E Pluribus Unum*.

You will succeed, on your terms, in whatever way you define success. If you don't, no excuses. OK—one excuse: catastrophic illness affecting you or one close to you, God forbid. Other than that, no excuses. Not for race, creed, color, national origin, physical disability, sexual orientation, make of car, affiliation with the wrong clubs, lack of popularity in junior high, or too much TV in early childhood. No excuses.

Success is not hard if you define it in a wholesome, realistic manner. Just don't set goals for yourself that are absolutely impossible to achieve, or goals that are not worth achieving. If your goal is to make a killing on the market so you can join a Republican country club and complain over martinis about the unions, the immigrants, and the tax laws—well, maybe you deserve to fail. I'm not going to feel sorry for you, especially if you're giving me excuses.

Success is something you work for—something you simply have to have—something that's worth the sweat and sacrifice.

And you'll have success if you have the talent to do the job and the desire to apply that talent to achieve what you want. People with talent and desire are in demand.

So, what's going to hold you back? Racial and sex discrimination? Well, you can count on it. And here's what you do about it. You make your complaint. No action? Then you sue them, and win or lose, you move on. Give your talents to an outfit that wants you and is worthy of you. If you've got the talent and desire, they'll find a spot for you and give you a chance to advance. But be honest with yourself. Don't claim discrimination or harassment if you know in your heart that you didn't have the goods. Because then it's just an excuse, and you know how I feel about excuses.

White people have excuses, too. Some are saying affirmative action is keeping them back. I'd bet that in most cases that claim is an excuse. I lost a job to affirmative action sixteen years ago last month. Best thing that ever happened to me. The network that passed me by has since fired more than half its news staff, lost much of its audience, and is currently in last place in the ratings.

So instead of working for that network, I stayed at NPR, where we've expanded our staff to about twenty times what it was sixteen years ago, and we have an audience greater than any of the morning TV programs.

Besides, if I had really shown that network some talent and desire, they'd have found a slot for me. No excuses.

It's your turn. Go realize your potential and know that your fellow man or woman is not your enemy. The one who can keep you from achieving your goal is the one you see in the mirror. I hope you like what you see there.

∽◦∾

Bryant Gumbel
Broadcaster
Providence College

You will find that the world is not inclined to gauge your intelligence by the strength of your grades. Rather, most will view your diploma as an indication that you possess intelligence.

It's a constant reminder to you of what you are capable of—a certified reminder of your curiosity, your perseverance. It indicates what you're about and it arms you with a formidable weapon with which to attack the future. You are armed, too, with the force of youth. You may think that a tired cliché and pooh-pooh the idea now, but later will, I guarantee you, come to appreciate it. Youth is not, as Shaw once suggested, wasted on the young . . . but only undervalued by those who don't recognize its worth. You're at a point thankfully where a mistake isn't a final note . . . where one error generally won't spoil a dream. Your youth provides you with the chance to be uncertain . . . to try, and if necessary, to fail. You may be anxious to rush up on your future, but youth guarantees you the luxury that the future won't rush up on you. . . .

I grew up thinking that some people—the famous, the strong, the caring, the dedicated, the involved—were somehow inherently better than I was. I grew up thinking them smarter, or wittier, or luckier, or harder-working than I ever thought I would be. Instead, what I've learned from daily on-air encounters is that those who influence my world and yours do so because they want to, and because they've dared to try.

They are the people you speak of and read about every day. Sometimes in headlines, ofttimes in whispers. They are players and they matter. In most cases, they've no more smarts than you . . . they're no less ambitious . . . have no more free time . . . they're just as selfish. But ultimately, they make a decision to be more than just a spectator in life because they have "graduated" to more than that. . . .

What you'll find is that being involved means taking some hits from people who say hosannas to your principles until those principles collide with their backdoor.

They'll tell you honesty's great until you tell them an unpleasant truth. They'll applaud your courage until it creates discomfort for them. They'll salute your loyalty until it's mistaken for acceptance of anything they do and they'll praise your pride until it outdistances their own. Be an empty glad-hander and everyone'll be your friend. Get involved . . . do what's right . . . be committed . . . "graduate" to all of that, and ultimately the small, the ignorant, the petty will try to reduce you in size. It's not a pleasant prospect, but I guarantee you it's much more attractive than joining their ranks without ever coming to bat.

Live your life with a purpose beyond yourself, and you'll find that the world is as bold and as broad as the interest that brought you here today. Live it only for yourself, and its limits will always be at arm's length, and if I've one wish for you today it's that you could understand how empty a fair-weather life eventually proves to be.

∽◦∽

1992

A new president and vice president stood poised to take over the White House: former Arkansas governor William Jefferson Clinton beat not only George Bush but a vaguely mean-spirited Texas billionaire named Ross Perot. It was Clinton's and Vice President Al Gore's youth that many voters found most extraordinary: both were born after World War II, and baby boomers everywhere, particularly women who were offended by the largely male and largely out-of-touch Senate during the Clarence Thomas–Anita Hill hearings, found themselves cheering the election of a youthful president. The only person not cheering was the baffled and disappointed sitting president, George Bush.

Following the breakup of Yugoslavia, three former Yugoslav republics—Croatia, Slovenia, and Bosnia-Herzegovina—were admitted to the U.N. in 1992. Disney opened EuroDisney, outside Paris, to typically mixed reviews from the French. Across the channel, John Major gained a fourth term for the Conservative Party. A wave of neo-Nazi violence erupted in Europe, largely in Germany, primarily against Turks, causing massive finger-pointing and inquiries about Europe's "character." Congress was torn in two by scandal, and Los Angeles experienced severe civil disorder. After nearly thirty years, Johnny Carson exited the airwaves, as did The Cosby Show. *The so-called Dream Team, a collection of all-star basketballers culled from the NBA who decimated the international competition, commandeered Olympic headlines, and ultimately walked away with the gold medal. The improbably named Boutros Boutros-Ghali began a five-year term as secretary general of the United Nations. Thousands upon thousands of Haitians escaping their country into America were repatriated; critics cried racism. Menachem Begin, who signed a peace treaty with Egypt, died in Jerusalem.*

Our dominant national problem—race—reared its head in 1992. In Simi Valley, California, a Superior Court jury acquitted four white police officers of all but one count in the case stemming from the beating of Rodney King in March 1991. A state of emergency was declared when looting and violence broke out in Los Angeles. Eventually, all four officers would be indicted once again on federal charges of violating Rodney King's civil rights. The Chicago Bulls won their second NBA league title in a row. The Washington Post *announced that approximately a dozen women had made allegations of sexual harassment against Oregon senator Bob Packwood; that same year saw nine women accuse Senator Daniel Inouye of a similar offense. South Africa witnessed continued strife and violence. Former Panamanian dictator Manuel Noriega was sentenced to prison in the United States. "Downsizing" was the operative word on Wall Street and within the business world. The exploits of* Murphy Brown *riveted television viewers.* Macy's and Trans World Airlines—TWA—filed for bankruptcy protection. In Indiana, Mike Tyson was convicted of rape. In December, just before the holidays, John Major, the head of Britain's Conservative Party, announced that Prince Charles and Princess Diana had "agreed to separate."

Politically, a torch had been passed.

❦

Ann Richards
Governor, Texas
University of Texas at Austin

We are just completing a period in our history that has come to be known as the "Me Decade."

There were images of people straight out of college making six figures . . . of young titans like Michael Milken running billion-dollar scams with other people's money . . . of elders like Leona Helmsley telling you that only the little people pay taxes.

But it was all an aberration.

Leona Helmsley never really looked happy to me anyway.

And she probably wasn't.

But the more serious problem was that millions of people were unhappy with themselves . . . because they were sitting there thinking that if they didn't rate a spot on *Lifestyles of the Rich and Famous,* it was because they were suckers or fools.

If that is true, there are an awful lot of us fools.

Because most of that grand new wealth, that outrageous affluence, went to less than 20 percent of the American population. The rest of us saw little of it or counted ourselves lucky to hold our economic ground.

And a lot of people didn't hold their ground. Millions of families in this country slipped into poverty during the Me Decade.

And we have begun this decade with a recession that reached well into the middle class . . . and beyond it, into the ranks of the white-collar workers who have lost their jobs and lost their businesses. And I know for a lot of you out there, it is really tough figuring out what you are going to do. That's the real world.

Even those who reaped the profits of the eighties are finding that money may buy the trappings of success, but it comes up short on personal satisfaction.

Hollywood is about as upscale as you can get . . . and if you saw the movie *The Player,* you heard one of the great comments on how the high life doesn't mean much if you haven't got a life.

One high-living young studio executive is talking to another as he is cruising down the boulevard in his expensive sports car . . . he mentions that he's on his way to an Alcoholics Anonymous meeting.

He's going there, even though he doesn't have a drinking problem, because "that's where all the big deals are made now."

There you have it. Megadollars changing hands while everyone is trying to make sense of their lives.

What's wrong with this picture?

∽o∽

DANIEL PATRICK MOYNIHAN
U.S. Senator
Hobart and William Smith Colleges

You may be part of the first generation in American history in which large portions of the population are worse off than their parents had been, something we have never known in our ten-generation history. Social progress is slow, but social regression can be rapid indeed. We see signs of social regression all over this nation, and especially in our cities, and we see signs of rising anger. Years ago, in *Civilization and Its Discontents*, Sigmund Freud wrote: "*Homo homini lupus*"—man is a wolf to man. "Civilized society," he said, "is perpetually menaced with disintegration through this primary hostility of men towards one another." If men and women can build a community of love, it is almost always by virtue of having an external enemy to hate. And so in the aftermath of the Cold War—the Long Peace, as it has been called—we look up and we find ethnic violence everywhere on earth. This century began with ethnic violence in Sarajevo in the Balkans; it's ending with bestiality and ethnic violence in Sarajevo in the Balkans.

Glum thoughts? Yes, but think, on the other hand of how much more open and promising the future is than it was forty years ago . . . when you had to think of living in a world totally beyond your control. This is not such a world. This is a world in which we can start out thinking, How do we control the outer atmosphere? and be serious. If we can do that, we can certainly control our lives here on earth, and we've got that chance.

☙◦❧

PATRICIA SCHROEDER
U.S. Congresswoman
Mount Holyoke College

Let me say that if you didn't think you are needed by the great country—just think about the headlines this week. I really encourage you to cut them out. Because I think twenty years from now, trying to explain them to your children will be very interesting. You can say this is the week that I graduated in America.

First of all, Dan Quayle attacked Murphy Brown. She had a baby and he had a cow! Your children will say, "What?" And you'll say not only that—the press had a picnic and it went on for five days, with everyone wading in and putting out all their issues that they wanted. And then Johnny Carson left. And then they'll say, "What?" And they'll say, "What was really going on when you graduated, again? What were the issues, again?"

∽ᴏᴏᴄ

WENDY KOPP
Founder and President, Teach for America
Syracuse University

My fear is that not enough of us—I would venture to say almost *no one*—really believes that significant change is possible. And I would say that *that* is the number one problem in America. . . .

How many people have questioned the fact that we place in one classroom twenty to thirty kids—all of whom have different needs, all of whom are motivated by different things, all of whom learn in different ways? We expect one teacher to engage all of these students simultaneously. And our schools are built, in fact, on the assumption that every single teacher can, for students in any particular class are subject to the strengths and weaknesses of whatever teacher happens to be standing in front of them.

How many people have questioned the fact that we grade students? Any school of education worth its salt teaches that all children can learn, and yet we have an education system built on the assumption that they can't. The theory behind the bell curve is, in fact, that as many kids fail as succeed. Can you imagine Toyota turning out cars, a third of which ran well, a third of which ran sort of, and a third of which didn't run at all?

How many people earnestly question the way our schools are funded? Does it really make sense—and is it *just*—that we spend $32,000 per student in the Bridgehampton public school system while we spend less than $7,000 per student in New York City?

Our schools are the way they are because too few people really believe that radical change is possible. How many times have we heard that the unions won't allow meaningful change, that the bureaucracy won't, that the teachers won't?

You and I have a responsibility to make this nation and this world a better place. When something is not how we want it to be, we must figure out how to change it, and then we must change it. If we cannot effect change within the system, we must start a new system. We cannot afford to be intimidated by change, and we shouldn't be. Radical change is simple if you just divorce yourself from convention and use logic. Realize, too, that change is not always a process of improvement. Sometimes it's a process of invention. When Thomas Edison invented the lightbulb, he didn't start by trying to improve the candle. He decided that he wanted better light and went from there.

∞

BERNADINE HEALY
President, American Red Cross
Ohio State University

If you're a male, you will most certainly need at least two pairs of socks. One pair should be black. It would be nice if the other pair was something other than green, but matching colors are better than nothing. And both pairs should be laundered more frequently than the phases of the moon.

If you are female, you will no longer be able to wear a pair of nylons with a run in them until you have time to get a new pair.

And regardless of where you work, no matter how great the temptation, you will not be allowed to hang profane slogans on your office wall about the geography of Ann Arbor or the genealogy of a Wolverine. The fact is, John Cougar Mellencamp notwithstanding, you are no longer Jack and Diane outside the Tastee-Freez with a chili dog. You are graduates with at least some obligation, and I admit it is not easy to begin masquerading as responsible adults. Mr. Mellencamp would put it this way: "Life goes on long after the thrill of living is gone." He would not only put it that way, he *has* put it that way. But you know, he's wrong. My message to you today is that life indeed goes on, but it will be as thrilling as you want to make it. . . .

Arthur Freed was a famous theatrical producer and he once gave this advice to Alan Jay Lerner, the man who cowrote the Broadway version of *Camelot*. He said, "Stop trying to be different. You don't have to be different to be good. To be good is different enough." So whatever you do, be good at what you do.

And be proud of it. Joseph Campbell, quoted in the book *The Power of Myth*, recalled his Catholic childhood somewhat ruefully. He remembered having to confess his sins and the apology that was always required first. Looking back, he thought the whole thing should have been turned around to read this way: "Bless me, Father, for I've been great. These are the good things I have done this week." I'm no theologian, but I can tell you for sure that a positive outlook, as long as it doesn't become arrogant, can go a long way.

Great life to each of you.

∽◦∾

Hillary Rodham Clinton
Lawyer
Wellesley College

When all is said and done, it is the people in your life, the friendships you form and the commitments you maintain, that give shape to your life. Your friends and your neighbors, the people at work or church, those who touch your daily lives. And if you choose, a marriage filled with love and respect. . . .

Second, your work. For some of you, that may overlap with your contributions to the community. For some of you, your future might not include work outside the home (and I don't mean involuntary unemployment); but most of you will at some point in your life work for pay, maybe in jobs that used to be off limits to women. You may choose to be a corporate executive or a rocket scientist, you may choose to run for public office, you may choose to stay at home and raise your children—you can now make any or all of these choices for the work of your life.

Third, your service. As students, we debated passionately what responsibility each individual had for the larger society, and just what the college's Latin motto—"Not to be ministered unto, but to minister"—actually meant. The most eloquent explanation I have found of what I believe now and what I argued then is from Václav Havel, the playwright and first freely elected president of Czechoslovakia. In a letter from prison to his wife, Olga, he wrote, "Everything meaningful in life is distinguished by a certain transcendence of individual human existence—beyond the limits of mere 'self-care' toward other people, toward society, toward the world . . . only by looking outward, by caring for things that, in terms of pure survival, you needn't bother with at all . . . and by throwing yourself over and over again into the tumult of the world with the intention of making your voice count—only thus will you really become a person."

∽o∽

1993

On January 20, former Arkansas governor William Jefferson Clinton was inaugurated as the forty-second president of the United States, an election that seemed less a transfer of presidential power than a generation passing of the mantle (or the buck).

There was no denying Clinton's personal and political power. A young president with a baby-boomer history and baby-boomer habits, Clinton brought to office his fiercely intelligent lawyer wife, Hillary Rodham Clinton, who made it clear early on that she was uninterested in the traditional First Lady role of baking cookies or beautifying highways; less than a week after his inauguration, Clinton named his wife as the chair of the President's Task Force on National Health Reform.

A youthful explosion was taking place abroad, too. Former playwright Václav Havel was named president of the Czech Republic, and in South Africa, African National Congress president Nelson Mandela and South African president F. W. de Klerk buried their differences and shared the 1993 Nobel Peace Prize for their efforts in eliminating South Africa's brutal, long-standing apartheid system. At a White House ceremony marking a new Middle East peace accord, two longtime enemies—Israel's prime minister, Yitzhak Rabin, and PLO chairman Yasser Arafat—shook hands. Twelve American soldiers were killed in Mogadishu, Somalia. "Don't Ask, Don't Tell" was the new mandate for homosexuals serving in the military, which struck many observers as business as usual. Deputy White House counsel Vincent Foster Jr. was found dead in Virginia, an apparent suicide.

In literature, Toni Morrison became the first black woman to be awarded the Nobel Prize. America's attention was riveted to Waco,

Texas, where a standoff between the FBI and members of the Branch Davidian religious cult, led by David Koresh, ended in arson and violence. NAFTA gained approval, as did the Brady Bill, which among other things mandated a five-day waiting period for gun purchases; and in Washington, D.C., the U.S. Holocaust Museum opened, offering visitors the chance to review history's most horrendous period. Rudolf Nureyev died in Paris of AIDS. A bomb exploded in an underground garage below the World Trade Center. Janet Reno was sworn in as attorney general. Unforgiven, a neo-Western directed by Clint Eastwood, was voted best picture of the year at Hollywood's annual self-congratulation fest. Tennis star Monica Seles was hospitalized after being stabbed in the back by an overzealous fan during a break in a German tennis match. In June, Clinton withdrew the nomination of Lani Guinier to head the Civil Rights Division of the U.S. Justice Department after several articles that she had written caused contention. Two Los Angeles cops, Stacey Koon and Laurence Powell, were sentenced to two and a half years in prison for their roles in violating Rodney King's civil rights.

One of President Bush's final acts in office was to sign the START II treaty with Russian president Boris Yeltsin, an agreement that called for both countries to reduce their long-range nuclear arsenals to approximately one-third of their current levels within a ten-year period, and completely eliminate land-based missiles.

∾

GWEN IFILL
Broadcaster
Simmons College

Life is all about choices.

I remember the choices that my mother, for instance, did not have the opportunity to make. And I know that my grandmother, who was born, raised, and buried on the island of Barbados, would not have dreamed of this.

I am grateful that my father told me I had choices. He pretended to be a sexist for all the years he lived, but he managed to raise feminist sons and accomplished daughters who were never told there was something they could not do. . . .

Choice is a powerful notion. Its definition has become polluted in recent years, wrapped up in contentious battles over abortion and taxpayer support of private schools. But all those things are argued in stark black-and-white. I have learned, and you are probably already discovering, that almost everything in life is painted in shades of gray.

You now face the most staggering array of choices that you may ever have before you in your life. Do not underestimate their range. The unhappiest people I know have become that way because they have imposed artificial limits on their lives.

I can tell you this: Take every choice you are offered. Have as much fun as you can, when you can. Do not shrink from life, and do not shrink from the choices.

∽∾

VERNON JORDAN
Civil Rights Leader
DePauw University

Wherever you go from this place, and whatever you do, I say to you there is no hiding place down here, and I would suggest, as you pursue your chosen profession, as your careers take hold, as you rear your families, as you plan your futures, that you become agents of change, that you play your part in building a better, more fair, more inclusive America. That you understand that every child that grows up hungry or homeless, every child that grows up uneducated, every young adult denied training and job opportunities represents precious human resources American cannot afford to lose. It is written, "to whom much is given, much is required." As witnessed here today, you have been given much and you will get much more, but I've come simply to ask that in return you share, you care, you dare, and you lead, for you can help America change for the better. You can help America live up to its vast potential as a beacon of world freedom and a land of plenty for all of its people.

This commencement marks the beginning of your acceptance of what has been called the terrific responsibility to human life. You now share that full responsibility for shaping your own lives and your country's destiny. And as you do, hear the words of Herman Melville, who wrote, "We cannot live for ourselves alone. Our lives are connected by a thousand invisible threads, and along these sympathetic fibers, our actions run as causes and return to us as results." Now, as you go down from this place, as you accept the responsibilities and duties of citizenship, be steadfast, be strong, be of good cheer, and as you go, may your own dreams be your only boundaries, henceforth, now and forever, amen.

∞

Mona Van Duyn[*]
Poet
Georgetown University

Some of you already know that you will be learning how to join the *visible* powers of the earth—as scientists, industrialists, politicians (even world leaders), engineers of all kinds, etc. These powers are very great. *They can change the world.* But I hope that all of you, whatever direction you choose for the joy and excitement of learning, will never forget or forgo your pleasure in the arts—particularly, since I am prejudiced in their favor, poem and story (including good film). *The arts are invisible powers;* they do not force themselves upon their subjects, who freely choose to submit to them. They *work* invisibly—they widen and deepen the human imagination, they increase empathy (without which no being is truly human), they train the emotions to employ themselves with more appropriateness and precision, they change or modify the very language in which human thought is formed. Like love, but stronger,

*Copyright © by Mona Van Duyn.

since love's power is limited by mortality, they are holders and keepers of what time would otherwise take away from us—the world, both the natural (its creatures who live with us, its colors, shapes, textures, sounds, smells, tastes) and the social (the others we love or hate or have never known, their voices, appearances, thoughts, motivations, the inner and outer contexts of their lives). These powers, too, are very great. *They can change the self.* Perhaps, in a democracy (particularly now that so much of the world wishes to remold itself into this form of government), these invisible powers may be more important than anyone ever dreamed.

∽◦∾

Marian Wright Edelman
Founder and Director, Children's Defense Fund
University of Illinois at Champaign-Urbana

There is no free lunch. Don't feel entitled to anything you don't sweat and struggle for. You must help our nation understand that it is not entitled to world leadership based on the past or on what we say, rather than how well we perform and meet changing world needs. For those young people among this class and among you who are African American or Latino or Asian American or Native American, I hope you will remember that you can never take anything for granted in this country. As racial intolerance resurges all over our land—some of it blatant and some of it subtle—we should be reminded of what Frederick Douglass told us, that "it's the same old snake which we must be mindful of and fight." For those of you who are white graduates who may feel entitled to leadership by accident of birth, I want to remind you that the world you face is already two-thirds nonwhite and poor and that our nation is becoming a mosaic of greater diversity that you are going to have to understand and respect. Only two out of every ten new labor force entrants in the 1990s will be white males born in America. I talk to my kids a lot about Frederick Douglass, who said something that you should never forget—that men (and women, let me add) may not get all they pay for in this world, but they will certainly pay for all they get. . . .

Never work for money. Money won't save your soul or build a decent family or help you sleep at night. We are the richest nation on earth with the highest incarceration, drug addiction, and child poverty rates in the world. Don't ever confuse wealth or fame with character. Don't tolerate or condone moral corruption whether it's found in high or low places, whatever its color or class. It is not OK to abuse alcohol or drugs even if every person in America is doing it. It is not OK to cheat or to lie even if everybody you know does. Be honest and demand that those who represent you be honest.

Don't ever confuse legality with morality. Dr. King once noted that everything Hitler did in Nazi Germany was legal. Don't ever give anybody the proxy for your conscience. . . .

Finally, never think that life is not worth living, or that you can't make a difference. I don't care how hard it gets, and it's going to get very hard sometimes. There's an old proverb that keeps me going that says, "When you get to your wit's end, remember that's where God lives." Harriet Beecher Stowe said that when you get into a tight place and everything goes against you till it seems as though you can't hang on another minute, never give up then. For that is just the place and the time when the tide will turn. Hang in with life. A lot of your discipline and a lot of your accomplishments today may not work or translate immediately into a good job. Hang on. Things will begin to change and get better.

∾○∾

LEE SMITH
Writer
Hollins College

In the address he gave upon receiving the Nobel Prize for literature in 1950, Faulkner said that the only thing worth writing about is "the problems of the human heart in conflict with itself." Faulkner also took that occasion to remind us that "man alone among creatures . . . has a soul, a spirit capable of compassion and sacrifice and endurance. The poet's, the writer's duty, is to write about these things. It is his privilege to help man endure by lifting his heart, by reminding him of the courage and honor and hope and pride and compassion and pity and sacrifice which have been the glory of his past."

Let me repeat this for emphasis—"the courage and honor and hope and pride and compassion and pity and sacrifice which have been the glory of his past." Now let me ask you this: How much do you know about your own past? How much time have you spent talking to your grandmothers? How much do you know about where your people came from, and why? And about what kind of people they were, anyway? Because the only story you have to tell is—finally—your own. . . .

The great mythology professor Joseph Campbell believed that our lives are like mythic journeys, following the oldest plot in literature—the quest. The Hero is the one who receives the Call, goes on the adventure, and brings back the Message. . . .

So you start out in the dark. You don't know where you're going. Strange little helpmates come along—a fairy, a gnome, an old man in the park. They give you clues and talismans, and you continue. Of course, you will run into danger, because no one else has ever taken this particular journey before. But all the stories tell us that where we stumble, there we may find our treasure. In *The Arabian Nights*, for instance, someone is plowing a field, and his plow gets caught. He digs down to see what it is, and finds a ring. With the aid of the ring, he finds the cave with all the jewels in it. Whenever your life seems hardest, in other words, there is the chance to find deeper and greater powers within yourself. Well, you go on. Your journey continues. You will have encounters with monsters and demons who symbolize your limitations—as each of these is conquered, your consciousness is enlarged, and your possibilities expand.

And so I say to you today: This is your life. This is your journey. You are the Hero. . . .

You're the writer now. Maybe you couldn't pick the setting, or the cast of characters at the beginning, or the conflicts you were born into. But this graduation ceremony is a ritual marking the transition from the beginning of your story into the middle, into the main part of the story. Now the plot is strictly up to you. And as you write your own story, the best that I can wish for you—speaking as one writer to another—is that you dip your pen in love and history before you face that blank sheet of paper, and that you write always with an open mind, a listening ear, and a ready heart.

ᶜᵒᵛᵕ

John Updike
Writer
University of Massachusetts at Amherst

Mine was, I can see now, a rather fortunate generation. . . . They called us, long ago, the Silent Generation. Now we are old enough to take early retirement and paint watercolors in Arizona, but many of us still cling to positions of power, and in our silence have carried forward the work of industry and the arts, agriculture and business, advertising and bureaucracy. Of course, I love my generation; I have spent my professional life mostly writing about myself and my peers—our gradual loss of sexual and political innocence, our experience of the last four decades of history, and of the timeless human experience of growth, work, change, and decay.

All generations, when the dust has finally settled, are mostly silent. The world is always with us, and is never without danger and woe. History tints us, like fish that swim through colored water; but our bones are all fishbones. The human species, with its drives and conflicts, is a constant. A Cro-Magnon man of thirty-five thousand years ago, were he dressed in academic garb and placed on this platform, would not look out of place. We are born into history, and graduate into it, but our animal optimism and our cerebral capacity to plan our own personal futures exist independently of history. The individual is the unit of measure and of national movement; nowhere is this more true than in the United States.

I was conditioned to believe that America has a heart of gold; mine may be the last generation that could believe this easily. But international events in the four years since you entered this university make it easier, it seems to me, and newly exciting, to be American.

We are no longer obliged to pour our strength into a Cold War of reaction and counterblow; we have moved from a dualistic to a pluralistic world, a world in which our national gifts are by no means obsolete. What are those national gifts? At a stab, they are good humor, optimism, the ability to improvise, willingness to learn, and respect for the individual.

Thanks to television and computers, you are savvy in ways my generation was not. What you know about the facts of life, and what you understand of tolerance and acceptance and multiform ways of being human, puts 1954 to shame. But your generational savviness, it could be, in our age of imagery and sound bites, is a matter more of imagery than of the heft of real things, of earth and the tools that bit by bit move it. You cannot but learn more of the world's heft, as you take it now into your hands. Take it up reverently, for it is an old piece of clay, with millions of thumbprints on it.

❦

JODIE FOSTER
Actor
Yale University

Let me tell you what I do for a living. . . . I put all my stuff—my history, my beliefs, my experiences, my passions and taboos and personal foibles, my weaknesses and unconscious agendas and eccentricities—I put them delicately and precisely on the tip of the proverbial arrow. I take careful aim, keep the target in my sight, and try desperately to communicate all that is me in a straight line toward an audience. But I am only human. My eyesight is faulty; my hands are shaky; a million things will distort the goal. And no matter how well I aim that arrow, I never completely connect with the other. But it's the process of trying that's significant. That's where all the messy, beautiful human stuff lies—in the space between the "you" and the "other," between the "you" and the "I."

❦

Jim Lehrer
Broadcaster
Williams College

Journalism in my opinion is being consumed before our very eyes and ears by a form of arrogance that I believe, if it is not arrested and stopped soon, could undermine the whole point of the exercise. Go with me please in your mind for a few moments . . . go with me to most of the radio and television talk shows—the ones at night and the ones in the morning, the ones on Sunday and Tuesday, and the ones on Thursday, the ones on most networks at most times. Go with me to the front and inside pages of most daily newspapers, to the columns of most newsmagazines. Go with me to televised news conferences from the White House, from the courthouse, and the World Trade Center in New York, from Waco, Texas, from most places where news is made. Go with me to most places where journalism is practiced and consumed these days. Have you ever seen, heard, read, or inhaled such snide arrogance in your life? It permeates the tone of the questions and the commentary. "Mr. President, you idiot . . . Senator, you fool . . . Madam Mayor, you jerk . . . Mr. Secretary, you ninny . . . Mr. and Mrs. and Ms. Public People of All Kinds, you crook, you fraud." There is a stench of contempt in the approach and the words, in the sneer, in the body language, and the message is there for all to see.

And this is the message: These people in public life, in public service, are creeps. They're scum. They're suspect. They're guilty until proven innocent. Only the journalists of America are smart enough to know what to do in Bosnia, in the economy, in health care, and Supreme Court appointments, in paving the streets, in all walks of all lives. Only the journalists of America are pure enough to judge all others . . . to tell you who are the good ones and the bad ones, to identify success and failure, to, through our words and actions, go thumbs up, thumbs down, on all ideas, all institutions, all conduct. And more importantly, pinpoint and identify motives. Don't believe politicians, government officials, or any other people when they say why they are doing something. They never tell the truth. We, the journalists, will tell you why the president, and members of Congress, and the city council, and the think tanks, and the college administrations, and the FBI agents, and the cops, and the teachers, and the social workers, and all other people do what they do. We are experts in motives because ours are so pure. That is because we care only about the public's right to know. We care only about what Thomas Jefferson said: "An informed electorate is a free electorate." We're the only ones in our society dedicated and capable enough to judge all others. And judge we must because God really did die and the journalists of America must take up the slack. There are no others who are capable or willing to do so.

From my perspective inside journalism, I think that this kind of snide arrogance is a plague on and in the newsrooms of America. I believe that unless something is done about it, the credibility of all of us in the business will continue to erode with all of you, the people who read and watch and listen to what we do.

∽◦◦∽

CORNEL WEST
Professor and Writer
Wesleyan University

I know your history. You've been through some struggles, and it's getting you ready for what the world has to offer. 'Cause even in this grand moment of celebration and jubilation, we're living in one of the most terrifying and frightening moments in the history of this country—unprecedented lethal linkage of economic decline and cultural decay and political malaise. Yes, the downward mobility and the poverty and the fear of poverty. Yes, the cultural consumption that promotes an addiction to stimulation that tries to convince us that we are vital and vibrant only when we're consuming. Down and out? Go to the mall. Feeling down and out? Turn on the television and reinforce that spectatorial passivity. Yes, that's so much of what this culture is about. And the political malaise—even given Brother Clinton in the White House and Sister Hillary (thank God for her)—this deep sense that maybe public institutions no longer have the wherewithal to respond to the deep problems. . . .

There is a need for audacious hope. And it's not optimism. I'm in no way an optimist. I've been black in America for thirty-nine years. No ground for optimism here, given the progress and regress and three steps forward and four steps backward. Optimism is a notion that there's sufficient evidence that would allow us to infer that if we keep doing what we're doing, things will get better. I don't believe that. I'm a prisoner of hope, that's something else. Cutting against the grain, against the evidence. William James said it so well in that grand and masterful essay of his of 1879 called "The Sentiment of Rationality," where he talked about faith being the courage to act when doubt is warranted. And that's what I'm talking about.

Of course, I come from a tradition, a black church tradition, in which we defined faith as stepping out on nothing and landing on something. That's the history of black folk in this country. Hope against hope. And yet still trying to sustain the notion that we world-weary and tired peoples, all peoples in this society, can be energized and galvanized around causes and principles and ideals that are bigger than us, that can appeal to the better angels of our nature, so that we, in fact, can reach the conclusion that the world is incomplete—that history is unfinished, that the future is open-ended, that what we think and what we do does make a difference.

∽○∼

RON BROWN
Politician
Howard University

Your challenge is to be our conscience, to keep the drumbeat of activism alive, to rouse those who have become too comfortable for the struggle, and to reinvigorate those too tired to fight.

∽○∼

ELLEN GOODMAN
Writer
Smith College

This afternoon, I solemnly promise you that these have *not* been the best years of your life. The truth is that people who look back to college as the peak experience have had the dreariest of adulthoods. I don't wish that on any of you.

∞

RONALD REAGAN
Former U.S. President
The Citadel

When life does get tough and the crisis is undeniably at hand, when we must, in an instant, look inward for strength of character to see us through, we will find nothing inside ourselves that we have not already put there.

∞

1994

Peace, or at the very least compromise, was in the air in 1994. Following scattered violence across South Africa, apartheid finally ended, and Nelson Mandela was elected his country's first black president. Two Israelis—Prime Minister Yitzhak Rabin and Foreign Minister Shimon Peres—and Palestinian leader Yasser Arafat, shared the Nobel Peace Prize. A doughy Republican with the unusual name of Newt Gingrich announced a Contract with America as his party gained control of both the Senate and the House of Representatives for the first time in forty years. But political miracles notwithstanding, America's attention was riveted to a murder case in Los Angeles, in which former Buffalo Bills running back, Hertz rental car pitchman, and occasional actor O.J. Simpson went on trial for the slaughter of his ex-wife and one of her friends.

Elsewhere in the world, discord and violence broke out between the Tutsi and Hutu ethnic groups in Rwanda, and Jean-Bertrand Aristide was restored as the president of Haiti. The IRA called for a ceasefire in Northern Ireland, though, to no one's surprise, it didn't last. Fifty years after Allied forces stormed ashore, D-Day was solemnly remembered by world leaders. The Russians invaded Chechnya. The United States hosted the World Cup soccer matches, but the game failed once again to catch on in America, whose cities and towns seemed much more interested in debating the case for and against public smoking. Moviegoers flocked to Forrest Gump and Pulp Fiction, and kids adored Disney's The Lion King. In March, Steven Spielberg's Schindler's List won the Academy Award. Jacqueline Kennedy Onassis, long perceived by the world as vaguely immortal, died of lymphoma in her apartment in New York City. On the other side of the country, Nirvana *front man Kurt Kobain fatally shot himself. Former President Richard Nixon died at age eighty-one, his funeral attended by five U.S. presidents. After being indicted on seventeen felony counts, Democratic representative Dan Rostenkowski relinquished his post at the House Ways and Means Committee.*

In Great Britain, Tony Blair was appointed the leader of the Labour Party, succeeding the late John Smith. In Yugoslavia, Serbian president Slobodan Milosevic declared that Yugoslavia was cutting its ties with the Bosnian Serb Republic. Kenneth Starr was appointed independent prosecutor to investigate the Whitewater affair. A man flying a small single-engine plane crash-landed on the lawn of the White House, killing himself. In South Carolina, Susan Smith, who had appeared distraught on television news stations, claiming that her two little boys had been carjacked, was arrested and charged with double homicide. Forty-five-year-old boxer George Foreman won the International Boxing Federation and World Boxing Association titles. In Brookline, Massachusetts, a lone gunman murdered two women working at abortion clinics, injuring five others in the process. U.S. surgeon general Jocelyn Elders was forced to resign her post, a victim of candor.

But it was the O.J. Simpson case that had most of the nation glued to their television sets, particularly following his arrest, when Simpson "escaped" in a white Ford Bronco owned and driven by his friend Al Cowlings, taking a near-suicidal joyride along the freeways of Los Angeles, with members of the public cheering him on. The blurring between reality and fantasy had seldom been so pronounced.

∽◦∾

LAMAR ALEXANDER
Governor, Tennessee
Coe College

It was 1980 when our family got to know Alex Haley. He was perhaps the most celebrated author in the world, and I was governor of the home state. He had homes in North Africa and Los Angeles. Everybody knew him. Walking with him in Philadelphia I heard, "Alex!"

And across the hotel lobby came Dr. J, Julius Erving. In Los Angeles, a couple of hoodlums accosted him until one looked up and said, "Hey, it's Mr. Roots," and they asked for his autograph instead of his money. But we don't remember him because he was famous or, for a while, rich. We remember him because he would walk into our house and pick up our daughter's school essay and say, "My goodness, Leslee, with a little more work that could win a prize." Or to Will, who was fooling around with a video recorder, he would say, "You know, Steven Spielberg started just that way." Or to all of us, "Do you know how lucky you are to have each other?" Find the good and praise it.

He always seemed to have time for anyone. Walking down the street in Knoxville, he met a man who couldn't read, helped him learn, and the man found himself the subject of a story in *Parade*. Find the good and praise it.

President Reagan, Elizabeth Taylor, even Captain Kangaroo stayed at our Governor's Mansion—but the one that all the employees who worked there most liked to see coming was Alex Haley, because he was as interested in them as they were in him. Find the good and praise it.

He had a sense of humor that would keep you on your toes. For example, if he were in my place today, first he would say to the graduates, "Congratulations, but you need to remember that if you see a turtle on top of a fence post, you know he had some help in getting there." And then he would explain with a twinkle in his eye the mystery of why grandparents and grandchildren get along so well. "It is," he would say, "because they have a common enemy." I rarely saw him angry, never heard him say an offending word about some other person's background or race. Find the good and praise it.

He especially liked to say those six words to people who were busy finding everything wrong with America. It was a powerful message coming from the grandson of slaves, from the man who wrote *Roots* and *The Autobiography of Malcolm X*. People forgot he helped write that one, too. I thought about those words in February two years ago on a bright chilly afternoon in Henning as an African flute played "Amazing Grace" and we buried Alex Haley next to the front porch where his grandma and great-aunts cooked in the summertime and told him those stories. On the marker there—which I hope you will visit some day—are those six words: FIND THE GOOD AND PRAISE IT.

∽o∽

Cokie Roberts
Broadcaster
Wellesley College

You will be the caretakers in this society. It's what we do. That's what women do. We're the nurturers, we're the carriers of the culture. And whether you run for president or run the Patriot's Day race or become editor in chief of the *New York Times* (though you might want to talk to me before you do that), whether you do, as Hillary said, "make policy or bake cookies" (it's been my experience that one generally does both), what you will be doing, no matter whatever else you do, will be being the caretakers.

Ronald Reagan offended people when he said that women should be honored as civilizers. That statement was offensive because he said it to a group of professional women and defined them in terms of their relationship to men. He said that we were civilizers of men. But he was right. We are. (I must say that men sometimes make it a little difficult, but this is what we do.) We can't avoid it. And as I say, in politics, it is the women who are constantly bringing the civilizing issues to the forefront, the caretaking issues, the issues of concern to families and children. . . .

But I have to tell you I don't just see this role of women as caretakers in the world that I cover, I see it in the world I work in. Slowly, slowly, slowly but definitely, the workplace is becoming a more humane place because of the presence of women. The idea that time can be taken for family, whether it's having children or caring for sick people or elderly parents in your family—that is becoming more possible for the men in the workplace as well as for the women in the workplace because of the fights that we have fought over the last several decades.

Life is long. You have many opportunities ahead of you. You have so many more opportunities than so many people. You are privileged and blessed. And you will have the opportunity to say yes to many different things, but you also will have the opportunity in the saying of yes to say no sometimes, to say, "No, it's not right for me and my family right now to take this great job offer." And you know what? Another one will come along. I'm living proof of that. You can do it all. There are times when you have to not do it all at once. There are times when you don't sleep. But you can have it if you have some sense about saying, "This is what's right now, this is where I am now, and this is the care I need to take right now." I think that it is important to look at the long view as you go out of here and realize that there's a long time ahead, and there is time to see it all, to do it all, and to do it in ways that make you proud and happy in the end.

∽○∾

HILLARY RODHAM CLINTON
First Lady
University of Illinois at Champaign-Urbana

A few days ago I was honored to be part of the American delegation that attended the inauguration of Nelson Mandela in South Africa. I wish every one of you in this arena could have been there with me. It was both an incredibly moving historical experience and also one that confronted those of us who were there with profound questions about our own commitment to and convictions about freedom and democracy.

I sat and watched a man take the oath of office, joined by two other men: one his comrade over many years, Deputy President Mbeki; the other his foe over many years, Deputy President de Klerk. Three men who, despite enormous differences in a faraway land torn by racial strife and hatred and violence that we cannot even imagine, joined together in a vision of a new South Africa. The inaugural ceremony was especially moving because of the speech that President Mandela gave, because the platform consisted of black and white and colored citizens of South Africa and the presidents of the military and security forces in their uniforms, and because of a twenty-one-gun salute and a flyover of the most advanced military contingent committing itself to the new South Africa. But the highlight of the entire inaugural for me came later, at a lunch where President Mandela stood and talked about how he had invited to his inaugural ceremony three of his former jailers.

This is a man who was in prison for twenty-seven years, longer than many of you have yet lived, in the constant confinement and under the watchful supervision of jailers. And yet, because he was a man who understood that real change must come from within, who understood and incorporated the message of love and forgiveness that too many of us only give lip service to, he learned to love his jailers, and they, in turn, learned to love him. They no longer saw each other as stereotypes, as people who came from different racial backgrounds; but they broke through the barriers that divide us, even in this country, to see each other in their full humanity.

When he stood there and said that, I thought of several things. I thought of what my husband has said repeatedly since he started his campaign for the presidency—that real change must come from the inside out; that government can do only so much; that institutions, even ones of excellence like this university, can lead only so far; that fundamental change must come from the hearts and minds and souls of individuals. And I thought, What an example the world now has of what that truly means, a new president who invites his jailers to his inauguration.

∞o∞

LANFORD WILSON
Playwright
Grinnell College

You're probably as well informed about what's out there as I am. You know the infrastructure sucks. (I hate that word. Not "sucks"— I like "sucks." "Infrastructure.") Our health care is relatively Third World, we rank twenty-seventh in infant mortality; you get a job based on who you know, not what you can do; lobbyists run the government; we worship youth and crush the young, despise and disregard the old; "family values" is a euphemism for prejudice; "the sanctity of the home" is about as sacred as most other religious practices; and the current state of society could best be described as "tribal."

About the only truism that's really true is a deadly bore, but has to be said: and that is, nobody nor any group nor any tribe is any better than anybody else or any other tribe, and as soon as you think you are, just set yourself down and say, I'm screwed up and wrong and I've got to get straight here. This is something you really will encounter in yourself and it's best to talk yourself out of it as soon as possible. Most of the conflict we read as racial or religious (just as in Northern Ireland) is economic, not racial or religious. Just remember: the only sin, the only sin, is knowingly to use someone for your own purpose.

∾○∾

BARBARA KINGSOLVER
Writer
DePauw University

The first thing I'm going to do is admit to you that I tried to get out of this ceremony seventeen years ago when I was graduating myself, because I was twenty-two and I was way too cool to put on a goofy Batman outfit and a paper plate on my head and march down to East College and listen to a bunch of boring geriatrics tell me how it was up to the youth of America to save the world. And so here I am now, in a Batman outfit for the first time on any stage, and so I guess the one sure thing that I can tell you is that sooner or later, they get you where they want you. . . .

I read that a couple of hundred years ago, the Iroquois really had their act together. The Iroquois Federation of tribes in the northeastern part of North America was a governing body that made all important decisions on the basis of one rule, and that was the seven-generations question. That is, they would ask, "How does this decision, how does this act that we are about to undertake today, affect the world seven generations from now?" That's a really long time. In modern times in America, we seem inclined to live as if there weren't even going to be a next week, much less a seventh generation. It's interesting that we build structures to last, we build them to meet earthquake codes, but we seem inclined to engineer without any thought to the future. If we did, we would be throwing everything we have into education, into the salvation of wildlands and natural resources, into libraries, into improved prenatal care, into preventive counseling and life opportunities for kids who are at risk of becoming gun owners later in life.

But we don't seem to be doing those things. It's very easy to claim that policy is just such a complicated matter that there's no way to tell what is the right thing to do. I think that's baloney. I think it's almost always really easy to know the right thing to do. If you take the seven-generations perspective, it's easy to know which is more important, a pile of paper and lumber and sawdust in buildings that are going to fall down, probably before we do, or a million acres of old-growth forest in the Pacific Northwest. There's no question.

If you doubt that a single person making a single decision can influence the future, think again, because that's almost all that ever does influence the future. All of history is the accumulation of single decisions. Rosa Parks decided to sit down on that public bus in the section reserved for white people, and she decided not to get up again, even if that meant being spat on and going to jail, and that was only one generation ago and the world is a whole lot better for it. Rachel Carson decided in 1963 to keep working on her book *Silent Spring*, even though she was being ridiculed as a hysterical female, and on top of all that, she was dying of cancer. But she did it anyway. She kept researching and writing, and she published her book, which led to the banning of DDT, and the beginning of the environmental movement; and it's only thirty-two years later now, or something like that, and it's almost impossible to imagine how awful the world would be right now if she hadn't put herself on the line for the sake of the future.

I haven't ever had the occasion to be so brave as Rachel Carson or Rosa Parks, but I have to make minor decisions every day in just the same way that you do, and I believe that they could accumulate into something heroic if I keep making decisions in the right direction. I think every day of my life, every time I have a choice between doing this thing or that one, I can think of the future, instead of my own convenience. I can vote yes on the school board election. I can vote for the person who supports health care rather than the person who supports tax cuts for novelists whose last names start with K. I can get out of the habit of selfishness and start acting like there is going to be a tomorrow.

One of the very first things I've figured out about life since I left here . . . is that it's better to be a hopeful person than a cynical, grumpy one, because you have to live in the same world either way, and if you're hopeful, you have more fun. You get invited to more parties. People like you better, and you like yourself better. And hope is a renewable option: if you run out of it at the end of the day, you get to start over in the morning. There's no cost.

I'm going to go out on a limb here and give you one little piece of advice, and that is: Like the idea of a future. Believe that you have it in you to make the world better, rather than worse, seven generations from now. Figure out what that could look like, and then if you're lucky, you'll find a way to live inside that hope, running down its hallways, touching the walls on both sides.

∽o∾

ANDREW GROVE

Chairman, Intel
Haas Business School, University of California at Berkeley

Accept that no matter where you go to work, you are not an employee—you are a business with one employee, you. Nobody owes you a career. You own it, as a sole proprietor.

∽o∾

Kurt Vonnegut
Writer
Syracuse University

I first declare to you that the most wonderful thing, the most valuable thing you can get from an education is this—the memory of one person who could really teach, whose lessons made life and yourselves much more interesting and full of possibilities than you had previously supposed possible. I ask this of everyone here, including all of us up here on the platform—how many of us, how many of you, had such a teacher? Kindergarten counts. Please hold up your hands. Hurray. You may want to remember the name of that great teacher.

For you freshly minted graduates, this is a puberty ceremony long overdue. We, whose principal achievement is that we are older than you, have to acknowledge at last that you are grown-ups, too. There are old poops, possibly among us on this very day, who will say that you are not grown-ups until you have somehow survived, as they have, some famous calamity—the Great Depression, World War II, Vietnam, whatever. Storytellers are responsible for this destructive, not to say suicidal, myth. Again and again, in stories, after some terrible mess, the character is able to say at last, "Today, I am a woman; today I am a man. The end."

When I got home from World War II, my uncle Dan clapped me on the back and he said, "You're a man now." So I killed him. Not really, but I certainly felt like doing it.

I apologize. I said I would apologize; I apologize now. I apologize because of the terrible mess the planet is in. But it has always been a mess. There have never been any "good old days," there have just been days. And as I say to my grandchildren, "Don't look at me. I just got here myself."

The teacher whose name I mentioned when we all remembered good teachers asked me one time, "What is it artists do?" And I mumbled something. "They do two things," he said. "First, they admit they can't straighten out the whole universe. And then second, they make at least one little part of it exactly as it should be. A blob of clay, a square of canvas, a piece of paper, or whatever."

As I have told you, I had a bad uncle named Dan, who said a male can't be a man unless he'd gone to war. But I had a good uncle named Alex, who said, when life was most agreeable—and it could be just a pitcher of lemonade in the shade—he would say, "If this isn't nice, what is?" So I say that about what we have achieved here right now. If he hadn't said that so regularly, maybe five or six times a month, we might not have paused to notice how rewarding life can be sometimes. Perhaps my good uncle Alex will live on in some of you members of the Syracuse class of 1994 if, in the future, you will pause to say out loud every so often, "If this isn't nice, what is?"

Now my time is up and I haven't even inspired you with heroic tales of the past—Teddy Roosevelt's cavalry charge up San Juan Hill, Desert Storm—or given you visions of a glorious future—computer programs, interactive TV, the information superhighway, speed the day. I spent too much time celebrating this very moment and place—once the future we dreamed of so long ago. This is *it*. We're here. How the heck did we do it?

A neighbor of mine, I hired him—he was a handyman—to build an ell on my house where I could write. He did the whole damn thing—he built the foundation, and then the side walls and the roof. He did it all by himself. And when it was all done, he stood back and he said, "How the *hell* did I ever do that?" How the hell did we ever do this? We did it! And if this isn't nice, what is?

I got a letter from a sappy woman awhile back—she knew I was sappy, too, which is to say, a lifelong Democrat. She was pregnant, and she wanted to know if I thought it was a mistake to bring a little baby into a world as troubled as this one is. And I replied, what made being alive almost worthwhile to me was the saints I met. They could be almost anywhere. By saints I meant people who behaved decently and honorably in societies which were so often obscene. Our own society is very frequently obscene. Perhaps many of us here, regardless of our ages or power or wealth, can be saints for her child to meet.

∽o∾

Judy Woodruff
Broadcaster
Duke University

Let me leave you with two simple challenges. First, no matter how busy you are in the years ahead, take time to find a young, less fortunate child in a single or nonparent home. Spend just two hours a week with that boy or girl, only a little more than one percent of your time. You can tutor them, take them to a ball game, a movie, out to get a hamburger, or just talk. Make a difference in that child's life. Some of you may be able to do a lot more; all of you should be able to do at least this.

The second challenge is that after this marvelous moment today, recall the words of Mark Twain, who wrote, "When I was a boy of fourteen, my father was so ignorant, I could hardly stand to have the old man around. But when I got to be twenty-one, I was astonished at how much the old man had learned in seven years." So find your mom or dad, give them a hug of appreciation, and let them know how delighted you are at how much they have learned over the past four years.

❧

Lowell Weicker
Governor, Connecticut
Wesleyan University

We are still casting ourselves in the roles of past American heroes without performing our own heroic acts. The fact in 1994 is that a revolutionary spirit is down to an ember. That ember has to be fanned into flame. That flame into a bonfire. The same bonfire of change that swept South Africa and the former Soviet Union.

As you men and women of newly acquired power take your place in the world, move us off the stage if we refuse to go gracefully.

Don't accept our views on race; rather, observe the smallest children.

Don't accept America as a finished product, because if it is truly America, it never will be.

Don't accept moralizing as a substitute for the sacrifice of money and activism.

Don't accept a negative stereotype of anyone. Make being different in America a badge of honor or a cause, rather than the trial it has become.

Change a nation at your rising and then change it again before the night falls. This is what your last four years was all about. Otherwise, it was just a ritual from the past and you are as much a part of a deception, academic, as my generation is a part of a deception, constitutional.

Change is the certainty.

Change the promise.

Change the purpose.

Of life. Of America.

∽

1995

Nineteen ninety-five brought hope, if not closure, on several international fronts, and yet the more news that filtered in from abroad, the less, it seemed, Americans cared about their foreign neighbors, though technology had brought the world closer than it had ever been. The Internet was everywhere, chat rooms having replaced hearths and town squares as centers of discussion and discord. Nineteen ninety-five witnessed the political ascendancy of Republican leader Newt Gingrich, who dominated the news as the GOP assumed control of both the House of Representatives and the Senate. A simmering debate between President Clinton and the GOP over balancing the federal budget left the nation without a budget for 1996, and partially shut down the federal government not once but twice.

Domestic terrorism—the worst ever—hit home when a car bomb exploded outside a federal office building in Oklahoma City, Oklahoma, killing numerous adults and children. Former U.S. secretary of defense Robert McNamara admitted that America's participation in Vietnam had been a mistake. State of California vs. O.J. Simpson, later dubbed the trial of the century, began with opening arguments, as the football hero was charged with the murders of his ex-wife, Nicole Brown Simpson, and her friend Ron Goldman.

In late 1995, the presidents of Bosnia and Herzegovina, Croatia, and Serbia inked an agreement to end the fighting in Bosnia. By year's end, some twenty thousand American NATO troops had shown up in Bosnia to monitor the truce. Elsewhere, discussions regarding the future of Northern Ireland proceeded apace. The agreement on the second phase of interim Palestine autonomy, between Israel's prime minister, Yitzhak Rabin, and PLO chairman Yasser Arafat, suffered a

*severe blow when Rabin was assassinated by a fellow Israeli who
objected strongly to Middle Eastern compromise.*

*Toy Story, the first movie to be animated by Pixel, a new technique
of computer animation, was a hit at the box office. A rock-and-roll
museum opened in Cleveland, Ohio, and the Ebola virus struck Zaire.
A baseball strike brought into question Americans' loyalty to baseball, as basketball, with its speed and momentum, seemed more
appropriate to our diminishing attention span. Coffee bars flour-
ished. President Clinton invoked emergency authority to provide a
$20 billion loan to Mexico in order to stabilize the peso and to help
Mexico avoid defaulting on its long-term debt. Michael Jordan
rejoined the Chicago Bulls following a two-year voluntary exile as a
so-so baseball player.*

*Domestically, a Senate committee began hearings into the so-called
Whitewater affair, the financial and real estate dealings of President
Clinton and his wife while they were living in Arkansas. Susan Smith
was found guilty of killing her two little boys. Disney bought Capital
Cities/ABC, the second-largest takeover in history, which was swiftly
followed by a merger between Chemical Bank and Chase Manhattan.
In New York City, ten Muslims, including Sheikh Omar Abd al-Rah-
man, were convicted of seditious conspiracy for their part in leading
the terrorist group responsible for the World Trade Center bombing.*

*In October, O.J. Simpson was acquitted of double murder. There
was cheering in many black neighborhoods, incredulity and anger
among most whites. The belief of many Americans that, as far as race
was concerned, we were (in Andrew Hacker's words) two separate
nations never seemed truer.*

∽०∾

GLORIA STEINEM
Publisher and Writer
Smith College

The double standard lives. For instance: men are actually praised as
self-sacrificing for leaving their families to fight for what they

believe in—no matter how distant or arcane their cause—but women are called selfish if we fail to sacrifice almost everything for our families, or even if we speak up for ourselves. We are urged to be so much more concerned with the welfare of others than with our own that "codependent," the term invented by twelve-step programs, is really just a well-socialized woman.

To paraphrase Marlo Thomas: For a male leader to be called ruthless, he has to take over your life or your country. For a female leader to be called ruthless, she has only to put you on hold.

The double standard will end only when gender roles end and we are finally allowed to be the unique and whole individuals we truly are.

We're halfway there. We've begun to raise daughters more like sons—so now, women are becoming whole people. But fewer of us have had the courage to raise our sons more like our daughters. Yet until men raise children as much as women do—and are raised to raise children, whether or not they become fathers—they will have a far harder time developing in themselves those human qualities that are wrongly called "feminine" but are really those necessary to raise children: empathy, flexibility, patience, compassion, and the ability to let go.

To put it another way, at my graduation, I thought we had to marry what we wished to become. Now you are becoming the men you once would have wanted to marry. But too few men are becoming the women they want to marry. So women have two jobs, children continue to have too much mother and too little father, and the gender roles continue to replicate themselves. Women can't combine career and family unless men combine career and family, too.

As Margaret Mead once said, "Marriage worked well in the nineteenth century because people only lived to be fifty." Because life expectancy has increased about thirty years since 1900, there are bound to be many different ways of living during each lifetime. Some people will marry and raise children young, then go off amicably for another life of a different accomplishment. Some will marry late—after their work lives are well under way—and have children later or not at all. Some will not marry, or will love and live with a partner of the same sex. Others will raise their children among a chosen family of friends, or find colleagues in work and shared ideals who are their spiritual family.

Kind of a relief—isn't it?—to find there's no one right way of living—and that there's life *after* happily-ever-after.

∽∾∾

BILL CLINTON
U.S. President
Dartmouth College

There are unparalleled opportunities for those of you with a wonderful education in this global economy in this Information Age. And you don't have to worry about things that your parents had to worry about all the time. I am very proud of the fact that in the last two years, for the first time since the dawn of the nuclear age, there are no Russian missiles pointed at the people of the United States. And I might add, there are no American missiles pointed at the people of Russia. . . .

What I wish to say to you is that you are going into the time of greatest human possibility in all history, but you must address the fact that all of our forces of opportunity have seeds of destruction. You must make sense and clarity out of complex problems. And I think you must do it with a much greater sense of optimism and hope than we are seeing in most debates today. There is nothing wrong with this country that cannot be solved by what is right with it, and you should never forget that. . . .

Yes, there's more ethnic and racial diversity in this country than in any other large country. Yes, there's more income differential, and that's getting worse, and it's troubling. But this is still, for my money, the country that's the best bet to keep alive hope and decency and opportunity for all different kinds of people well into the next century. . . .

Do not let people make you cynical. And do not think for a minute that you can have a good, full life if you don't care about what happens to the other people who share this nation and this planet with you.

Good luck and God bless you.

M. L. Flynn
Television Producer
Hollins College

As a public service, and after a totally unscientific polling of my class, here, with our apologies to David Letterman's top ten list, are some guideposts from the class of 1973, as you search for the meaning of life.

- *Don't panic.* The waves of self-doubt and anxiety you have been suffering from and will continue to be paralyzed by for weeks, months—though I trust not years—is known as postcollege depression. We have all had it. You will survive.
- When your parents ask you, *What do you plan to do with the rest of your life?* take a deep breath . . . and realize that this is the first in a series of questions they will soon be asking you. The next two questions up are: When are you going to get married? followed by, When are you going to have children?
- *Don't be afraid to fail.* There are plenty of second, third, and countless chances to change careers, cities, and sweethearts.
- *Promise you won't "dress for success"* in those prim dark suits that seem to come with tucked shirts and silk bow ties. And as an addendum, if you come to New York, show courage and wear colors other than *just black.*
- *Stand up and be counted.* This is still a man's world you are going into, but the more women who express their opinions, contribute ideas, and roll up their sleeves and play to win will make it a better workplace for all of us. Sitting on the sidelines, playing the part of a meek and passive young girl, will make you very frustrated when you hear your brilliant idea expressed by someone else.
- *Get a real life.* Don't make work an obsession. Climbing the corporate ladder does not mean you have to be a one-dimensional person. Find a hobby, do volunteer work, even take a step class— but do something that pushes you outside of the office.
- *Learn to balance a checkbook.* Save your money, and enroll in a retirement program. It's scary how fast it all catches up with you.
- *Don't try to be an overnight wonder at work.* Don't pretend to

know more about something than you do. Listen and learn from others.

- *Don't die because you are having a bad hair day.* This is, after all, why God invented headbands and baseball hats.
- *Keep a journal.* Something I really regret that I didn't keep.
- *Don't apologize for not having a career,* or not being married, not having children, or not staying married. These are your choices— be proud of them. Don't let your life be defined by other people's labels.
- *Don't feel you have to be the total woman.* The consensus in my class is that being the total woman is too exhausting, and you don't get to really enjoy life while you are juggling all those balls in the air.
- *Spend time with your families.* Life is very short, and you will soon find out that your parents, sisters, brothers are actually interesting people . . . and are also your best friends in life.
- And finally, *follow your dream*—even if it seems risky and the odds seem overwhelming—whatever it may be. You will always regret it if you didn't give it your best shot. Remember, gut instincts are usually right.

∽∘∾

Hugh Sidey
Writer
Coe College

My counsel is, above all else go out with a sense of humor. It is needed armor. Joy in one's heart and some laughter on one's lips is a sign that the person down deep has a pretty good grasp of life. Humor after all is only the outcropping of deeper understanding of how difficult and absurd human beings can get from time to time. You will encounter it all and if you can put life in perspective with a bit of joy and laughter, you will survive. No person or society can prosper on a steady diet of despair.

I recall one of my final talks with Secretary of State Henry

Kissinger, in which I asked him what was the most important quality he brought to his job, which he had done very well through two presidencies. He answered that it might seem a bit frivolous but the fact was that he felt having a sense of humor was absolutely vital to success. A diplomat like himself just had to understand and roll with the ridiculous events that came along. He told me how he tried to deflect anger when negotiating with the Soviets back then. If they made rash statements in front of others, their pride would not let them back down, thus leading to deadlock. So whenever he noted anger rising, Kissinger would attempt a joke. Once, negotiating the complex disarmament treaty with Defense Minister Marshal Andrei Grechko, he noted the marshal getting red in the face. A bit of humor was in order. Kissinger suggested that the Soviets could put their big missiles on their submarines and under the new formula, when the missile was fired and sank the sub, they could build new ones.

There was no laughter. Bad joke, thought Kissinger, and he changed the subject. Three days later, he felt Grechko's elbow in his ribs, and the big marshal leaned down and said, "Vee are going to put our missiles on our submarines. Ha, ha, ha." It had taken three days, noted Kissinger, but the Soviets had decided to laugh.

Carry laughter with you wherever you go.

∽∘∾

VÁCLAV HAVEL[*]
President of the Czech Republic
Harvard University

We now live in a single global civilization. The identity of this civilization does not lie merely in similar forms of dress, or similar drinks, or in the constant buzz of the same commercial music all around the world, or even in international advertising. It lies in something deeper: thanks to the modern idea of constant progress, with its inherent expansionism, and to the rapid evolution of science

[*]Translated by Paul Wilson.

that comes directly from it, our planet has, for the first time in the long history of the human race, been covered in the space of a very few decades by a single civilization—one that is essentially techno-logical. . . . Thanks to the accomplishments of this civilization, prac-tically all of us know what checks, bonds, bills of exchange, and stocks are. We are familiar with CNN and Chernobyl, and we know who the Rolling Stones, or Nelson Mandela, or Salman Rushdie are.

But I want to focus today on the source of the dangers that threaten humanity in spite of this global civilization, and often directly because of it.

Many of the great problems we face today, as far as I understand them, have their origin in the fact that this global civilization, though in evidence everywhere, is no more than a thin veneer over the sum total of human awareness, if I may put it that way. This civilization is immensely fresh, young, new, and fragile, and the human spirit has accepted it with dizzying alacrity, without itself changing in any essential way. Humanity has gradually, and in very diverse ways, shaped our habits of mind, our relationship to the world, our models of behavior, and the values we accept and recognize. In essence, this new, single epidermis of world civilization merely covers or con-ceals the immense variety of cultures, of peoples, of religious worlds, of historical traditions and historically formed attitudes, all of which in a sense lie "beneath" it. At the same time, even as the veneer of world civilization expands, this "underside" of humanity, this hidden dimension of it, demands more and more clearly to be heard and to be granted a right to life.

And thus, while the world as a whole increasingly accepts the new habits of global civilization, another contradictory process is taking place: ancient traditions are reviving, different religions and cultures are awakening to new ways of being, seeking new room to exist, and struggling with growing fervor to realize what is unique to them, and what makes them different from others. . . .

It is often said that in our time, every valley cries out for its own independence or will even fight for it. Many nations, or parts of them at least, are struggling against modern civilization or its main proponents for the right to worship their ancient gods and obey the ancient divine injunctions. They carry on their struggle using weapons provided by the very civilization they oppose. They employ radar, computers, lasers, nerve gases, and perhaps, in the future, even nuclear weapons—all products of the world they challenge—to help defend their ancient heritage against the erosions of modern civilization. In contrast with these technological inventions, other products of this civilization—like democracy or the idea of human rights—are not accepted in many places in the world because they are deemed to be hostile to local traditions.

In other words, the Euro-American world has equipped other parts of the globe with instruments that not only could effectively destroy the enlightened values which, among other things, made possible the invention of precisely these instruments, but which could well cripple the capacity of people to live together on this earth.

∽○∾

DAN RATHER
Broadcaster
University of Texas at Austin

Being a Texan, for better and for worse, means you're going to be special for the rest of your lives. Special things are going to be expected of you. Determined, proud, tough. You remember that during World War II, Winston Churchill used to flash the V for "victory" sign, like this? Who knows? If Churchill had flashed the hook-'em-horns instead, he might've won the war in half the time.

Being a Texan means daring. It means dreaming. It means doing. It means thinking of your community, which is your family, your town, your state, and your country. . . .

What do *you* think about the genocide in Yugoslavia and Rwanda? And what do *you* plan to *do* about it? Do you or don't you plan to inform yourself about it and, at the very least, speak out about it? Similar to what the Nazis did in World War II, reminiscent of the ghastly Holocaust—today, now, in your time, on your *watch*, science and history are again being used to justify the slaughter of thousands and the humiliation of many other thousands. Women are raped and tortured; children are maimed. Their only crime, so called, is that they are of the "wrong" tribe or race or religion. These things I have seen and these things I bear witness before you tonight.

This is a murderous outrage. I respectfully submit that it is un-American, certainly un-Texan, to duck it, dodge it, or cop out by saying, "Well, it is a long way from here, Dan Rather, and from anything I care about," or by saying, "I don't know about it and I don't want to know."

In Rwanda, in what's left of Yugoslavia, the time to be a Texan is now.

Across Europe—in Russia, in Germany, even in France—some of the old demons of fascism, including anti-Semitism, are dancing tonight. Fascism—like communism—is totalitarian, rooted in the belief that might means right, that a few can rule not by law but by violence and terrorism. In this, the comparative comfort of the post-communist era, as we revel in the triumph of the end of the Cold War, it is easy, too easy, to overlook.

Do you know *what* fascism is? Do you know why your grand-fathers and grandmothers were willing to lay down their lives to defeat it? What *do* you think about the dangerous potential for its revival? What *do* you plan to do, to say about it?

In the face of fascism, the time to be a Texan is now.

And terror at home, on our own shores, in our own land, this land of the Pilgrims' pride, this land where our fathers died, by some of our own fellow Americans? With the sickening outrage of the Okla-homa City bombing murders still in the headlines and fresh in our minds and in our hearts, where do *you* stand on *these* questions: How and why were such fires of hatred lighted? And who lit them?

In the face of terror and hate and demagoguery, the time to be a Texan is now.

Then there is the question of race relations in our country, this great historical experiment in multireligious, multiracial, multieth-nic self-government. Are we still committed to the idea, and the ideal it represents? Are you? What are *you* prepared to do to pre-serve it? *Can* we, with our uniquely American blend of races and cultural heritage, get along? Can we preserve our Constitution and our unity? These, my young friends, are *not* rhetorical questions. They are real. They are fundamental, and go straight to the vitals of ourselves as a nation, as a people, as Americans, and as Texans.

In our beloved United States of America, the time to be a Texan is now.

∽○∽

MADELEINE ALBRIGHT
U.S. Secretary of State
Barnard College

Fifty years ago this spring, the American army liberated Buchenwald. They found eighteen hundred naked bodies, stacked like cordwood alongside an incinerator; they watched thousands of those freed die because starvation and disease and abuse had gone on too long; crying themselves, they embraced hollow-eyed children who had forgotten how to cry.

Eleanor Roosevelt said once that "within all of us there are two sides. One reaches for the stars, the other descends to the level of beasts."

That is not only a statement of fact. It is a presentation of choice.

∽○∽

ANNETTE BENING
Actor
San Francisco State University

I wish you the ability to trust your instincts, follow your passions, and to find the ability to pursue a life where love of work and love of self are combined.

∽○∽

Donna Shalala
U.S. Secretary of Health and Human Services
Syracuse University

Your graduation comes at a crucial juncture in our nation's history. How ironic that at a time when the Cold War has ended and democracy is replacing totalitarianism throughout the world, we see fault lines of division ripping through our country.

No matter what your political beliefs, all of us can agree that the political debate has become too polarized. Antipathy has replaced empathy. Sound bites have replaced substance. Division has replaced discourse. And simplistic solutions have replaced thoughtful answers. . . .

Twenty-five years ago, as I sat where you are sitting today, I promised myself only one thing: That I would never play it safe. That I would take risks, personally and professionally. I've kept that promise in some of the world's greatest universities, in the roughneck politics of New York and Washington, and while even hanging from a rope in the Himalayas.

I expect nothing less from each member of the graduating class of 1995. Don't play it safe. Get involved in the world. More than I believe in anything on this earth, I believe in each of you. I believe in your generation. And therefore I come today to wish you only great adventures, great love, and, I hope, wildly uncomfortable lives and happy futures.

∽∘∾

Joan Konner
Dean, Columbia University Graduate School of Journalism
Sarah Lawrence College

Ancient cultures had rituals based on myth to mark life's important changes from one season to another—from childhood to adulthood, from ordinary reality to spiritual awareness. The ceremony marks the change, and the ability, to evolve beyond self-interest to share the burden of the larger society. The transformation requires some acceptance and identification with something larger than yourself— the clan, the tribe, the community. Without such passages, there is no civilization.

We see the remnants of such rituals today in the ceremonies that occur when a lawyer becomes a judge, an immigrant becomes a citizen, or when a citizen puts on a uniform and becomes a soldier. Without the uniform and the ritual of commitment to the larger whole, a soldier is simply a murderer, or a vigilante in a private militia, an example that is all too real for us today.

Graduation retains some of the features of these more ancient rites: the gathering of elders (your families, the alumni) and priests (your teachers) to welcome you back from your books and experiences, and to celebrate with ceremonies and feasts.

[Joseph] Campbell's seminal work, *The Hero's Journey*, . . . is one of the most compelling works in our culture, in movies, books, and religions. The story endures because it entertains and it inspires us. I think of it today as you begin your journey into the larger world. The hero usually emerges from humble beginnings, but is called to a path of trials and suffering. He survives a series of ordeals and returns to the community carrying a gift, a message from which everyone in the culture can learn. In fact, the hero's journey is like the journey of life itself. It's a mystery and a challenge, and in the process, you find something of value in the experience and about yourself. . . .

Campbell viewed the world around him as the consequence of a society without rituals of maturation, a society of untamed, immature, unsocialized barbarians, a society without the guideposts of myth to work out passages in life. . . . Acknowledging the hardship and drama of life, he would ask of it: "Is this a private fight, or can anyone get into it?" Or, to quote from the Shinto text: "The processes of nature cannot be evil. You participate in the world. Participation is a key to the experience of being alive."

∽o∾

Ann Richards
Governor, Texas
Mount Holyoke College

The first rule of life is: Cherish your friends and your family as if your life depended on it . . . because it does.

Number two: Love people more than things. You know those T-shirts that say "He who has the most toys when he dies wins"? I'm going to promise you that over the years I've spent my life collecting a great number of things I thought I was going to die if I didn't have. And I wouldn't give you a nickel for most of it today.

Number three: Indulge the fool in you. Encourage the clown and the laughter that is inside of you. You know? Go ahead and do it. Make time now for play, for the impractical, for the absurd, and make a rule to do it. Not just every now and then. Let your heart overrule your head once in a while. Never turn down a new experience unless it's against the law or it's going to get you in real serious trouble.

Number four: Don't spend a lot of time worrying about your failures. I've learned a whole lot more from my mistakes than from all of my successes.

And number five: Have some sense about work. No one ever died muttering, "I wish I had spent more time at the office."

✑

1996

Nineteen ninety-six may well be remembered for a terrible incident involving an airplane: TWA flight 800, heading toward Paris from New York's John F. Kennedy Airport, crashed mysteriously off the coast of Long Island, killing all 230 passengers; for weeks afterward, debris drifted ashore onto the beaches of the Hamptons. Was it terrorism? No one was able to say for sure.

Certainly, terrorism had been in the news all year: violence in the Middle East; more bombings in Northern Ireland; a bomb exploding during the Summer Olympic Games in Atlanta, Georgia; a truck bomb exploding in Saudi Arabia, killing nineteen U.S. servicemen. All of a sudden, the world seemed terribly unsafe.

Despite a cloud of allegations about his character, Bill Clinton won a second term in the White House, beating Robert Dole, though the GOP retained control of both congressional houses. In Russia, President Boris Yeltsin was also elected to a second term. Benjamin Netanyahu was elected prime minister of Israel, an election that cast significant doubts about that country's desire for peace. Job insecurity rose, as increasingly it seemed that the notion of corporate loyalty and longevity was a thing of the past. Theodore Kaczynski, a suspect in the Unabomber case, was arrested in Montana. Fidel Castro met with Pope John Paul II at the Vatican. Rent captured the attention of theatergoers, and Madonna engaged in her umpteenth reinvention by taking the lead role in the movie version of Evita. Teenagers danced to the macarena. Tiger Woods dominated golf, and at the end of the year, as the northeastern United States buckled under a blizzard that dropped nearly two feet of snow on New York City, Christmas shoppers went nuts for the Tickle Me Elmo doll. Gene Kelly died at age eighty-three,

Ella Fitzgerald died at age seventy-nine, and comedian George Burns died at age one hundred.

In Dunblane, Scotland, a gunman opened fire on a kindergarten class, killing sixteen children; American violence was blamed. Erik and Lyle Menendez were found guilty of the first-degree murders of their parents in Beverly Hills, California. Seven-year-old pilot Jessica Dubroff was killed when her single-engine plane went down in Wyoming. A ValuJet flight crashed in the Florida Everglades. The U.S. Supreme Court ruled that women could attend the Virginia Military Institute. Buckingham Palace announced that Prince Charles and Princess Diana had agreed to the terms of their divorce. Rap singer Tupac Shakur was killed in Las Vegas. For the first time ever, the Dow Jones Industrial Average swelled past the 6,000 mark. Alger Hiss died in New York. Truck drivers struck in France by simply parking their trucks along the highways in and out of Paris and refusing to budge. In Oakland, California, the local school board announced that it would be the first school district to recognize Ebonics, or black English, as an independent language.

In South Africa there was optimism, finally, as President Nelson Mandela signed into law a new constitution.

∞◦∞

WENDY WALKER WHITWORTH
Television Producer
Hollins College

If your goal is to have a successful career . . .

Work harder than the next guy—come early and stay late.

Keep a good attitude; don't be moody.

If you don't understand something, don't fake it. Ask questions and more questions. Your education is just beginning.

Take any job to get a foot in the door. Nothing should be beneath you—don't take shortcuts to get that promotion. Work at building a strong foundation and the promotions will follow.

Don't be hung up on that you're-a-woman-and-he's-a-guy stuff. Just work harder than the guys, and you will be fine.

Along the way, treat all people the same. Don't just suck up to the boss. Treat your peers with respect and help them as much as you can. Everything you do is a self-portrait. The way you treat people above you, and below you, paints a picture of what kind of person you are. And besides, you never know when that desk assistant is going to become the host of the *Today* show, or when that guy dispatching camera crews is going to be cohosting *Dateline NBC*, or even when the secretary may become an executive producer.

Ronald Reagan has a sign on his desk that I put on mine. It says, "There is no limit what you can do or where you can go as long as you don't mind who gets the credit."

༚༠༚

STEVE KROFT

Broadcaster

Syracuse University

The first lesson I often offer is life is full of second chances. Remember that. Sometimes even third and fourth chances. Occasionally even fifth and sixth chances, if you make enough money to afford a good lawyer. . . .

I think you're going to be pleasantly surprised that you're much better prepared than most for the challenges that await you. After you get that first job, nobody is going to pay attention to your grades, they're not going to be looking at your transcripts, they're going to be looking at you. You may discover, as Al McGuire once said, that much of the world is run by C students. . . .

I'm not saying that life is going to be easy; if it were, Zantac, a pill for heartburn, and Prozac, a pill for depression, would not be two of the biggest-selling drugs in America. . . .

The world is changing much faster than at any prior point in my lifetime and probably faster than at any point in the last century, when the automobile and electricity and the telephone changed people's lives. There are revolutions under way in cybernetics, telecommunications, genetics, optics, physics, environmental sciences, medicine—and there are more opportunities than ever before. If you have a great idea, pursue it. Stay informed and be ready, because before you know it, you're going to be running the place. You're going to inherit a great country with a lot of tough problems. Don't screw it up any worse than it's already screwed up. If you see something that's wrong, don't be afraid to try and fix it. . . .

If you love adventure and you want to see the world, find a way to do it. It's becoming a smaller and smaller place, and by the time you reach my age, you'll require a much more intimate knowledge of it. If you don't speak a foreign language, I'd suggest learning one even if it means listening to tapes on your way to work. It's the best way I know right now to job security.

Your schooling, for many of you, is over, but your education is still continuing. And I would tell you to reproduce. Not tonight. But you are the best we have, and we need all of you that we can get.

∽∘∼

GEORGE BUSH
Former U.S. President
Williams College

Don't be afraid of trying—of dreaming. Don't be afraid of failure—or tears. We all stumble, we all face fear—that's what makes us human. But none of us should ever regret. None of us should ever sit at a grandchild's graduation and think, I wish that were me starting out all over again. There's so much I'd do differently.

Don't even worry if you are not 100 percent sure what you want to do for the rest of your life—what you want to be thirty years from now. . . . I'm here simply to say that while the road ahead may look unclear, today the future is brighter than at any time in our nation's history. You can take heart that the world today is much different from the one in which your parents and grandparents grew up.

Your grandparents know what it was like to live in a world at war—but today the world is at peace.

Your parents know what it was like to hide under their desks as young students, practicing for a possible nuclear attack—but today the superpower conflict is no more and the threat of nuclear holocaust has receded.

And I think each of you is old enough to remember what it was like before the Berlin Wall fell or the Soviet Union was replaced by a democratic Russia—but today we see more people are living in freedom and democracy.

So when you look at how far we've come, then maybe you can understand why I am an optimist about the future. I sincerely believe our best days are yet to come.

∽⚭∾

Andy Rooney
Television Commentator
Colgate University

One of the things you have to face . . . is the unpleasant fact that you will not ever arrive at any condition of life with which you are totally satisfied and happy. It seems unfortunate, but it's true, that to experience real happiness, you first, or occasionally anyway, have to be unhappy. So you're going to be unhappy sometimes. Just accept it as part of the process. Ambition and satisfaction are at war. If you're ambitious, you aren't satisfied, and if you're satisfied, you aren't ambitious.

∽⚭∾

Anna Quindlen
Writer
Smith College

Twenty-five years ago today, I had just graduated from Barnard College. . . . There had never been a woman justice of the Supreme Court. There had never been a woman rabbi or a woman Episcopal priest. There was no Emily's List, and there was no women's campaign fund. There were no girls in Little League. There were no altar girls in Catholic churches. There had never been a female astronaut. Most large law firms had never had a woman partner, and most hospitals had never had a female surgical resident. Great Britain had never had a woman prime minister. That year one in four American women worked outside the home. The woman known as Jane Roe had had a baby and given her up for adoption, and the woman known as Hillary Rodham was still talked about at Wellesley as someone who might be president of the United States one day. And some days I wish she were. There were thirteen women in the United States House of Representatives. There was one woman in the Senate; literally everything written about her included an account of what she wore.

I could never have imagined how different the world would be just twenty-five years later. I could never have imagined that we would come to take for granted women rabbis and women ministers, women senators and women judges, women partners and women surgeons, women editors and women columnists.

[But] once we entered men's arenas we discovered a dirty little secret, and that is that work, influence, even power, with no countervailing forces, no intimacy, no family, no sense of connection to others, is for many of us no kind of life at all. Part of that synthesis has been a recognition of the truth that while parity and equality are critical, and we will have them, as important are recognizing and not fearing the admission of the ways in which we women may be inclined for whatever reason to make different choices, different life decisions, than our male counterparts.

The great social revolution of the last twenty-five years meant that we rebelled against the indiscriminate taking of those things we had to give. We rebelled against being taken for granted as support and as caregiver. We rebelled against being seen as second-class citizens because we had done the discredited work of creating and launching an entire new generation of human beings every twenty years. . . . But with great gains we must always be careful of our potential losses. And if we become the sort of people who believe as a group that the position of your name on the page or the letterhead is the most important thing about you, we will, as the Bible verse goes, have gained the whole world and lost our own souls. The things that last are not set down on paper.

What does it profit us if we have gained so much but have not love toward our fellow without? Doesn't that mean essentially that the price of equality will have been the loss not of femininity but of humanity? The wonderful thing, of course, is that we won't let that happen—any of us, any of you—as we search for that new paradigm. . . . It's fine to want to do well, but if we do not do good, too, doing well is simply not good enough.

∽º∾

CORNEL WEST
Professor and Writer
DePauw University

Even on this day of celebration and jubilation, let us not forget that we are coming to the end of a ghastly century. A century in which we have witnessed unprecedented levels of vulgarity and bestiality and brutality. The Nazism at the heart of so-called civilized Europe. The Stalinism at the core of the so-called emancipatory Soviet Union. The European colonialism in the name of Christianity and civilization that would leave such scars and bruises on Asians and Africans. The Jim Crow and Jane Crow in America, the city on the hill. The patriarchy that leaves such wounds on women of all colors across social systems. The homophobia that loses sight of gay brothers and lesbian sisters; or all forms of ideology and practices that lose sight of humanity, whether it be the elderly or the disabled. What a century it has been, and yet here we sit in the sun. . . .

If with our sense of history we can expand the scope of empathy, accenting nonmarket values—not just like love and care and empathy, but parenting, friendship, support of others, companionship—and in the larger context, creating public spaces that we can enter without humiliation such that citizenship has real content and substance, so that we view ourselves not simply as bearers of an identity or clients of a constituency or as consumers, but rather as citizens, democrats—small *d*—involved in the making and remaking of democracy in the face of the legacies of evil that steal, permeate our souls, our society, our hearts and homes, then maybe we have a chance.

ᦂᦂ

David Halberstam
Writer
Dartmouth College

The choices for you out there are not simple. It is, for example, possible to be immensely successful in your chosen field and yet in some curious way to fail at life, to get to the top and yet fail to enrich yourself. A few years ago my colleague Russell Baker, the distinguished *New York Times* columnist and humorist, was asked by the *Times* in-house magazine to write a piece about a colleague who had just been promoted to a powerful new position. Baker went to see his own great mentor, James Reston, then the *Times* bureau chief. He mentioned the colleague's name to Reston.

"Tell me about his life," Baker asked Reston.

"That's not a life—that's a career," Reston said with great disdain.

He meant that the colleague had at once done everything right, but had somehow missed the point of what he had done; he had covered the requisite big stories, had made the front page the requisite number of times, but he had in some way failed in the elemental human involvement so necessary for real pleasure in this career. He won all the prizes save the real ones, the friendships and all the fun that are at the core of what we do. . . .

In all things in life, choose your conscience, and trust your instincts, and lead your lives without regrets. It's simply easier that way. I mention that because life, under the best circumstances, even if you're lucky, as I have been, to choose the right profession, is very hard. First you have to choose the right profession—and then you have to work hard for the rest of your lives to sustain yourself in this choice which you happen to love. As the noted philosopher, basketball player, and sports commentator Julius Erving—Dr. J—once said, "Being a professional is doing the things you love to do on the days when you don't feel like doing them."

∽o∽

Mary Higgins Clark*
Writer
Providence College

In a suspense novel, the protagonist has faith that he or she will emerge triumphant. I wish you the kind of abiding faith that knows that God is there waiting and watching even when at times he seems very far away. . . .

Yeats, being Irish, had an abiding sense of tragedy which sustained him through transient periods of joy. With all due respect I suggest you reverse the order—have an abiding sense of joy.

The protagonist in a book often has a good buddy, a best friend, a sidekick. I wish you good friends, people who will celebrate your victories with you, and who will be around when you feel as though the sky is falling in.

A good novel should be a page-turner, something to be gulped at

*Copyright © 2000 by Mary Higgins Clark. Used by permission of McIntosh & Otis, Inc.

one sitting. Fortunately, or unfortunately, life is like that. It goes by very swiftly. You will find that your twenties will disappear in a blur, then it will be your thirties and your forties.

A year ago I was at a significant reunion of Villa Maria Academy, the high school I attended more than four decades ago. My classmates and I all felt the same way. It was yesterday that we were together in our school uniforms, talking about our Friday night dates. One of us plaintively said, "But I'm still seventeen inside." We all expressed that feeling . . . inside still young, still doing the Lindy to the tune of "Dance with the dolly with the hole in her stocking . . ."

But the months have become seasons; and the seasons, years; and that was a very long time ago.

I beg you, cherish the day, live it, enjoy it, savor it.

∽◦∾

Nora Ephron
Director and Writer
Wellesley College

I've written about my years at Wellesley, and I don't want to repeat myself any more than is necessary. But I do want to retell one anecdote from the piece I did about my tenth Wellesley reunion . . . which was that, during my junior year, when I was engaged for a very short period of time, I thought I might transfer to Barnard my senior year. I went to see my class dean and she said to me, "Let me give you some advice. You've worked so hard at Wellesley; when you marry, take a year off. Devote yourself to your husband and your marriage." Of course, it was a stunning piece of advice to give me because I'd always intended to work after college. My mother was a career woman, and all of us, her four daughters, grew up understanding that the question "What do you want to be when you grow up?" was as valid for girls as for boys. Take a year off being a wife. I always wondered what I was supposed to do in that year. Iron? I repeated the story for years, as proof that Wellesley wanted its graduates to be merely housewives. But I turned out to be wrong, because years later I met another Wellesley graduate who had been as hell-bent on domesticity as I had been on a career. And she had gone to the same dean with the same problem, and the dean had said to her, "Don't have children right away. Take a year to work." And so I saw that what Wellesley wanted was for us to avoid the extremes. To be, instead, that thing in the middle. A lady. We were to take the fabulous education we had received here and use it to preside at dinner table or at a committee meeting, and when two people disagreed, we would be intelligent enough to step in and point out the remarkable similarities between their two opposing positions. We were to spend our lives making nice.

Many of my classmates did exactly what they were supposed to when they graduated from Wellesley, and some of them, by the way, lived happily ever after. But many of them didn't. All sorts of things happened that no one expected. They needed money so they had to work. They got divorced, so they had to work. They were bored witless, so they had to work. The women's movement came along and made harsh value judgments about their lives—judgments that caught them by surprise, because they were doing what they were supposed to be doing, weren't they? The rules had changed, and they were caught in some sort of strange time warp. They had never intended to be the heroines of their own lives; they had intended to be—what? First ladies, I guess; first ladies in the lives of big men. They ended up feeling like victims. They ended up, and this is really sad, thinking that their years in college were the best years of their lives.

Why am I telling you this? It was a long time ago, right? Things have changed, haven't they? Yes, they have. But I mention it because I want to remind you of the undertow, of the specific gravity. American society has a remarkable ability to resist change, or to take whatever change has taken place and attempt to make it go away. Things are different for you than they were for us. Just the fact that you chose to come to a single-sex college makes you smarter than we were—we came because it's what you did in those days—and the college you are graduating from is a very different place. . . . The women's movement has made a huge difference, too, particularly for young women like you. There are women doctors and women lawyers. There are anchorwomen, although most of them are blond. But at the same time, the pay differential between men and women has barely changed. In my business, the movie business, there are many more women directors, but it's just as hard to make a movie about women as it ever was, and look at the parts the Oscar-nominated actresses played this year: hooker, hooker, hooker, hooker, and nun. It's 1996, and you are graduating from Wellesley in the year of the Wonderbra. The Wonderbra is not a step forward for women. Nothing that hurts that much is a step forward for women.

∽◦∽

1997

Exactly twenty-five years after the Watergate scandal, 1997 was a year in which grandeur, and in some cases bombast, made a comeback, culturally, socially, and in the case of the death of Princess Diana, royally.

Politically, we were reminded as well of greatness, the past intruding more than usual into the present. The transfer of Hong Kong from British to Chinese control evoked both the might and the diminution of Great Britain. In Scotland, a Finn Dorset lamb named Dolly was cloned. James Cameron's Titanic packed teenaged moviegoers into seats with a turn-of-the-century world populated with fairy-tale polarities of good and bad, and such words as "bravery" and "courage," a theme that Tom Brokaw would profit from a couple of years later with his book The Greatest Generation.

But it was the abrupt death of Princess Diana in a car crash in a Paris tunnel, surrounded by paparazzi and attempting to escape with putative new beau Dodi Al Fayed, that shattered the English reserve and caused genuine, immense sorrow around the world. Conspiracy theories abounded, but the crash was later ruled the product of a drunken chauffeur named Henri Paul. Though Mother Teresa died five days after Princess Diana, her death was nearly buried by the world outpouring of sorrow for Diana; predictably, editorial writers had a fine time discussing where the world's priorities lay, and their sons and daughters momentarily put aside their Tamagotchis and Beanie Babies to send letters and postcards to the young princes William and Harry. Nineteen ninety-seven was also a year in which children seemed to be maturing too fast; the increased media savviness of kids ages five to eight made one Disney marketeer suggest aloud that the days of *movies in which a cricket and a hound went on a journey together were over; kids wouldn't stand for it anymore. Many parents disagreed.*

Internationally, the past intruded into the present. In response to claims that Swiss banks held approximately $7 billion of assets unfairly swindled from Holocaust victims, the Swiss government and a cabal of Swiss banks agreed to establish a fund to pay back victims who were unable to retrieve assets that they or their relatives had deposited in Swiss banks during the Second World War. Tony Blair, the head of the Labour Party, took office, Britain's claim to youth and vitality. The phantasmagoria of American life continued: thirty-nine members of an obscure southern California cult committed mass suicide in Rancho Santa Fe, California. Tiger Woods continued to dominate golf. Timothy McVeigh was sentenced to death. Mike Tyson bit off a chunk of Evander Holyfield's ear. A civil trial in Santa Monica found O.J. Simpson liable for the stabbing death of his ex-wife and Ron Goldman. While Simpson's career as an actor and a spokesman was effectively over, the decision struck many people as too little, too late. A drifter named Andrew Cunanan shot and killed designer Gianni Versace in Miami, Florida.

Diana, princess of Wales, was thirty-six.

⟋⟍

Marian Wright Edelman
Founder and Director, Children's Defense Fund
Smith College

We are living at an incredible moral moment in history. Few human beings are blessed to anticipate or experience both the beginning of a new century and a millennium. How will we say thanks for the life and earth and nation and children that God has entrusted to our care? What legacies, principles, and values will we stand for and send to the future through our children to their children and to a spiritually confused, vulcanized, and violent nation and world desperately hungry for moral leadership? How will progress be measured over a hundred and thousand years if we survive them? By the kill power and number of weapons of destruction we can produce and traffic at home or abroad, or by our willingness to shrink, indeed destroy, the prison of violence constructed in the name of peace and security? Will we be remembered in these last years of the twentieth century by how many material things we can manufacture, advertise, sell, and consume? Or by our rediscovery of more lasting, nonmaterial measures of success? A new Dow Jones for the purpose and quality of life and our families, neighborhoods, and national community. Will we be remembered by how rapidly technology and corporate merger mania can render human beings and human work obsolete? Or by a better balance between corporate profits and corporate caring for children, families, and communities? Will we be remembered by how much a few at the top can get at the expense of the many at the bottom and the middle? Or by our struggle for a concept of enough for all Americans? Will we be remembered by the glitz and violence and style and banality of too much of our culture? Or by the substance of our struggle to rekindle an ethic of caring, community, and justice in a world driven too much by money, power, and weaponry?

∽◦∾

MADELEINE ALBRIGHT
U.S. Secretary of State
Mount Holyoke College

As you go along your own road in life, you will, if you aim high enough, also meet resistance, for as Robert Kennedy once said, "If there's nobody in your way, it's because you're not going anywhere." But no matter how tough the opposition may seem, have courage still—and persevere.

There is no doubt, if you aim high enough, that you will be confronted by those who say that your efforts to change the world or improve the lot of those around you do not mean much in the grand scheme of things. But no matter how impotent you may sometimes feel, have courage still—and persevere.

It is certain, if you aim high, that you will find your strongest beliefs ridiculed and challenged; principles that you cherish may be derisively dismissed by those claiming to be more practical or realistic than you. But no matter how weary you may become in persuading others to see the value in what you value, have courage still—and persevere.

Inevitably, if you aim high enough, you will be buffeted by demands of family, friends, and employment that will conspire to distract you from your course. But no matter how difficult it may be to meet the commitments you have made, have courage still—and persevere.

It has been said that all work that is worth anything is done in faith.

ᔆᔆ

Bob Newhart
Comedian
Catholic University

Humor makes us free. That may seem like an odd conclusion, but as long as the tyrant cannot control the minds of free men, they remain free. Humor abounded behind the Iron Curtain and in POW camps. Humor is also our way of dealing with the inexplicable. We had an earthquake a couple of years ago in Los Angeles, and it wasn't more than three or four days later that I heard the first earthquake joke. Someone said, "The traffic is stopped, but the freeways are moving."

ᔆᔆ

ANNA QUINDLEN
Writer
Barnard College

I realize that there is something broader, ultimately more important to me than religious affiliation, which has determined how I feel about myself and about the people I love and have come to admire. And that is something I think of as my attitude. Perhaps you could call it a worldview. Perhaps you could call it a spiritual identity. It has to do with what you are made of, with how you approach the world around you, and ultimately, whether you perceive it as a worthwhile place and those who inhabit it as worthwhile human beings.

Fortunately, I came by my attitude pretty young. Unfortunately, I came by it in the worst possible way. I was nineteen years old when I was told that my mother had stage four ovarian cancer, a diagnosis which meant she was not going to live much longer. . . .

I learned something enduring, in a very short period of time, about life. And that was that it was glorious, and that you had no business taking it for granted. I went home in September and my mother died in January, leaving a handful of jewelry to be divided among her children and an index card on which she had written the words to that section of St. Paul's letter to the Corinthians which begins, "Though I speak with the tongues of men and angels and have not love . . . " And by April, I realized I had salvaged one thing out of the ruin of my life as I had known it. And that was that I was still alive, and that it was so wonderful that I could actually take pleasure in the feeling of my lungs filling and emptying again. I looked at the daffodils and the azaleas in our suburban neighborhood and, Lord, they were beautiful. . . . I was never again going to be able to see life as anything except a great gift.

Oh, I've lost that, from time to time. Bad days and good days. Life cycles and dark moods. But it always comes back and, in some ways, has separated me from some of my peers. . . .

One Thanksgiving I wrote a column about this, about being thankful, about life being good, and I wrote it more gingerly than I've written about abortion, or the death penalty, or gay rights, because I was afraid of it. I was afraid of being seen as a Pollyanna. I was afraid of speaking of plenty in the midst of want. I was afraid of being off the beaten path of anomie and disaffection.

But I wrote it anyhow, because I felt it. And the mail that followed was amazing. Because what people said, again and again, was: *I almost forgot. I almost forgot it was true.*

∽∘∾

MARK SHIELDS
Political Commentator
University of Notre Dame

Rule number one: call your mother. And then call her again.

Number two: if and when you do become mothers and fathers, please remember to spend more time with your children than you judge to be reasonable. You will never regret that time. And please know that nobody in recorded history, on his or her deathbed, ever said, "Gee, I wish I'd spent more time at the office."

Please pay off your student loans. If you don't, the only people you are hurting are those kids coming behind you. The loan money has been there for you because those who went before you paid off their own student loans.

In every political campaign or public professional debate you will ever be involved in, there will inevitably and always be somebody on your side that you wish devoutly was on the other side.

In addition, perhaps the most fundamental truth of all: life is not like college. You have heard it time and again, that is true. Life is not like college. Life is a lot more like high school.

If you remember nothing else, try and recall the wisdom of Walker Percy, who wrote, "Do not be the kind of person who gets all A's but flunks ordinary living."

Finally, remember that the fear of failure is the most paralyzing of all human emotions. Fear of failure stops more people from trying and from doing good, from daring, from succeeding. It truly is to be avoided at all costs. Will Rogers once said of these United States, "It's a great country, but you can't live in it for nothing."

DENISE DI NOVI
Film Producer
Simmons College

When you are deciding what to do, don't do it because it's safe and sensible or because others expect it. Though we all need to pay the bills, the biggest mistake you can make is to do something only for the money. Do something because you love it so much you'll be miserable if you don't. Try helping others to reach their potential. Like magic, it will come back tenfold and help you find your own. If you decide to do something different from what your education prepared you for, don't worry. As Albert Einstein said, "Education is what remains after we forget what we're taught."

Society has to understand that we must help good workers to be good mothers, too. Trying to be a good mother has underlined something profoundly important for me: being a good human being is more important than being good at my job.

∽o∼

ART BUCHWALD
Newspaper Columnist
University of North Carolina at Greensboro

Another bit of advice I have for you when looking for a job is, how does one get through to a person on the phone when you are being stonewalled by a snooty secretary? And here are a few suggestions that might make you get through. Whenever a secretary asks what I'm calling about, I say, "Please tell Mr. Goldstone I just crashed into his car in the parking lot and I want to give him my insurance company's name." And if that doesn't work, this one usually does: "Please tell Mr. Goldstone we just got his test back from the lab." And if that one fails, this one never has failed: "Tell Mr. Goldstone I just found his American Express card on a water bed at the Silk Pussy Cat Motel. Does he want me to mail it in, or bring it to him?"

Michael Dirda
Writer
Washington College

Words matter. Totalitarian regimes—the experts at realpolitik—ban books, imprison, exile, and kill writers, do everything to control what people read so they can control what they think, control what they do. For centuries, rhetoric—the power of language to persuade and inspire—lay at the very heart of education. The great Russian short-story writer Isaac Babel once pointed out the devastating power of language in a remark about punctuation, of all things. "There is no iron," said Babel, "which can enter the human heart with such stupefying effect as a period placed at just the right moment."

Words have power. When King Lear bends over the body of his daughter Cordelia, he expresses what anyone who has experienced the death of a loved one has felt: "Why should a dog, a horse, a rat, have life / And thou no breath at all? O thou wilt come no more. / Never, never, never. . . ." Almost anybody past forty can be reduced to maudlin wistfulness by the lyrics of some old rock song or other. . . .

For a long time now people have bemoaned the decline of reading in this country. Books have been done in by television, the movies, VCRs, CD-ROMs, the Internet. I'm not so sure. Certainly new media such as these may alter the form of books—but poetry and fiction will certainly survive. People need stories, to exalt us when young with dreams, to help us to understand ourselves and our world as adults, to comfort us in our old age, to give us pleasure.

I implore you to remember [Walt] Whitman's plea: take up books that matter. The philosopher Schopenhauer once wrote, "A precondition for reading good books is not reading bad ones: for life is short." Or as Whitman's contemporary Thoreau remarked, with his usual succinctness, "Read the best books first, or you may not get a chance to read them at all."

∽∘∾

TIM RUSSERT
Broadcaster
Catholic University, The Columbus School of Law

People with backgrounds like yours and mine can make a difference. Believe me, you will have more of a role in determining whether true justice prevails in this country than the superlawyer/lobbyists on K Street, or so-called rainmakers of Wall Street.

In Poland, it was a young electrician named Lech Walesa, the son of a carpenter, who transformed a nation from communism to democracy. In Czechoslovakia, a writer named Václav Havel, the son of an office clerk, who traded his pen for a podium and rallied his people to freedom. In South Africa, Nelson Mandela, a brave black man who worked his way through law school as a police officer, spent more than twenty-seven years in jail to make one central point: we are all created equal.

All these leaders have one thing in common with you. Like the past, the future leaders of this country, of this world, and of the legal profession will not be born to the blood of kings, but to the blood of immigrants and pioneers. . . .

Remember the words of the U.S. hockey coach at the 1980 Winter Olympics. He told his team, "You were born to be a player. You were meant to be here, at this moment. Do it." And, against all odds, the United States won the gold medal.

So, go climb that ladder of success and work and live in comfort and enjoy yourself. You earned it. For that is the American dream.

But please do this world and your honorable profession one small favor. Give back. Remember the people struggling alongside you and below you. The people who haven't had the same opportunity, the same blessings, the same education, the same degree. . . .

Whatever your ideology, reach down and see if there isn't someone you can't pull up a rung or two—someone old, someone sick, someone lonely, someone uneducated, someone defenseless. Give them a hand. Give them a chance. Give them a start, give them protection. Give them their dignity.

∽०∽

ROBERT COLES
Psychiatrist and Writer
Syracuse University

I want to conclude with something . . . that my mother used to tell me. She had read about William James's son, whose name was also William James—Billy, who became an artist. And Billy wrote to his uncle, the great novelist Henry James, asked him what he ought to do with his life. He was about your age. He was twenty, twenty-one, twenty-two, wondering where and whither and why. And the great novelist wrote back to his nephew, "Three things, Bill, three things I tell you to do in life. The first thing is to be kind. The second thing is to be kind. And the third thing is to be kind."

So, be kind, be kind as you leave here, be kind to one another. Reach out beyond the confines of your own life and your own background, reach out to one another to make this a country united, united by our willingness to link arms with one another, to trust one another, and to love one another, and to be part of one another's lives. Again, world without end.

∾ͻͽ∾

DIANE SAWYER
Broadcaster
University of Illinois at Champaign-Urbana

Survival tip number one for going into the real world is to bring a map with you—a map, by the way, of yourself. Don't listen to others for directions about who you are. I have a perfect illustration of why this is a bad idea, something that happened to me awhile back. I was in a store in New York City and all of a sudden the clerk came streaming toward me, and he was jumping up and down and he was squealing, and he said, "I just can't believe it, I can't believe it. This is so exciting." And people were gathering around me, maybe twenty or thirty people gathered around, and at the top of his voice he said to me, "Are you who I think you are?" And, well, I puffed up a little bit and I said, "I suppose so." Whereupon he shouted, "I loved you in *Out of Africa.*" I did the honorable thing and said, "Robert Redford was great," and slinked away.

Bring your own map and on it make sure that you have pin-pointed three things. They were the three things my father said to me when I stumbled back from college and had no idea what I wanted to do. And he said, "Let's just begin here. First, tell me what you love. And then tell me the most daring place to do it. And then tell me if that place has heart—if you can be guaranteed that in some way you are serving others. It's what they say about businessmen, 'that managers do things right, leaders do the right things.'" So I told my father I loved writing and that television seemed adventurous, and it was a place for me to talk about what I thought really matters. So I pass his formula on to you. Know what you love and even if you can't begin in the work you love, find what you love in the work you're doing, and it will be like a star that will guide you to the next place. . . .

Beware of things that go "Duh" in the night. I don't know if evil and ignorance are in fact twins, but I can tell you this. Of all the people I have interviewed, and I have interviewed murderers—Charles Manson—and I have interviewed bigots and racists and tyrants like Saddam Hussein—and the one thing they have all had in common is profound ignorance about the world. Sometimes it's willed, sometimes it's pathological. But if you don't keep growing and learning, the danger is not just being boring. The danger is being unwittingly cruel.

∞

1998

Nineteen ninety-eight witnessed a political scandal that would not go away, and in that sense, proved to be a culmination of trivia over real issues, a triumph of television ratings over substance, a victory of prurience over politics. On one hand was President Bill Clinton, only the second president in history to face impeachment, for obstructing justice as well as lying under oath about his relationship with a plump, immature Beverly Hills–born White House intern named Monica Lewinsky. Facing him was a doggedly uncharismatic Texas-born prosecutor with the paradoxically magnetic name of Ken Starr. Laughing, but more often than not rustling with annoyed impatience, was a fed-up American public, a group more forgiving and compassionate than most pollsters had taken them for.

Culturally, 1998 was a mixed bag. Titanic continued its surge, capitalizing neatly on the "Nobody understands me" ethos of the American adolescent, despite a tin-eared script. In the end, it would gross more than a billion dollars. Hollywood's absurd, albeit solidly business-minded, emphasis on youth intensified; a writer for the television show Felicity was fired when it was revealed that she had falsified her age, and was in fact thirty-two years old, and not twenty-three. Baseball came back from a fallow period with a home-run contest between the St. Louis Cardinals' Mark McGwire and the Chicago Cubs' Sammy Sosa, which McGwire won in the end with seventy homers. The Winter Olympics got under way in Nagano, Japan. James Earl Ray, assassin of Martin Luther King Jr., died in Tennessee. The Chicago Bulls won the NBA title for the third consecutive year, and a gunman killed two policemen in the U.S. Capitol, in Washington, D.C.

In Germany, Gerhard Schröder of the Social Democrat Party was elected chancellor, thus putting an end to the Helmut Kohl era. Newt Gingrich resigned his speakership, as well as his House seat. The U.S. economy forged ahead. Exxon and Mobil joined forces. Helen Hunt won both an Emmy and an Oscar. E-commerce was the new trend in shopping, and Seinfeld bowed off the airwaves.

Elsewhere, life and death went on as usual. Frank Sinatra died, with virtually no comparable male singers in the wings to take his place. Viagra was touted as the new male impotence drug, and Internet stocks soared, based on an oxygenated belief in a technologically interconnected future. India and Pakistan conducted underground nuclear tests. In Kosovo, the Serbian army and police force enforced a full-force crackdown against ethnic Albanians desiring independence. Weathercasters prattled on incessantly about El Niño. Swissair proved that even an airline with a near-matchless safety record can falter; on September 2, Swissair flight 111 crashed into the North Atlantic, killing 229 people.

In August, President Clinton testified before a grand jury regarding his relationship with Monica Lewinsky. Later, in a televised address, the president admitted to the country that he and Miss Lewinsky had had a relationship that was "not appropriate." In November, Clinton agreed to pay nearly $1 million to settle a sexual harassment lawsuit brought by Paula Jones. As ever, the European press was scathing: what was so shattering about Clinton's behavior anyway?

John Glenn, seventy-one, returned to space, with many of us wishing we could go with him.

❧

RUTH BADER GINSBURG
U.S. Supreme Court Justice
Northwestern University

On the Jewish New Year, Rosh Hashanah, a special prayer is read in some synagogues. The prayer was called to my attention by Cincinnati, Ohio, U.S. district judge Susan J. Dlott. It contains these lines:

Birth is a beginning
And death is a destination.
And life is a journey:
From ignorance to knowing;
From foolishness to discretion.
And then, perhaps, to
Wisdom.

∾○∾

JOYCE PURNICK
Columnist, Former Metro Editor, *New York Times*
Barnard College

You first have to know a little bit about me for any of this to make sense. The short version of my life is this: I grew up in a struggling but proud middle-class family in Queens, the daughter of devoted parents—especially my mother, who encouraged me to write, because, being an avid reader, I always wrote pretty well. . . .

I always worked nonstop, found a profession that encouraged good writers and workaholics, and starting out as a clerk, moved up in classic newspaper style from clerk to reporter to columnist to editor—from the *New York Post* to *New York* magazine to the *New York Times.*

Along the way, without realizing what I was doing to myself until it was too late, I forfeited the chance to have children, but found love when I was forty and got married at forty-two to a wonderful man who understands driven women—at least this one—and the demands of journalism.

So, what can you learn from this?

One thing is this: *you CANNOT have it all.* It doesn't happen unless you are really, really wealthy, and even then it's hard and rare. "Having it all" is a phrase for books and speeches by political cheerleaders.

The point is that all along the way, you make choices; that was an easy one.

A very difficult one: family versus profession.

I made a choice there, too, albeit a passive one, and I confess I will always regret it. I wish I'd thought earlier about having a family because then I probably would have done something about it. . . . But though I did have some options, I was so dogged and driven about my career—in a profession that, as I said before, welcomes and rewards overachievers—that as weird as this sounds, I didn't think much about the time that was passing me by until I reached my late thirties and then, suddenly, it happens that fast, I passed forty.

The flip side of my experience is that I am absolutely convinced I would not be the metro editor of the *Times* if I had a family. I love the *Times,* I love the city desk, and my job is very much a part of my identity—a proud part.

Still, this is where "having it all" comes in. With rare exceptions—in nearly all competitive professions—women who have children get off the track and lose ground. I see it all the time in my business. There is no way in an all-consuming profession like journalism that a woman with children can devote as much time and energy as a man can.

Whether it should be or not, raising children is still mostly a woman's job. We have many more devoted fathers today than in the past, for sure. More and more men on my staff ask for paternity leaves, special hours so that they can share child care time with their wives and ex-wives. But the responsibility of fathers and mothers is not usually equal. Moreover, very few women want to put their professional ambitions ahead of their family today.

It is another sign of how far we have come that those women who feel strongly about the importance of raising children can candidly acknowledge the feeling and act on it. But let us not pretend there are no consequences.

It is still true in most fields—affirmative action notwithstanding—that a woman has to be better at her job than a man and work harder to compete. Working less puts a woman at a disadvantage; it's that simple.

If I had left the *Times* to have children, and then come back to work a four-day week the way some women reporters on my staff now do, or if I had taken long vacations and leaves to be with my family, or left the office at six o'clock instead of eight or nine—I wouldn't be the metro editor.

I wouldn't be out on the street. I'd be a reporter, or a lower-level editor. I might even be happier. But I doubt I would be able to work twelve-hour days, sometimes seven-day weeks. I am the first woman to run the largest news department at the *New York Times* not only because I am qualified—which I confess I am—but because the course of my career allowed me to *become qualified* and stay qualified.

∾∾∾

Norman B. Rice
Professor
Whitman College

If I can leave you with only one thought out of this entire speech, it's the idea that you *can* make a difference in this world.

One individual—one child of light—can make a difference.

There will be times when the crisis is going to feel overwhelming.

But whenever it starts to get you down, just remember one thing. Remember that the Chinese word for "crisis" is composed of two picture characters—one for the word "danger" and one for the word "opportunity."

Yes, we live in difficult, even dangerous times. Yes, we face bewildering challenges in the years ahead.

But these are also times of great opportunity. Political, social, and scientific advances have opened up new opportunities that previous generations could not even imagine.

We have the knowledge and the resources to create a better world, if only we have the *will* to do it.

Every one of you can play a role. Every one of you can help seize the *opportunity* that these perilous times present.

But only if we have the courage to throw off our blinders and set aside our fears.

Only if we are able to see the needs and hopes and dreams of men and women all around us.

So today, I'm asking you to join me, and dare to believe that one person really *can* make a difference.

Dare to dream. Dare to fail.

Dare to make a few mistakes along the way.

And most of all, dare to reach out your hand into the darkness, to pull another hand into the light.

Because when you do, you'll find that it's your own hand.

∽○∾

Louis V. Gerstner Jr.
Chairman/CEO, IBM
Wake Forest University

Consider that Americans spend more on PCs than TVs. The Ford Taurus contains more computing power than the first lunar landing module. And the chips inside today's Sega video games are more powerful than the supercomputers of 1976, the year most of you were born.

Of course, we're now riding the next great technology wave—the rise of powerful global networks like the Internet. Something very important is happening here. Networks are collapsing the physical barriers between nations, markets, cultures, and people. This connectivity will change everything: the way we access entertainment, replace a lost driver's license, book a seat on an airplane, bank, and interact with one another. . . . Our society is at the very beginning of profound change. I think that five or ten years from now we'll see that information technology has transformed nearly every institution and enterprise in the world and, by extension, every aspect of society.

Having said that, however, I'm beginning to wonder if some people are taking all of this too far, and far too seriously. I'm not talking about just the Internet junkies. And you know who you are out there: people who can't call their mom, because she doesn't have a modem; know more about the browser war than the Boer War; and who want to stay at Wake Forest for another year or two just for the free Internet access.

No, I'm not referring to all of you. I'm really referring to all of us. Yes, we should be impressed by this technology. But we shouldn't be distracted by it. Or fooled into thinking that technology, unto itself, is the solution to anything.

Look at the attention that was drawn to the match between IBM's Deep Blue supercomputer and Gary Kasparov. It was quite a contest. Kasparov is certainly the greatest living chess grand master, and many people say he's the best ever. He estimates that he can think about two chess moves a second. Deep Blue can consider 200 million moves a second. That's astounding.

But that's not what people were stirred up about. That's not what they wrote about and argued over. A lot of people characterized the match as the modern incarnation of John Henry against the steam drill—with nothing less than human worth hanging in the balance. Personally, I was pulling for Deep Blue. After all, you know, it's like family. But part of me, I confess, was rooting for Kasparov. I think almost everyone feels that way about technology—about its potential and limitations, and what defines what humans uniquely do best. . . .

Computers are magnificent tools for the realization of our dreams, but they will never replace the dreamers. No machine can replace the human spark: spirit, compassion, love, and understanding.

A word processor might have made it easier to write the Declaration of Independence, but it required the genius of Thomas Jefferson to capture the American cause. Sophisticated technology made possible the triumph of the moon landing. It did not instill in us the dream to go there. Yes, computers may someday simulate nuclear explosions, and help preserve the sanctity of the international test ban. But no computer has the humanity to know why civilization needed that ban, or the insight to negotiate the treaty.

And . . . I can assure you that no computer—even one that can process 200 million possible brush strokes, or scan 200 million notes per second—will ever paint a Monet, compose a Beethoven symphony, or write with the eloquence of Toni Morrison or Maya Angelou. And we shouldn't ask them to.

Let us use this very powerful, amazing technology to help us with the problems it can solve. But let us as people choose the problems we must solve.

∽✼∾

Marian Wright Edelman
Founder and Director, Children's Defense Fund
University of North Carolina at Chapel Hill

How can each of us make a difference? I hope we will take parenting and family life seriously. I hope you will plan for being a good father or mother if you choose to have children, or a good aunt and uncle or a good neighbor, as seriously as you think about your career. And I hope you will join with us in insisting that those you work for and who represent you take parenting and family life seriously. I hope your generation will have the same high expectations of your girls as for your boys, and raise your sons to be fair to other people's daughters. Young men, remember that your wife is not your mother, and recognize that your children need strong fathers *and* strong mothers. Superwoman has simply collapsed of exhaustion.

I hope that you will stress family rituals and be moral examples for your children and not have them until you are emotionally and economically ready to meet their needs.

I hope you will provide the moral example that you want them to reflect. If you lie, they will lie. If you don't value hard work, they won't either. If you spend all of your money and time on yourself and not for civic causes, they won't either. And if you tell or snicker at racial and gender jokes or try to demean any other human being, they will pass on the poison we must eradicate from this land.

Do not make hate, violence, and intolerance family values in your home—that is the most important thing we can do to transform America.

Let me end with a prayer, asking God to forgive our rich and powerful nation, where small babies die cold quite legally. God forgive our rich nation, where small children suffer from hunger quite legally. God forgive our rich nation, where toddlers and schoolchild-ren die from guns sold quite legally. God forgive our rich nation that lets children be the poorest group of citizens quite legally. Oh God, forgive our rich nation that lets the rich continue to get more at the expense of the poor quite legally. Forgive our rich nation, which thinks security rests in missiles rather than in mothers, and in bombs rather than in babies. Oh God, forgive our rich nation for not giving you sufficient thanks by giving to others their daily bread. Lord, help us never to confuse what is quite legal with what is just and right in your sight.

∽∾∾

KURT VONNEGUT
Writer
Rice University

Have we met before? No. But I have thought a lot about people like you. You men here are Adam. You women are Eve. Who hasn't thought a lot about Adam and Eve?

This is Eden, and you're about to be kicked out. Why? You ate the knowledge apple. It's in your tummies now.

And who am I? I used to be Adam. But now I am Methuselah.

And who is a serpent among us? Anyone who would strike a child.

So what does this Methuselah have to say to you, since he has lived so long? I'll pass on to you what another Methuselah said to me. He's Joe Heller, author, as you know, of *Catch-22*. We were at a party thrown by a multibillionaire out on Long Island, and I said, "Joe, how does it make you feel to realize that only yesterday our host probably made more money than *Catch-22*, one of the most popular books of all time, has grossed worldwide over the past forty years?"

Joe said to me, "I have something he can never have."

I said, "What's that, Joe?"

And he said, "The knowledge that I've got enough."

His example may be of comfort to many of you Adams and Eves, who in later years will have to admit that something has gone terribly wrong—and that, despite the education you received here, you have somehow failed to become billionaires.

This can happen to people who are interested in something other than money, other than the bottom line. We call such people saints—or I do.

∾⚬∾

Johnnetta Cole
Anthropologist
Mount Holyoke College

There was a group of young boys who decided to play a trick on an old lady. They would ask her a question, said they, and she would be incapable of answering it. With the arrogance and brashness of some of our youth, they were convinced that they were far wiser than she. So they called for the interrogator, the one who would pose the impossible questions, and asked him to practice.

"I've got it," he said. "I know exactly what to say and do. I will go up to the old lady and say, 'Old lady, old lady, this bird that I hold behind my back, is it dead, or is it alive?' And if the old lady says, 'Why, the bird is alive,' then I crush it. And if the old lady says, 'Why, the bird is dead,' I release my hand and the bird flies away."

Absolutely convinced that she would be stumped by the question, they approached her. With the graciousness that is often associated with our elders, she consented to respond to the question.

"Old lady, old lady," said the interrogator, "this bird that I hold in my hands, is it dead, or is it alive?"

The old lady, with wisdom, looked up and said, "The bird, why it's in your hands."

Indeed . . . the task of helping to make our world better is in your hands, and mine. It's in the hands of all of us.

∾⚬∾

DORIS KEARNS GOODWIN
Writer
Dartmouth College

I would like to share with you at the outset the experience I had with President Lyndon Johnson in the last years of his life during his retirement at his ranch, as he looked back on the choices he had made, wishing he had chosen differently, feeling despair and terror at the thought of death. . . .

The man I saw in retirement had spent so many years in pursuit of work, power, and individual success that he had absolutely no psychic or emotional resources left to commit himself to anything once the presidency was gone. . . . He was drained of his vitality. Years of concentration solely on work meant that in his retirement he could find no solace in recreation, sports, or hobbies. As his spirits sagged, his body deteriorated, until, I believe, he slowly brought about his own death. . . . Despite all his money and power he was completely alone when he died, his ultimate terror realized. As I understand the implication of this story, it reinforces a central wisdom I learned years ago at a seminar taught by the great Harvard psychologist Erik Erikson. And he taught us that the richest and fullest lives attain an inner balance of work, love, and play, in equal order; that to pursue one to the disregard of others is to open oneself to ultimate sadness in older age, whereas to pursue all three with equal dedication is to make possible an old age filled with serenity, peace, and fulfillment. . . .

I would leave each of you with the hope that as you make your own choices over time, you will choose in such a way that allows your drive for achievement to be balanced by an equal commitment to love, and to play, to family, to friends, and community. I hope that none of you, no matter how successful you become, ever have to experience the sadness and the loneliness that Lyndon Johnson experienced. For nothing, no amount of power or success, is worth that. I hope instead that when you are "old and gray and full of sleep," as the poet William Butler Yeats once wrote, you can say that your goal in life was not the perfection of work alone but the perfection of a life.

✺

STEPHEN BREYER
U.S. Supreme Court Justice
Colby College

Let me mention a metaphor that was helpful to me when I, like you, had to decide "What next?" When I graduated from college, I heard much advice: "Join the army," "Give blood," "Travel east," "Stay west," and (if you've seen *The Graduate*), "The future is plastics." Of course, advice sometimes reflects the tunnel vision of one's own career. Supposedly someone asked Conrad Hilton what he might pass on to others after fifty years in the hotel business. He replied, "Always keep the shower curtain inside the bathtub."

But the best advice I received was from a former law school dean, Bayless Manning. He pointed out that, when we make an important personal decision, we rarely know more than 10 percent of all we would like to know about it, let alone about the other options that the decision precludes. Sometimes agonizing does not help; sometimes we must simply choose. And our lives then shape themselves around the choices that we make. Those choices create a story—and that is the metaphor I have found so useful. Every person's life is a story of passion, with its moments of joy and happiness, of tragedy and sorrow. And each person's story is different, one from the other.

The external circumstances, the material circumstances, of that story are often beyond our control, but they often matter less than we think. We all know many people who complain, even when their glass is full to overflowing. And my wife, who works with children at Dana Farber Cancer Institute, could tell you of many families who bring joy to themselves and others through their ability to see half full a glass that many might find almost empty.

The most important parts of the story are personal. Your own story will include family and friends, not just career. And it will include your own justifications for choices made. What we do and how we explain it tells us who we are. We cannot escape the negative meaning that a failure of integrity—a failure to live up to our standards of right and wrong—will give to the stories we ourselves shape. I agree with the philosopher who said that money can vanish

overnight, power disappear, reputation can evaporate, but character—personal integrity—is a rock that stays secure.

A hope, I confess, is weaker than a prediction. Casey Stengel said,
"I never make predictions—at least not about the future." And I can
see why. Consider . . . 1895: The president of the British Royal Society predicts, "Heavier-than-air flying machines are impossible." 1899:
The chief of the U.S. Patent Office announces: "Everything that can
be invented has been invented." 1927: The head of Warner Brothers
asks, "Who . . . wants to hear actors talk?" 1943: Tom Watson, the
president of IBM, announces, "I think there is a world market for
maybe five computers." 1949: *Popular Mechanics* points out: "Computers in the future may weigh no more than 1.5 tons." Neither I nor
you can be certain how your lives will unfold; we cannot predict.

But we can hope. And my hope is that you will remember, as you
create your lives' story, to devote time and effort—to commit yourselves—not only to your personal lives, your careers, but also to the
public affairs of your communities and your nation—in a word, that
you will participate in community life.

∽o∾

THE DALAI LAMA
Spiritual Leader
Emory University

I believe that education is like an instrument. Whether that instrument, that device, is used properly or constructively or in a different
way depends on the user. We have education on the one hand; on the
other hand, we have a good person. A good person means someone
with a good heart, a sense of caring for the welfare of others, a commitment, a sense of responsibility. Education and the warm heart,
the compassionate heart—if you combine these two, then your education, your knowledge, will be constructive. Then you yourself
become a happy person.

If you only have education and knowledge and lack the other side,
then you will not be a happy person, but a person with mental unrest,

of frustration. If you combine these two, education with a good heart, your whole life will be constructive and happy. And certainly you can make immense benefit for society and the betterment of humanity. It is one of my fundamental beliefs that a good heart, a warm heart, a compassionate heart, is still teachable. Please combine the two.

Then there is another thing I want to tell you. You have achieved your goal, and now you are ready to begin another chapter. Now you really start life. Real life may be more complicated. You are bound to face some unhappy things and hindrances and obstacles, complications. So it is important to have determination and optimism and patience. If you lack patience, even when you face some small obstacle, you lose courage. There is a Tibetan saying, "Even if you have failed at something nine times, you must continue and not lose hope." I think that is important. Use your brain to analyze the situation. Do not rush through it, but think. Once you decide what to do about that obstacle, then there is a possibility to achieve your goal.

∽∘∾

1999

Why were we all so fascinated with the marriage of Bill and Hillary Clinton? Why, as 1999 came around, did so many articles and books on the Clinton marriage appear, and why were pundits so naively fixated on what they assumed was a Faustian marital pact? Again and again, however, the public showed how willing they were to grant that marriages can involve infidelity, the cold shoulder, dancing on an outdoor deck in Martha's Vineyard, an only child—you name it—and that in the end, these components combine as, well, marriage or something. The world, or so it appeared, was not as black-and-white as our screenplays, and our pro wrestlers, might have us believe.

Nineteen ninety-nine saw more than its share of violence and gun mania. Every week, it seemed, there was another horrific shooting. In "the close-knit community" of Littleton, Colorado, members of the Trench Coat Mafia blew up their high school, and in Atlanta, Georgia, a day trader announced, Clint Eastwood—style, "I hope this doesn't ruin your trading day," before spraying gunfire at his colleagues—the last a vivid glimpse at how, in our culture, reality and the movies had become depressingly intertwined. "Grimly familiar," moaned the commentators over footage of the memorial services, though as ever, no real steps were made regarding America's love affair with guns; the NRA reasserted that restricting firearms would do nothing to deter lunatics, and moreover, that individual freedoms would be padlocked if guns were taken away.

Elsewhere, Woodstock '99 took place, ending in rape, bonfires, and looting, and Tina Brown started a new magazine called Talk. AOL Instant Messenger supplanted the telephone in the lives of many adolescents as the communication device of choice. The Blair Witch Project, a low-budget documentary-style horror movie, became the most profitable movie ever made. Pokémon cards were the latest craze among the under-twelve set, and the world worried about the upcoming Y2K crisis, which seemed less a reality than a symptom of premillennium anxiety. Presidential candidates prepared for the November elections, with George W. Bush leading the Republican race and Bill Bradley and Al Gore leading the Democrats.

One of the most tragic incidents of the year took place when John F. Kennedy Jr., his wife, Carolyn Bessette, and her sister Lauren Bessette were killed when the plane Kennedy was flying crashed in the waters off Martha's Vineyard. Ironically, pieces of the plane's fuselage would eventually wash up on the beach of JFK Jr.'s late mother, Jacqueline Onassis. As the country and the world looked on, the television cameras seemed to take lewd delight in poking their lenses into the life of a person who had long protected his privacy and normalcy. The television ratings, one twenty-four-hour-news-channel executive was later heard gloating, were bigger than when Princess Diana died. Inevitably, on the fourth day of media saturation, came the television shows devoted to the question, why do we care? Has television coverage become obsessive? The media snake, as ever, had found its tail. It nibbled a little, let go, and then all of us moved on.

With our memories of the past so slight that many people were able to look back longingly at the seventies as a time of pastel naivete, and the eighties as a period when a benevolent grandfather figure ran the White House, we prepared, none the wiser, for the year 2000.

∽∘∾

Madeleine Albright
U.S. Secretary of State
University of Arizona

I happen to be someone who was born not in this country, but in what was then called Czechoslovakia. I am female, Caucasian, somewhat height-challenged, and a Taurus.

Each of you could provide your own list of personal characteristics.

These kinds of distinctions, or at least some of them, do make a difference.

For it is natural that we should feel kinship for those with whom we have something in common. Solidarity with others can help redress social grievances. And respect for heritage helps us to preserve identity and honor the past.

But as we have been so tragically reminded in recent months, when pride in "us" descends into hatred of "them," the grounds for pride vanish and terrible violence can result.

In my job, I have seen the heartrending consequences in places such as Bosnia and Rwanda, the Middle East, and now a brutal campaign of ethnic cleansing in Kosovo.

America is right to oppose intolerance abroad. . . .

We are all proud of the groups to which we belong, but it's what comes after the hyphen in "European-American," "African-American," "Latino-American," "Asian-American," or any other kind of American that truly matters.

After the tornadoes in Oklahoma, we did not reach out to help our neighbors as hyphenated Americans. After what happened at Littleton, we did not grieve and search our souls as hyphenated Americans. After the killing began in Kosovo, our servicemen and -women did not answer NATO's call as hyphenated Americans.

We are different one from the other. But we are all bound together by a single premise—that every individual counts. We each have a right to be judged not by where we come from or by who our parents are, but by our own actions and character.

∽o∾

TERRY TEMPEST WILLIAMS
Writer
College of the Atlantic

See, feel, question, explore, experience, walk, dance, run, play, eat, love, learn, dare, taste, touch, smell, listen, argue, speak, write, read, draw, provoke, emote, scream, cry, kneel, pray, pray often, bow, rise, stand, look, sing, embrace the questions, be wary of answers, create, cajole, confront, confound, walk backward, walk forward, circle, hide, seek, say no, say yes, embrace, follow your heart, trust your heart, engage love again and again on this beautiful, broken world.

∽◦∾

BILL BRADLEY
Politician
University of North Carolina at Chapel Hill

On this day that officially marks your entering the world of adults, I'm going to ask you to take a moment and think about children. With the recent tragedy in Littleton, Colorado, America's thinking once again about the pressures on our families and our children. What happened in Littleton was a horrific tragedy, as it was in Springfield, Paducah, Jonesboro, Edinboro—in all, twenty-eight children killed and seventy-one injured in a scourge of school shooting—as it is all across America, every day, when thirteen of our children every day are killed by gun violence.

Too many children are growing up with too little support or guidance. Parents struggle valiantly, but too often their children's values have been shaped by television, shopping malls, video games, and the street corner as much as by them. . . . Something is wrong when our children are abandoned to a high school subculture so segregated that the adults don't see the implication of the Trench Coat Mafia. Something is wrong when we allow children to commit murder in video games. We cannot consign so many of our children to a life of meaninglessness. We cannot turn away from the responsibility of salvaging their precious lives. When tragedies like Littleton occur, we come together as one nation, one family. And then too often we go our separate ways once again. But we can't afford to do that anymore. We must take responsibility for the society that our children live in.

∽◦∾

JULES FEIFFER
Cartoonist
Southampton College

We Americans are a people who have given failure a bad name. If you are not a winner, you're a loser. If you're not a player, you're a doofus or a nerd. If you're not number one or part of the winner's circle that dotes on and teases and genuflects before number one, then there is no circle for you. Losers *do* hang out, but one nod from the winning circle and it's "What did you say your name was? Do I know you?"

But in the writing and other arts, no one—well, almost no one—commits a perfect first draft. John Updike, maybe. Joyce Carol Oates. But I doubt it. James Baldwin once said, "I don't write, I rewrite." And that goes for every other field of endeavor.

We are all continually embarking on first drafts, in every aspect of our lives, in whatever line of work, and to succumb to the frustration of failure is to undercut the very purpose of a first draft. Get it down. Get it all down. Then go back, and get it right. If not the second time, then the third or fourth or fifth—and as you do this, you come to understand that there's a logic to this. You are learning, always learning—learning by following a trail, very much like a private eye, that leads you down one cul-de-sac—oops, wrong!—and then another, and then another. You begin to appreciate this kind of work—hard work, but interesting—as a process. A process, the demands of which teach you in time that while inspiration and luck are nice things to have, they are strategically negotiable.

You develop a nose for the right chain of events, and an ear for the order of words that will best tell and illuminate your story. And rather than this becoming formulaic and dry as dust as a way of doing things, it frees, it liberates.

There's nothing you can't take a stab at, because who's gonna know? You screw up. You cross out. You delete. You find one sentence or paragraph in this mess that's on the money, you get rid of the rest—or follow the lead of that one sentence or paragraph and figure out how to tame the rest of these out-of-control ramblings, so that they begin to take shape and make sense.

And while doing this, you don't make judgments on yourself. "I can't do this, I'm no good, this is too hard, whatever made me think that I, of all people—I loathe myself."

Well, of course, all creative people loathe themselves at one time or another. That, too, is part of the process. Then after indulging in glorious self-hate and self-pity, you get back in and go at it again. And again.

And you work, and you curse, and you suffer, and you understand, at bottom, that there is nothing, absolutely nothing, that's as much fun as this.

∽○∽

Bill Richardson
U.S. Secretary of Energy
Colorado College

What does the world hold for you? You will take your spirit of community service and your degree from this great college into a nation of virtually unprecedented economic prosperity and into a world offering almost unlimited opportunity.

As you enter that world, I offer you four simple suggestions:

- Find a job—no matter how large or small—that means something to you.
- Be generous with your advantages; and all of you have a lot of advantages. Give to others.
- Stand up for what you believe in. Take a stand no matter how unpopular that stand may be. The world does not honor fence-sitters.
- Remember where you came from—your community, your neighborhood, your school, your friends.

At this moment in history, you have the opportunity to shape the world. But you have a responsibility to create a better one. So I would ask you to add a fifth suggestion, and that is to think of yourselves as citizens of the world, thinking of yourselves in a global community, thinking of yourselves as someone who will make a difference for all mankind, not just yourselves and your country.

∽o∾

CHRISTOPHER REEVE
Actor
Williams College (unrehearsed remarks)

A lot of people have said to me, "Well, how do you get through this? I mean, something really terrible happened in 1995, it changed your life." I said, "Well, if I had to describe it in a nutshell, yeah, I'm not going to have nearly as much fun as I used to have, there's going to be a lot that I can't do, but how do I get through it? Because there's a platform that was built after twenty-eight years of being an actor, facing rejection, learning the discipline of giving your best eight times a week, having made that commitment for something that I wanted to do with my life."

I had a platform. Now, it took me a little while, but I saw that there was an opportunity, not something I would have chosen, but something that's absolutely fascinating, because I was injured at a time when research into the nervous system and the brain is progressing very rapidly and will ease a tremendous amount of human suffering.

So I don't fight just to get myself out of a chair, but to help push science and to find the funding to allow our best researchers to conquer inner space, the frontier of inner space, which involves Parkinson's, Alzheimer's, MS, ALS, stroke; and it's going to be a truly fascinating journey, because there's going to be a vaccine for diabetes, there's going to be a vaccine for AIDS, we will be able to stop the spread of Parkinson's, we will be able to remyelinate nerves in MS, and we will be able to regenerate the spinal cord.

It's an incredible time—incredible moment of opportunity—and I feel that if I hadn't built a base a long time ago, I wouldn't be able to deal with it. But along with my family and friends, the support of so many people around the world, I'm able to go forth in a way that I never would have thought possible. And we all have this inner strength within us—nothing special about me. Anybody can do it if they just rely on that solid base or foundation that you start building now with the education you've received.

∽∘∾

JANE ALEXANDER
Actor
Smith College

Our world is finite; we are not. "Oh brave new world that has such people in't," exclaims Miranda in *The Tempest*. It is a brave new world. The old rules don't apply; all the oceans have been crossed, the lands have been mapped, the mountains have been climbed. What was done in the name of possession is now done in the name of tourism—for fun. The last frontier today, other than the distant reaches of the stars, is the human brain. It is our brains, not our brawn, that will move us forward.

I believe in the transcendent powers of science. Science has been good to us in the twentieth century, giving us wings to take to the air, pills to quell the body's ills, images and sounds to delight the eye and ear, life in a petri dish, and Velcro—so many things that they can't be counted, coming at us so rapidly that we can hardly keep up. But watch how young children grasp the nature of new things, as if the circuits of their brains are channels longing to be filled; they have none of the informational overload I experience from decades of cramming. . . .

I also believe in art. The educator Ernest Boyer said that "the arts are one of humankind's most vital forms of language. . . . In most respects the human species is far less equipped than other creatures on the planet: we are no match for the lion in strength; we're outstripped by the ostrich in speed; we can't outswim the dolphin; we see less acutely than the hawk. And yet, as humans, we excel in the exquisite use of symbols which empowers us to outdistance all other forms of life in what we see and feel and know." These symbols have made all forms of communication possible, from simple hand gestures, which convey information and feelings, to the most intricate combinations, which gave us the computer and take us to the stars. . . .

As Daniel Boorstin says, art "awakens us to our own possibilities." If religion teaches us that love is all-encompassing, art teaches us that anything is possible, and science shows us how to get there.

I spent four years trying to get a bunch of troglodytes in Congress to understand that cutting the budget of the National Endowment for the Arts was like cutting out the best part of our brains. Rather than invest in a future of possibilities for young people, such as arts programs after school nationwide, they decided to build more prisons. Rather than celebrate the millennium through the arts, sciences, and humanities, they are devoting millions to a new version of Star Wars. Over and over again I felt their priorities were all wrong. One man said to me, "My God, we don't want any more artists in the world, we have too many already!" That's like saying we have too much imagination and beauty running amok in the world—let's get rid of it!

∽∾∾

BRIAN LAMB
President and CEO, C-SPAN
Ursinus College

Dr. Harry S. Wright last night at baccalaureate . . . gave a great speech, and he told a story. For those of you who weren't there, I'll just fill you in on it. He told a story about getting caught in a snowstorm, in Texarkana, Arkansas-Texas, two towns of the same name right there across the border. He had to go to Dallas because . . . he was the president of this school and had to be there for a meeting. And the truck drivers in the truck stop said, "You just follow us, keep our lights in front of you, and we'll get you there." And then, at the end, he said, "And for the rest of your life, keep your heroes in view all the time, and it'll get you through life."

I've interviewed in my lifetime thousands of people, and I've got to tell you that I've asked this question so often: "Who's your hero?

Who do you admire the most?" And almost ninety-nine out of a hundred times, the answer is not what you might think it might be, but the hero turns out to be people right here in this audience—both behind me and in front of me. It's almost always a parent, a grand-parent, an uncle, an aunt, or it's a teacher. So you don't have to go very far to see where those headlights are going to be for the rest of your life. They're right here around you. . . .

I had an experience that I'll never forget. And I tell you this story because you ought to do this kind of thing earlier than I did. I'm fifty-seven years old, and about fifteen years ago, I started to think about some of the teachers that had meant a lot to me. And I was home in Lafayette, Indiana, one day, and my favorite teacher of phi-losophy, Eric Clitherow, who did so much for us, was somewhere in that town. He still lived there, retired, and I looked for him and I found him, finally, in a nursing home. So I called him up—hadn't talked to him in years—and I said, "Dr. Clitherow, I wanted to call you today. I have no other reason to call you but to just tell you how much you meant to me and how much you did for me when I was in school, and I want to thank you."

And then came something that I was totally not expecting. He said, "No, Brian, I want to thank you. For you see, the most impor-tant thing in my life was reading." And he said, "I'm now blind, and with C-SPAN, at least I've been able to keep my mind active." Well, I barely could get off the phone. I mean, tears were running down my eyes. Every time I tell this story to friends, the same thing hap-pens. The message of all that was—and Dr. Clitherow is not alive any longer—the simple message of all that was, thank them today. Find them in this audience. And if you don't thank them today, call them on the phone.

∽o∽

DAVID McCULLOUGH
Writer
University of Connecticut

I have some calculations for you to consider: reportedly, the average American watches twenty-eight hours of television every week, or approximately four hours a day. The average person, I'm told, reads at a rate of 250 words per minute.

So, based on these statistics, were the average American to spend those four hours a day with a book instead of watching television, the average American could, in a week, read

- the complete poems of T. S. Eliot
- two plays by Thornton Wilder, including *Our Town*
- the complete poems of Maya Angelou
- *The Great Gatsby*, and
- the book of Psalms

That's all in one week.
Read, read, read, is my commencement advice.

✺

MUMIA ABU-JAMAL
Activist and Writer
Evergreen State College

(Mumia Abu-Jamal's speech was delivered via audiotape from jail, where he is on death row for the murder of a Philadelphia policeman. The policeman's widow was in attendance. Abu-Jamal's sentence is currently on appeal.)

A life lived deliberately has been the example of people I admire and respect . . . people, although of quite diverse beliefs, ideologies, and lifestyles, share something in common: a commitment to revolution and a determination to live that commitment deliberately in the face of staggering state repression.

No doubt some of you are disconcerted by my use of the term "revolution." It's telling that people who claim with pride to be proud Americans would disclaim the very process that made such a nationality possible, even if it was a bourgeois revolution. Why was it right for people to revolt against the British because of "taxation without representation," and somehow wrong for truly unrepresented Africans in America to revolt against America? For any oppressed people, revolution, according to the Declaration of Independence, is a right.

Malcolm X, although now widely acclaimed as a black nationalist martyr, was vilified at the time of his assassination by *Time* magazine as "an unashamed demagogue" who "was a disaster to the civil rights movement." The *New York Times* would describe him as a "twisted man" who used his brains and oratorical skills for "an evil purpose." Today, there are schools named for him, and recently a postage stamp was even issued in his honor.

Dr. Huey P. Newton, Ph.D., founded the Black Panther Party in October of 1966 and created one of the most militant, principled organizations American blacks had ever seen. J. Edgar Hoover of the FBI targeted the party, using every foul and underhanded method they could conceive of to neutralize the group, which they described as the "number one threat to national security." . . .

These people dared to dissent, dared to speak out, dared to reject the status quo by becoming rebels against it. They lived—and some of them continue to live—lives of deliberate will, of willed resistance to a system that is killing us. Remember them. Honor their highest moments. Learn from them. Are these not lives lived deliberately? This system's greatest fear has been that folks like you, young people, people who have begun to critically examine the world around them, some perhaps for the first time, people who have yet to have the spark of life snuffed out, will do just that: learn from these lives, be inspired, and then live lives of opposition to the deadening status quo. . . .

The great historians Will and Ariel Durant teach us that history in the large is the conflict of minorities. The majority applauds the victor and supplies the human material of social experiment. Now, I take that to mean that social movements are begun by relatively small numbers of people who, as catalysts, inspire, provoke, and move larger numbers to see and share their vision. Social movements can then become social forces that expand our perspectives, open up new social possibilities, and create the consciousness for change. To begin this process, we must first sense that (1) the status quo is wrong, and (2) the existing order is not amenable to real, meaningful, and substantive transformation. Out of the many here assembled, it is the heart of him or her that I seek who looks at a life of vapid materialism, of capitalist excess, and finds it simply intolerable. It may be one hundred of you, or fifty, or even ten, or even one of you who makes that choice. I'm here to honor and applaud that choice, and to warn you that, though the suffering may indeed be great, it is nothing to the joy of doing the right thing.

∽∘∽

ZOE CALDWELL
Actor
Barnard College

One hundred and twenty-five thousand years ago, Neanderthal man lived in caves, worshiped fire, hunted in packs, and spent an inordinate amount of time on tools and weapons. There was no music, no dance, no theater. Thirty-five thousand years ago, Cro-Magnon man lived in caves, worshiped fire, hunted in packs, and spent an inordinate amount of time on tools and weapons. There was no music, no dance, no theater—but there was painting. These men went deep, deep into the dark of the inside of a mountain—so dark that they had to take fire with them—and with sharpened stones drew on the walls of the caves the most elegant drawings. If they needed color, they used oxide of iron and manganese, and burnt bone was used for black. But they found it difficult to stick the black to the rock, so they took the burnt bone into their mouths and chewed until it was mixed with their saliva and spat it onto the walls. I find that thrilling.

And why did they do all this? Because they had souls that were heavy and in pain and they were frightened and needed to assuage their spirits. And as man evolved and became more aware of the need to assuage his soul, he discovered music and dance and theater and many different forms of painting. When we realized that we needed a god to bring all this to, we created God. Who, strangely enough, has created us. And so we were safe and well.

The Greeks really understood the need to serve what makes us feel well. They created huge amphitheaters where from sunup to sunset all the people sat on stone seats in the sunlight, drinking, eating—whole families, young, old, rich, poor—to observe specially trained priests who could dance and sing and act out all the stuff we secretly thought about but didn't dare do. Kill the king, your father, your mother, the kids. Make love to the king, your father, your mother, the kids. But because these people were called actors, and were doing it in the daylight in front of everyone, you were able to laugh, to cry, and rid yourself of the need to do it. In other words, your soul was calmed and your humanity restored. Acting is a very godly thing to do.

So for thousands of years, with a few blank spaces, that is what actors have done. But lately, we have become confused. Instead of the personal involvement of spitting on the wall, we have become involved in technological separation. We have put barriers between ourselves and direct contact with other humans. Our theaters, because of electricity, operate mostly in the dark. Therefore we give our power to the marvelously talented men and women who can light us and make us heard. But it comes to the audience secondhand. I won't get into films, television, and the Internet. This is the age of communication—*www.com*. I have seen people on dates talking on cell phones. To whom? To each other? I just know that we have become more lonely. What does it mean: "communicate"? I looked it up in my old Oxford dictionary: "To give, to receive, to connect, by gesture, expression, words. To receive holy communion." Everything human. Then my son said, "What about *Webster's Tenth*?" So I went to *Webster's Tenth*. "To transmit information, thought, or feeling so that it is satisfactorily received or understood." Maybe that's why they use cell phones on dates.

I still think it is the actor's job to rush the playwright's word out of the temple to the people and make them feel human again. Today,

Neanderthal man lives in Washington, D.C., and his needs are pretty much the same. He lives in swell caves, worships firepower, hunts in packs, and spends an inordinate amount of time and money on tools and weapons. Music, dance, theater, painting to him are not vital. When will he understand that if we are to evolve and become truly great, there must be an amphitheater big enough to hold every-one—young, old, rich, poor, black, white, yellow, blue, brindle, laughing, crying, and feeling safe together?

∞○∞

Permission to use the following excerpts was granted by the copyright holders:

1975
May Sarton
Vincent Barnett

1976
Vernon Jordan
Andrew Hacker

1977
George Plimpton
Madeleine L'Engle
Studs Terkel

1978
Anthony Lewis
Edward O. Wilson
Francine du Plessix Gray
George Plimpton
Ramsey Clark

1979
E. L. Doctorow
Tom Brokaw
Toni Morrison
Joseph Califano

1980
Alan Alda
Elie Wiesel
Francine du Plessix Gray
Maya Angelou

1981
William Styron
Christopher Lasch
Elizabeth Holtzman
Jane Bryant Quinn
Sam Nunn
Sissela Bok

1982
Frances FitzGerald
Elie Wiesel
Ted Koppel

1983
Margaret Atwood
Meryl Streep
Wyndham Robertson
Lewis Thomas
E. L. Doctorow
Robert Thurman
Coretta Scott King

1984
Mario Cuomo
Julius Lester
Jane Alexander
Dan Rather
Howard Baker
Robert Coles
Neil Simon

1985
Beverly Sills
Thomas Winship

1986
Tracy Kidder
Lee Iacocca
Ellen Goodman
David McCullough
Henry Cisneros
Mario Cuomo
James Baldwin
Flora Lewis

1987
Ted Koppel
Thomas Kean
Ken Burns
Riccardo Muti
Maya Angelou
Mario Cuomo

1988
Malcolm Forbes
Marian Wright Edelman
Sissela Bok
Toni Morrison
William Zinsser
Stephen King

1989
Patricia Schroeder
Tracy Kidder
Sandra Day O'Connor
Michael Eisner
Johnnetta Cole
Richard T. Cunningham
Joseph Brodsky
Wendell Berry
James B. Stewart
Helen Vendler

1990
Tom Brokaw

Desmond Tutu
Jill Ker Conway
Ben Cohen
Johnnetta Cole
Paul Newman
Cathleen Black
Carl Sagan
Wendy Wasserstein

1991
John Naisbitt
Chinua Achebe
Madeleine L'Engle
Barbara Ehrenreich
William Chace
Bob Edwards
Bryant Gumbel

1992
Ann Richards
Daniel Patrick Moynihan
Patricia Schroeder
Wendy Kopp
Bernadine Healy

1993
Gwen Ifill
Mona Van Duyn
Marian Wright Edelman
Lee Smith
John Updike
Jodie Foster
Jim Lehrer
Cornel West
Ellen Goodman

1994
Lamar Alexander
Cokie Roberts
Lanford Wilson
Barbara Kingsolver
Kurt Vonnegut
Judy Woodruff
Lowell Weicker

1995
Gloria Steinem
M. L. Flynn
Hugh Sidey
Václav Havel
Dan Rather
Joan Konner
Ann Richards

1996
Wendy Walker Whitworth
Steve Kroft
Anna Quindlen
Cornel West
David Halberstam
Mary Higgins Clark
Nora Ephron

1997
Marian Wright Edelman
Bob Newhart
Anna Quindlen
Mark Shields
Denise Di Novi

Art Buchwald
Michael Dirda
Tim Russert
Robert Coles
Diane Sawyer

1998
Ruth Bader Ginsburg
Joyce Purnick
Norman B. Rice
Louise V. Gerstner
Marian Wright Edelman
Kurt Vonnegut
Johnnetta Cole
Doris Kearns Goodwin

Stephen Breyer
The Dalai Lama

1999
Terry Tempest Williams
Bill Bradley
Jules Feiffer
Christopher Reeve
Jane Alexander
Brian Lamb
David McCullough
Mumia Abu-Jamal
Zoe Caldwell

ABOUT THE AUTHOR

Peter J. Smith is a novelist, short-story writer, and journalist. He is the author of *A Good Family* and his writing has appeared in a variety of magazines, including the *New Yorker,* the *New York Times Magazine, New York,* and *Life.* He lives with his family in Massachusetts.

Dew